DATE DUE

DEMCO 38-296

CONGRESSIONAL CAUCUSES IN NATIONAL POLICY MAKING

Congressional Caucuses in National Policy Making

Susan Webb Hammond

The Johns Hopkins University Press
Baltimore & London

© 1998 The Johns Hopkins University Press
All rights reserved. Published 1998
Printed in the United States of America on acid-free paper
07 06 05 04 03 02 01 00 99 98   5 4 3 2 1

The Johns Hopkins University Press
2715 North Charles Street
Baltimore, Maryland 21218–4319
The Johns Hopkins Press Ltd., London

Library of Congress Cataloging-in-Publication Data will be found at the end of this book.
A catalog record for this book is available from the British Library.

ISBN 0–8018-5682–5

To Susan and David

CONTENTS

Figure and Tables

Figure

Tables

Preface and Acknowledgments

This book looks closely at the congressional caucus system, an important development of the late-twentieth-century Congress. In earlier times, affinity groups within Congress were either loose social groups or boardinghouse groups and were very rarely involved in the business of lawmaking. Other ad hoc and ephemeral groups had a brief life span. In the contemporary era, the caucus system has arisen as an important adjunct to the formal committee system and the political party system within Congress. Members have used congressional caucuses to do what they could not otherwise accomplish: organizing, reviewing, and balancing information and expressing and advocating policy concerns. This study surveys how caucuses do this, describing and analyzing caucus organization, work, and impact. Certain patterns emerge, illuminating differences among the various types of caucus. Certain changes are seen over time, and these illustrate how caucuses have affected and reacted to events as experienced in Congress.

Caucuses have become an important link in the policy chain for everyone—government official or staffer, private citizen or group—who is engaged in the business of federal Washington. Caucuses have, on occasion, initiated or resolved major policy actions, but more important, their work has touched upon the range of government activity and of citizen involvement in public affairs. This is the real significance of caucuses—not as centers of power that rival the traditional and permanent centers of power but as familiar, everyday tools of the trade of federal lawmaking, to which lawmakers and policy players turn again and again as they pursue their goals. As such, caucuses are fundamentally important and can be expected to continue as actors in national policy making.

This study draws upon (1) semifocused interviews with senators and representatives and with caucus staff and other congressional staff from the Ninety-seventh Congress through the 104th Congress, (2) a telephone survey of all caucuses active during the 100th Congress, (3) election, constituency, caucus membership, and roll call data for representatives in the

Ninety-seventh and 104th Congresses, (4) congressional documents, including caucus materials, and (5) media reports and other printed sources. The data are discussed in more detail in the appendix.

I am grateful to the American Enterprise Institute, the Everett McKinley Dirksen Congressional Center, and American University for grants that assisted the research; and to the Brookings Institution for appointments as a guest scholar and to colleagues there who helped shape my thinking about caucuses.

The early stages of this project were a collaborative effort with Arthur G. Stevens Jr. and Daniel P. Mulhollan. Interviews with caucus staff directors and some representatives during the Ninety-seventh and Ninety-eighth Congresses were jointly developed and conducted. We coauthored three papers and two articles reporting the early research. Art Stevens and I developed the caucus typology (see chap. 2). Dan Mulhollan participated in the survey of caucus activities and operations conducted during the 100th Congress. This book owes a great deal to my work with these colleagues.

Numerous scholars have offered encouragement, comments, and guidance and have contributed to my thinking about congressional caucuses. I am particularly grateful to Sarah Binder, Jon Bond, Janet Breslin, Joe Cooper, Nancy Davidson, Roger Davidson, Christine de Gregorio, Larry Dodd, Dick Fenno, Chris Foreman, Chuck Jones, John Kingdon, Laura Langbein, Burdett Loomis, Tom Mann, Gary McKissick, Eric Patashnik, Bob Peabody, Sula Richardson, Cathy Rudder, Barbara Sinclair, Jim Thurber, Kent Weaver, Margaret Weir, Joe White, and Rick Wilson, as well as colleagues who were panel discussants or anonymous reviewers for caucus papers or articles.

I am grateful to the many members and staff of Congress who gave so generously of their time and expertise to discuss and explain caucus work. They were promised anonymity; I very much appreciate their help. Students in my classes commented on aspects of the study as it took shape. I am also grateful to the doctoral students at American University who served as research assistants: Muriel Bowser, Carol de Frances, Bob Goehrig, Cindy McKinney, Kerry Mullins, Joung Park, and Scott Rudolf; to Susan Waite Hammond and David Shields Hammond, who handled the initial coding of the staff director interviews; and to Julie Dolan and Martha Kropf, research assistants during the final stages of manuscript preparation. I owe particular thanks to Timothy Huelskamp, who so ably handled much of the statistical analysis, and to David Shields Hammond, whose editing assistance throughout the project vastly improved the final product. And I would like to thank Henry Tom, editor at the Johns Hopkins University Press, for his suggestions and efficiency. My husband, Bob, provided much-appreciated encouragement and advice throughout.

Parts of chapter 6 first appeared in "Informal Congressional Caucuses and Agenda Setting," coauthored with Daniel P. Mulhollan and Arthur G. Stevens Jr., *Western Political Quarterly* 38 (Dec. 1985), published by the University of Utah. Parts of chapter 7 appeared in my article, "Congressional Caucuses and Party Leaders in the U.S. House of Representatives," *Political Science Quarterly* 106 (summer 1991). They are reprinted with permission.

PROLOGUE

In September 1959, a group of moderate-to-liberal Democrats in the House of Representatives, who were frustrated by conservative senior Democrats dominating the committee system, founded the Democratic Study Group. DSG members, working together as a caucus, hoped to loosen conservative Democratic control and to push through moderate-to-liberal policies. Early meetings focused on briefings and strategy about pending floor legislation. Later, the DSG began to distribute information on legislation scheduled for the floor and to put in place a whip system to obtain support from members on floor votes of interest to the caucus.

In the mid-1970s, the DSG developed, built coalitions for, and achieved passage of major changes in Democratic caucus and House rules, designed to facilitate approval of legislation supported by DSG members. The Subcommittee Bill of Rights, which gave House subcommittees permanent jurisdictions, separate staff and budgets, and more independence from chairs' control, was one result. Operating out of an office on the top floor of the Longworth House Office Building, DSG staff briefing papers and information on scheduled floor legislation filled an information gap left open by party leaders. Even Republicans subscribed to the DSG *Legislative Report* for its detailed, balanced descriptions of bills and proposed amendments scheduled for floor action and for information on the rules setting the terms of floor debate. By 1977, 37 percent of House members and 66 percent of legislative assistants surveyed by the House Commission on Administrative Review reported relying heavily on DSG material for information on legislation scheduled for floor action. An even higher proportion of legislative assistants used DSG information for committee work and to keep up-to-date on public issues (Maisel 1981).

At the start of each Congress, the DSG proposed changes to House and Democratic caucus rules. DSG staff director, Dick Conlon, earned respect as an adviser to representatives and other senior staffers. By 1984 a senior leadership aide was asserting that "party caucuses [e.g., the DSG] have to be listened to by leadership. . . . The DSG has very influential members."[1]

1

During the 1980s and into the 1990s, the DSG coordinated legislative strategy, produced background briefing papers and information on pending legislation, and drafted bills and amendments such as the 1981 Udall-Obey alternative tax plan and a 1987 amendment delaying President Ronald Reagan's action to reflag Kuwaiti oil tankers. The caucus refused a request to become part of the Democratic leadership, believing it could be more independent and more useful if it continued to operate outside the formal committee and party systems. As the DSG matured, the original Young Turks gained seniority and committee and party leadership power. For example, Thomas P. (Tip) O'Neill (D-Mass.) moved from majority whip to majority leader and, in 1977, to speaker of the House. Liberal Democrats who had gained some seniority became leaders of the DSG, and recent study group chairs served on the caucus's executive committee. In 1995–96 these included David Obey (D-Wis.), the ranking minority member and former chair of the Appropriations Committee; Bob Wise (D-W.Va.) and James Oberstar (D-Minn.), both ranking minority members of subcommittees of the Committee on Transportation and Infrastructure; and Martin Sabo (D-Minn.), ranking minority member and former chair of the Budget Committee. The DSG had become an influential and important informal group within the House.

In early 1995, the DSG lost its office and separate staff because of new regulations governing informal caucuses. Its publications on legislation were first spun off to a new nonprofit organization and then were sold to the *Congressional Quarterly*. Some publication functions were taken over by the House Democratic leadership. While the study group continued as a caucus, the Democratic Caucus, made up of all House Democrats, elected the DSG chair and officers. During the 104th Congress, David Skaggs, a fifth-term liberal Democrat from Colorado, chaired the study group. The DSG continued its mission to serve as "an organization for Democratic members of the U.S. House of Representatives who wish to join together in a common effort to develop policy options; to assure more effective communication and coordination of efforts to enact programs and policies supported by DSG members; and to make Congress a more effective institution responsive to the needs of the nation" (Brownson 1995, 809). Nevertheless, its operations were different from earlier years. Its previous activities were split among three organizations, one of them in the private sector. Without caucus dues, which were abolished in 1995 under House Oversight Committee regulations, it became difficult to define caucus membership. In mid-1996, the DSG was continuing to search for a structure and activities with which to carry out its mission as an independent policy actor.

In 1983 the Conservative Opportunity Society (COS) was founded in the House by Republican Young Turks, led by Vin Weber (R-Minn.) and Newt Gingrich (R-Ga.). The group, like its earlier DSG counterpart, was dissatisfied with what they considered accommodationist leadership of their party in the House. They sought a change in party operations from accommodation to confrontation and in party viewpoint from minority to majority outlook. The group met regularly to map out strategy, with a focus on speeches and floor procedures. Almost immediately, the COS organized a series of short speeches to oppose the nuclear freeze bill, which were televised by C-Span and given after the House finished the day's legislative business. It also offered numerous amendments that delayed passage of the bill and "denied freeze sponsors a quick and stunning victory" (Waller 1987, 289, quoted in Pitney 1988a, 13). In the next year, the COS targeted the school prayer issue and the Democrats' foreign policy. Many of the speeches infuriated Democratic members. Eventually, as COS member Robert Walker (R-Pa.) read the text of a foreign policy report by the Republican Study Committee as part of his speech, Speaker O'Neill ordered TV cameras to scan the House chamber so that the television audience could see that the chamber was nearly empty. COS members were furious. An exchange on the House floor between O'Neill and Gingrich resulted in a ruling that O'Neill's words were out of order, the first such ruling against a speaker in nearly two hundred years. News reports focused on the O'Neill-Gingrich battle, and both Gingrich and the COS became hot topics (Pitney 1988a, 14–15; see also Pitney 1988b).

The COS was instrumental in bringing to the House floor the 1985 fight over whether to seat Republican Rick McIntyre or Democrat Frank McCloskey, the incumbent, as representative from the Eighth District in Indiana. The vote, as reported in Indiana, shifted back and forth. At the opening of the Congress, McIntyre had been certified as the winner, but the Democrats refused to seat him. The COS pushed the case and worked with Republican leaders to bring it to the floor, "making it a big issue." The COS argued that "if they can do it to McIntyre they can do it to anyone." The House voted to establish a committee of two Democrats and one Republican to decide the winner. The vote tally continued to shift as ballots, including absentee ones, were recounted. Eventually, McCloskey was declared the winner and seated. Republicans were outraged and briefly walked off the House floor. The matter left a legacy of bitterness between the parties.

In the mid-1980s, the COS pushed for Republican congressional party conferences, to be held away from Capitol Hill, to discuss the Republican agenda, congressional elections, and "what face to present to the voters." It worked with leaders and other caucuses to develop agendas for achieving their party program and with outside groups to plot GOP strategy. It joined other coalitions, like the Moral Majority, in calling for the resignation of Secretary of State George Shultz. Weber, then chair of the COS, claimed that Shultz had become "a liability to the president" (*Maine Sunday Telegram*, July 28, 1985). COS members regularly proposed amendments, some successful, to change programs or to strike funding. An amendment to the FY1987 supplemental appropriations measure, proposed by Walker, to cut $300 million from various foreign assistance programs was passed twice, the second time after Democrats demanded a second vote (Conservative Opportunity Society n.d.). In 1988, Gingrich, supported by the COS, filed ethics charges against Speaker Jim Wright (D-Tex.), which led to Wright's resignation from the speakership and the House.

Campaign finance reform, the extension of private sector laws to cover congressional employees, and a strong military and foreign policy have been consistent COS themes. Led by Gingrich, the COS continued to develop programs and strategies and, in 1994, announced its "Contract with America," to win control of the House. Weber said in late 1993 that the probable ascension of Gingrich to the speakership "means the triumph of the Conservative Opportunity Society insurgency [we] both began in the House a decade ago" (Gigot 1993). House Republicans had elected Gingrich Republican whip in 1989. At the start of the 104th Congress in January 1995, he was elected speaker of the House—and the Republican revolution was launched.

Even after the Republicans gained control of the House in 1995, the COS continued to focus on traditional issues. Concerned about budget deficits, members opposed appropriations to revive the SR-71 Blackbird, a supersonic "spy plane," arguing in a letter to the chairs of the Budget and Appropriations Committees that "in today's budget climate, we believe this is too much money to spend on a program of dubious worth" (Morrison 1995). Speaker Gingrich served on the caucus's executive committee, even though at the start of the 104th he also supported actions to constrain the operations of caucuses. The COS statement of purpose captures the caucus's focus and style: "The COS is an activist group of more than 100 Republican Members of Congress who are dedicated to formulating the conservative agenda on the House floor and throughout the United States. COS focuses on action, themes and programs to promote the conservative agenda" (*Congressional Yellow Book 1996*, VI-50). Before 1995, in a Democratic-controlled House, the caucus could be credited with major achievement. It had brought about significant changes in the party's operating style, had been successful in various legislative battles, and had launched an agenda and a strategy for taking Republican control of the House. In 1995 it installed a Republican speaker for the first time in forty years.

Also in the early 1980s, the Senate Rail Caucus was established by senators from states dependent on railroads. One senior staffer described the caucus's purposes as follows.

> A year ago a lot of us found that rail issues began to dominate our agendas because they were so important to our states. We weren't on the Commerce Committee [which has jurisdiction over railroads]. We went through the deregulation bill last year, and it occurred to us that if we were going to handle these issues properly, we had to acquire a deeper knowledge of the intricacies of rail operation. . . . So, we decided that we would form a caucus that would work toward that purpose. . . . We wanted it to be non-partisan, because we're dealing with the needs of an industry and the people who depend upon it. If the caucus were partisan, we'd get into vying over alternate solutions and we'd be distracted from our central purpose, which was increasing everyone's knowledge of the system. Also, the issue is a part of a much larger agenda in [existing] committees. The caucus gives us the ability to focus on one sub-issue.

The caucus stuck to its purpose of informing members about rail issues. It invited representatives of various consumer and provider groups, even bringing adversaries together to discuss questions affecting the senators' states. Individuals with differing views, "to get a good clash," made brief presentations, followed by general discussion. Members and staff from as many as forty-eight Senate offices attended these meetings. The caucus did not take positions on pending legislation. Indeed, members of the caucus often disagreed. But the meetings produced a more educated constituency in the Senate and made it easier to deal with the problems because senators understood more about the perspectives of other senators and their aides.

In the 1990s, after the Republicans gained control of Congress, the Coalition, also known as the Blue Dog Democrats, a group of moderate-to-conservative House Democrats, formed to develop and pursue middle-of-the-road policy proposals, particularly on welfare and budget matters.[2] Its members shared some Republican concerns, such as a balanced budget amendment and the line-item veto, both of which were included in the "Contract with America." Coalition members, more conservative than many of their Democratic colleagues, formed a possible swing group of about two dozen votes, a critical number in a House with only a small GOP majority. The Coalition developed a Democratic alternative to the Republican welfare reform bill. It also developed an alternative budget, which, although defeated on the floor in late 1995, drew support from both Democrats and Republicans and, in the second session of the 104th Congress, became a central factor in ongoing budget debates and negotiations.

Coalition members met with President Clinton and regularly with Democratic leaders. Some held meetings with Republican leaders to explore the possibility of a centrist, bipartisan compromise on the FY1996 budget resolution. Coalition members were experienced and skilled in substantive issues and House procedures as a result of their committee work and activity in other caucuses. Charles Stenholm (D-Tex.), as a leader of the Conservative Democratic Forum, had worked long and hard in previous congresses on a balanced budget amendment. The Coalition occupied centrist positions in the House on several major issues, and both parties sought the group's votes.

After the Republican takeover of Congress in 1995, senators and representatives continued to launch new caucuses. Social conservatives founded the bipartisan Family Caucus to pursue an agenda that included "returning voluntary school prayer, reaffirming parental rights, establishing abstinence-based sex education, enacting tougher laws against obscenity and child pornography, and eliminating federal financing of abortion" (*Congressional Yellow Book 1996*, VI-37). By August 1996, the Family Caucus could call on seventy-five senators and representatives, primarily first- and second-termers.

In March 1996 the Internet Caucus was formed. Senators Patrick Leahy (D-Vt.) and Larry Pressler (R-S.D.) and Representatives Rick White (R-Wash.) and Rick Boucher (D-Va.) launched this caucus as a bipartisan and bicameral group to increase understanding among their colleagues of the new technology, including issues of access and control, and to encourage use of the Internet to reach out to constituents. White told *Roll Call* that "the Internet Caucus exists because most of Congress is lost in cyberspace" (Apr. 22, 1996, 12).

These brief vignettes illustrate the range of caucus interests and activities, suggest factors driving caucus establishment, and demonstrate their organizational variety. They may be partisan or bipartisan, bicameral or unicameral. They provide information to their members, affect agendas, draft bills and amendments, develop legislative strategy, build supporting coalitions, form voting blocs, and even launch congressional leadership careers. They precipitate, and participate in, battles on the floor but affect policy with varying success. The strong Democratic Study Group and Conservative Opportunity Society sought change and innovation and successfully caused dramatic shifts in committee and party power.

This powerful system of informal, policy-interested, congressional caucuses has only recently developed. During the 104th Congress, 161 caucuses were active. Their rapid increase, their shift in focus, and their varied activities raise a number of questions: Why has the caucus system developed? And why now, after nearly two hundred congressional years without caucuses? Who joins caucuses? And why? How are caucuses organized? And what do they do? Are caucuses linked to the formal committee and party systems? And if so, how? Do caucuses differ? Do they assist or inhibit the traditional legislative, representational, and oversight functions of Congress? How powerful are caucuses? Are they likely to continue? What can be learned about the power and influence of the caucus system from the career of Speaker Gingrich, who used a caucus as a springboard to the speakership and then, as speaker, supported congressional actions to make operating a caucus more difficult?

To answer these questions, this book seeks to be comprehensive, covering all caucuses and the caucus system.[3] It is comparative among caucus types, between the two chambers of Congress, and over time. The focus is on factors that lead to caucus formation; their establishment, purposes, goals, and organization; their issue interests and activities; and their interaction with individuals, other congressional subunits, and the existing party and committee systems. This study seeks to assess not only the impact of the caucus system on Congress as an institution and on the individual member but also the power and influence of the caucus system and its individual subunits.

The congressional caucuses in this study are informal member groups, outside of the formal system. Although caucuses are not subunits of the formal structure of either the Senate or the House, each caucus is a boundaried subunit. Each is ongoing, has formally stated goals, and has a stable structure. The formal organization of individual caucuses contrasts with their informal status within each chamber. They are different from organized party groups: the House Democratic Caucus, the Senate Democratic Conference, the Senate and House Republican Conferences. The caucuses that are my focus are voluntary associations of members of Congress that have no recognition in chamber rules or line-item appropriations, even though they seek to influence the policy process. Their influence may be through research, information exchange, agenda setting, policy formulation, and coalition building. They differ from formally constituted committee or party subunits and informal social groups. (The primary purpose of the social clubs of the House, such as the Chowder and Marching Society, the Acorns, and the SOS Society, is sociability, and although policy benefits may result, the major benefit is solidarity. These social groups are not included in this study.)

Quasi-official groups are also excluded. One such group is the Task Force on Missing in Action in Asia, which was chaired by a minority party member of the House, directed by a personal staff aide, and operated as a semiofficial unit of the House Foreign Affairs Subcommittee on Southeast Asia and the Pacific, with its members drawn from that subcommittee. Another is the International Drug Control Caucus, a task force funded by a House line-item appropriation and, therefore, an official House entity. The National Security Caucus is, however, included in the analysis, even though much of the staff work is handled by personnel of the Coalition for Peace through Strength, a noncongressional group, because caucus membership is drawn solely from Congress and congressional leaders of the caucus provide some staff work. Very informal groups that are organized and managed by entities outside of Congress, such as the German Study Group, and ad hoc, unorganized groups of members that arise from time to time are excluded. The few state delegations that have formally organized and that were designated legislative service organizations under House Administration Committee rules in effect between 1979 and 1995 are included in this book's analysis.

This study analyzes the relationship of caucus formation and operation to factors in the wider political environment, their institutionalization and organizational maturation, their operations and activities, and their linkages and interaction with other actors in the policy-making process.

As a corollary to understanding the development, operation, and effect of the caucus system, the analysis should also contribute to understanding how Congress changes and adapts and how the caucus system reflects and manages the tension between individual and collective goals. A study of the congressional caucus system is particularly timely as Congress seeks to come to terms with the consequences of a decade of institutional reform and the changes of the postreform era.

1/ CONGRESSIONAL CAUCUSES AND CONGRESSIONAL CHANGE

A powerful caucus system now operates in the U.S. Congress. This informal system has links to, but operates outside of, the two most prominent institutional features of Congress's formal structure: the committee and party systems. Congressional caucuses—voluntary, organized associations of members of Congress, without recognition in chamber rules or line-item appropriations and that seek to play a role in the policy process—are a unique development of the late-twentieth-century Congress. Various ad hoc and temporary groups of members have been active since the early years of the Republic. Some continuity exists between the earlier prototypes and the caucuses of today, but the differences are more striking. Contemporary caucuses are organized, stable, and continuous. They often work on more than one issue or piece of legislation, and some have quite broad ranges of continuing interests. Their links to the committee and party systems, too, are often ongoing and stable.

How can the emergence of caucuses as significant entities in the late-twentieth-century Congress be explained? Does the caucus system fit into current theories about the organization of Congress? Or can current theories be extended to explain caucuses?

According to distributive theories, legislators seek benefits for their constituents to get re-elected, and legislative organization is designed to ensure stability in capturing "gains from trade" (see, e.g., Mayhew 1974; Shepsle 1986; Shepsle and Weingast 1987a, 1987b). Stability is enforced by rules, such as closed rules for floor consideration of committee bills, which give parliamentary rights to committees. These rules help committee members—who hold intense and sometimes extreme preferences—achieve their preferred policy outcomes. In this perspective, committee to committee logrolls occur: Committee A brings legislation to the floor under a closed rule; Committee B does not fight the rule and defers to the preferences of Committee A embodied in the bill because Committee A will behave similarly on Committee B's legislation.

However, this perspective as currently developed does not seem to account for the caucus system. Caucuses are not part of committee or parliamentary rights systems, and although they seek to influence voting outcomes, they cannot be relied on to achieve policies compatible with committee preferences.

From the perspective of informational theory (e.g., Krehbiel 1991; Gilligan and Krehbiel 1988, 1989, 1990), committees develop to provide information and expertise. Committees capture "gains from specialization" (Krehbiel 1991, 5) and are granted parliamentary rights because committee members share their information and use their policy expertise to produce policies that are preferred by the majority of chamber members. It is an efficient system, linking individual expertise and committee specialization to collective goals. But this does not seem to account for the caucus system, either. Committees may satisfy the informational needs and policy interests of members, but many caucuses were established specifically to gather and disseminate to caucus members reliable information not obtainable elsewhere and to pursue policy interests not being handled by the committee system.

Nor do party theories, at least as currently developed, account for the caucus system. More traditional macro approaches to studying parties focus on electoral-legislative linkages and normative explanations for congressional change (see Cooper and Wilson 1994). Electoral-legislative linkage research includes macro change (realignment theories) and constituency or presidential influence on members' voting (e.g., Miller and Stokes 1963; Hurley and Wilson 1989; Bond and Fleischer 1990; and see Asher 1983). Other party perspective studies analyze party voting in Congress or the context and operations of congressional party leaders (e.g., Cooper and Brady 1981; Sinclair 1983; Smith 1989). The more traditional studies may offer insights into congressional operations and change, but these do not account for caucuses.

The rational choice party approach is, like distributive theories, based on individuals' goals, but like the informational viewpoint, there is linkage between individuals and the collectivity; in the party perspective, the collectivity is the party (Cox and McCubbins 1993; also see Aldrich 1989; Rohde 1991). The actions of parties in Congress can improve the re-election chances of all party members. The "collective character" of a party, defined as its public record (actions, beliefs, and outcomes), is a major factor in how voters judge candidates (Cox and McCubbins 1993, 108, 110). Party members within Congress will organize and choose leaders because there are advancement rewards within Congress for being of the majority party and for serving as a leader. Party members, coordinated and overseen by their leaders, support the party position even on legislation of general benefit to build a record that voters will endorse and that will increase party members' re-election chances. Parties act as legislative cartels, affecting the committee system and setting the agenda of floor debate. Party theories, then, could allow for caucuses. Most proponents of these theories argue that parties exist as important organizational elements within Congress, but they do not claim that parties entirely explain congressional organization. However, party perspectives ignore caucuses. Many caucuses are established precisely because the party system has failed in various ways, including addressing issues important to members and providing needed legislative information or coordination regarding legislation.

Although these theories do not account for the caucus system, they do explain some aspects of the system. Some caucuses do act like distributive committees and achieve benefits for regions or industries they represent. Some caucuses act much as informative committees do: developing expertise, gathering information, and drafting policies that are later supported by a chamber majority. And some caucuses, made up of members of only one party, work within that party to influence its leaders or to develop legislation that can reduce party divisiveness.

A fuller explanation of the caucus system, however, must combine member goals, contextual (exogenous) factors, and the organizational characteristics and structure of Congress. Their interaction precipitated the development of the contemporary caucus system. Congressional characteristics facilitated the formation of caucuses as an adaptive response to contextual and goal demand. The internal congressional structure was a given at the start of the caucus era, but it was not necessarily stable; the structure changed later, in part due to caucus activity. Member goals or the exogenous context may both change; one of these *must* change to elicit a congressional response.

Changes in the external environment resulted in, among other things, a significant increase in the demands on Congress. Because of Congress's permeability, articulation of demand occurred at all organizational levels and at all stages of the legislative process. Cooper and Collie (1981) cite an increase in demand stress in Congress's environment; among the indicators are more national mail, more broadcast stations, more research and development outlays, and more freight and passenger miles (ibid., tables 3, 4). Explosive changes occurred in the late 1960s to 1979. Walker (1991) cites the rapid growth of the interest group system in this same period, which "led to a dramatic increase in the range of interests being represented and the number of issues being debated in Washington" (39–40; see also Berry 1989; Schlozman and Tierney 1986). Demand stress increased throughout the caucus era but particularly in the decade before the dramatic growth of the caucus system. Demands led to structural stress (Haas and Drabek 1973; Cooper 1977, 1981; and see Collie 1994). Role expectation increased, and output capacity was strained (see Cooper and Collie 1981). Faced with these stresses, Congress adopted procedures such as multiple referral and increased the number of subcommittees and staff. In spite of these changes, as long as it used traditional structures and procedures, Congress had difficulty processing the growing number and complexity of demands. As deficiencies in the formal system continued, it became more difficult for members to achieve their goals. The characteristics of Congress as an organization were conducive to the establishment of caucuses as an adaptive response.

Caucuses are a logical response to this juxtaposition of external and internal factors and members' goals. During the 1970s reform era, internal changes resulted in slack resources (such as staff) controlled by individual members and increasing structural decentralization. When party leaders failed to address sufficiently issue or policy coordination concerns of members, members had the reason and the opportunity to form caucuses. Organizational attributes of collegiality, structural fluidity, low integrative authority, and permeability and ease of access facilitated caucus formation.[1]

In the external environment, complex issues cut across traditional party and committee jurisdiction divisions, and constituent demands and expectations of congressional action increased. Caucuses were first established, and now persist, because they help achieve the goals of both individual members and the institution. They assist members in achieving career and policy goals, and in carrying out their legislative, oversight, and representational duties. Caucuses also support Congress in its institutional functions and responsibilities, including institutional maintenance.

THE EXTERNAL CONTEXT

Changes in the polity during the 1970s and 1980s affected Congress's workload and the individual member's job. An increasing number of complex, crosscutting, and interconnected issues began to occupy the congressional agenda. Trade, for example, has domestic as well as international impact. Economic questions such as industrial productivity affect diverse groups—labor, management, and consumers. Subjects such as the environment raise both health and economic concerns. To consider these, members need additional, more detailed, and complicated information. Such issues are not easily handled through traditional party mechanisms. Nor, in many cases, are committees and subcommittees equipped to deal comprehensively with them; they either fall into jurisdictional cracks or are spread among committees and subcommittees. It may be impractical or impossible to mobilize a coalition. In such cases, oversight is also more difficult.

Although some procedures were changed, and the House, for example, began to use multiple referrals for complex bills, many members found that committee jurisdictions, the requirements of fixed agendas on committee calendars, and traditional adversarial procedures stood in the way of handling these changed issues. Party leaders were not prepared to change further procedures or structure to meet these new demands.

In recent years, constituent demands for policy responsiveness, representation, and accountability have also increased. At the same time, the congressional reforms of the 1970s created the expectation that a member, even a junior one, ought to be effective. Members also represent increasingly heterogeneous constituencies, due to apportionment changes, population mobility, and economic differentiation. Thus policy and symbolic expectations within a constituency have expanded. Similarly, expectations regarding Congress's role as an institution grew. It is expected to achieve policy agreements on increasingly complex issues and to oversee the efficiency and effectiveness of government programs more completely. Voters perceived that both members of Congress and the institution itself could not effectively meet these challenges.

THE GOALS OF CONGRESSIONAL MEMBERS

Congressional members pursue goals of re-election, policy, and power in the institution (Fenno 1973). Although a change in members' goals is not necessary to explain caucus formation, it may have contributed to the development of the caucus system. The little research that has been done suggests that the balance among goals has shifted and that, since the mid-1970s, members have been more concerned with policy issues. Loomis (1988) describes the election of 1974, the year of Watergate, as a watershed election and the members of the class of 1974 who entered the House of Representatives in January 1975 as independent policy entrepreneurs. They were different from more senior members of Congress because they were issue-oriented politicians who "helped to alter radically the role of the rank-and-file legislator" (9). Later cohorts emulated them. By the mid-1980s, most members of the class who were still in the House operated as "independent, policy-activist" subcommittee chairs (10).

Freshman members of the 103d (1993–94) and 104th (1995–96) Congresses showed a similar character. Democrats and Republicans of the 103d began their terms with specific reform agendas and immediately sought to craft legislation to bring about change. The 104th freshman Republicans were a cohesive group with a conservative agenda. They even became a problem for Speaker Gingrich when they refused to support bills with provisions that, in their view, diluted their agenda. On these and other issues they operated as independent policy entrepreneurs. Members of Congress now are more individualistic and less likely to "go along to get along" (Sinclair 1995). They are more likely to emphasize policy issues. If the formal congressional system does not produce policies in accord with members' preferences, the caucus system becomes a logical consequence. Members formed caucuses and developed the informal caucus system when deficiencies in the formal committee and party systems made achievement of individual goals difficult. Caucuses offer members an opportunity to pursue policy and other goals and to do so earlier in a congressional career than is possible within the formal system.

CONGRESSIONAL CHARACTERISTICS AND STRUCTURE

Like any complex, formal organization, Congress has organizational goals and outputs, and its organizational structure is shaped by the political and societal environment within which it operates. Congress's responsibilities of policy making and representation and its organizational attributes of collegiality, structural decentralization, and openness are important in facilitating caucus establishment and activity.

Congress is an organization of equals whose collegial decision making is based on the democratic values of the polity (Cooper 1977, 147). Each member has one vote, and each is accountable to constituents who control the senator's or representative's membership in the institution. The collegiality of the institution is manifested in a general absence of hierarchy and integrative mechanisms, although the accumulation of greater authority with seniority and the formal election of congressional leaders do modify these egalitarian characteristics somewhat. Decision making at each stage of the legislative process is collegial. Participants at one level of decision making also are participants at the next level, and unlike the typical bureaucratic organization, in which the number of decision makers decreases as an issue moves up the hierarchy, in Congress the number of formal decision makers increases as an issue moves through the legislative process. This requires continued negotiation and compromise and, in the absence of rigid decision procedures such as closed rules, offers individuals and groups opportunities to influence outcomes.

The committee system, which permits the division and specialization of labor, not only enables members to handle the congressional workload more efficiently but also brings about structural decentralization. This, too, creates opportunities for individuals and groups to influence outcomes. Integration—that is, the coordination of decision processes and subunit output—is necessary. Party leaders are instrumental in this integration, but their input must not conflict with the norms of collegiality.

Caucuses are thus a logical response to the interaction of external change, members' goals, and the internal environment of Congress; "the composition that results from interactions and transactions of participants," that is, of either persons or groups (Eulau and McCluggage 1981, 17), is more fluid than that of many organizations. Organizational fluidity is increased by Congress's high level of collegiality. There are few incentives or sanctions available through an authority system. Congressional norms favor inclusion in group processes, a tendency that has been strengthened in recent years. Both Senate and House leaders have increasingly practiced "leadership by inclusion" (the phrase is from Sinclair 1983; see also Sinclair 1995). Members of Congress hold multiple committee and subcommittee assignments, and in both chambers—but especially in the Senate—there are networks of overlapping memberships that, to some extent, integrate jurisdictions, coordinate complex issues, and cut across party and ideological lines. Members can fulfill different personal goals by serving on different types of committees.

In a more hierarchical organization, further differentiation of existing subunits of the formal structure might occur in response to external or internal changes. For Congress, this is not so obvious a response. It is difficult to change the formal system, which is not immediately responsive to context or goal shifts. Changes in the formal structure require the approval of the Democrats or Republicans in each chamber or, for some committee changes, a vote of the full Senate or House. Establishing informal subunits is a more viable option.

Congress is also a typical innovative organization: lines of authority are not rigid, there is a low level of coordination and a high level of vertical communication (e.g., member of Congress to staff aide), employees are highly committed and have a high degree of discretion, interpersonal relationships are highly affective, and productivity is high. Such organizations, especially those like Congress, whose members control individual offices and office resources, are most likely to develop new structural forms to handle increased demand and organizational stress (G. Bell 1967). Congress, as a representative institution, is also uniquely permeable. It is organized for ease of access by those in the general polity. Multiple subunits and procedures such as hearings assist permeability on policy concerns. Representatives and senators as individuals are attuned to the concerns of constituents, and elections serve as referenda.

These organizational attributes allow Congress to respond to new issues as they enter the political arena and to develop new structures as necessary. They support, and even encourage, the establishment of caucuses.

WHY CAUCUSES NOW?

Why has the caucus system developed in the contemporary Congress, rather than in earlier eras? Previous responses to deficiencies in the organization of Congress had resulted in new organizational forms, such as the standing committees of the nineteenth century and the articulated party system, with more party leaders and increasingly complex, specialized, and differentiated party groups, of the early twentieth century. Both these systems arose out of deficiencies in the structure of Congress; each was an adaptive response to external demands that members believed were not being properly addressed by the existing structure. Both systems developed within the parameters set by the characteristics of a democratic legislature: a collegial, nonhierarchical institution whose members were accountable to constituents, rather than to institutional leaders (see, e.g., Cooper 1981).

The committee system divided and processed the workload of Congress and developed specialization and expertise (Cooper 1970; Krehbiel 1991). Committees became the congressional subunits that crafted legislation and operated as policy innovators. The party system coordinated the work of the Congress, even if at different times it gave varying attention to monitoring the progress and the substance of legislation. Since about the 1970s in the House, political party operations have gradually become more inclusive through the use of leadership task forces and a larger whip system (Sinclair 1995). Because of Senate rules, Senate leadership has been typically more inclusive and participatory.

Over time, members of Congress have sought to respond to the demands of the polity within a legislature that balances the need for institutional coordination and centralization with the decentralizing pressures of representation and accountability to constituents. Members pursue their goals within this context (see, e.g., Dodd 1977, 1981, 1986a, 1986b, 1993, 1995).

By the late twentieth century, Congress operated in a vastly changed environment: increased issue complexity, new systems of political participation, increased constituent demands, technological change, and an internal structure that was dynamic and increasingly complex. In this period, as the systems in place failed members, the caucus system emerged. Members sought new mechanisms to achieve their goals. They were willing to give up some autonomy to party leaders to overcome collective action and collective choice problems (see, e.g., Rohde 1991; Cox and McCubbins 1993), and they voted to reduce committee system fragmentation but were not willing to rely on these systems entirely.

Thus, a search by members for new organizations in the late twentieth century to advance careers and policy interests led to the formation of caucuses. Given the difficulty of reforming the formal system and overcoming perceived formal system deficiencies, major changes were required elsewhere. Caucuses are easy to establish and operate and do not require formal system approval. They are vehicles for information, education, and the development of new policy options, and they can coordinate across party lines and bring adversarial groups together. For these reasons, caucuses have become increasingly important to members' personal careers and to policy making. Entrepreneurs like Newt Gingrich have used caucuses to develop expertise, influence policy, gain visibility within the House, and launch leadership careers in the formal congressional system. The prevalence of caucuses, their importance in policy making, and their contributions to members' careers suggest that they may be difficult to regulate and control and that they likely will persist even in a period of congressional centralization. The caucus system supplements—but also competes with—existing party and committee systems. It works because it serves members' interests.

2/ An Overview of Caucuses

Caucuses of the caucus system vary in membership, range of interests, issue focus, activities, and strategies. Yet they also share characteristics.

To give some examples, the hundred-member Conservative Opportunity Society developed confrontational politics into an art form. It was instrumental in bringing about Republican control of the House in 1995 and propelled Newt Gingrich into the speakership. The Coalition (the Blue Dogs), with twenty-two members, developed budget and welfare bills during the 104th Congress that became Democratic alternatives to committee-approved bills. The Coalition participated in constructing compromises acceptable to a majority of House members on major legislation and was wooed by both parties for their votes. The eighteen-member Hispanic Caucus was an important player on immigration and welfare legislation approved by the 104th Congress, especially when the caucus opposed provisions denying legal immigrants key welfare benefits. The Textile Caucus achieved passage of the Textile Trade Bill of 1985. Caucus chair Ed Jenkins (D-Ga.), also a member of the Ways and Means Committee's Subcommittee on Trade handling the legislation, introduced the bill.[1] The Military Reform Caucus sought to change the way Congress and the Pentagon approached weapons funding. The Senate Rail Caucus did not develop or advocate legislation but served as an information and issue-education mechanism. The Congressional Friends of Human Rights Monitors also focused on coordinating information and protesting human rights abuses rather than on initiating legislation.

Caucuses, whether in Senate or House, intersect the formal committee and party systems and are organized and situated to pursue policy purposes. As caucus members, senators and representatives seek to affect policy outcomes: they take part in activities that link to the formal committee and party systems, interact with other policy makers, and design activities to overcome perceived deficiencies in the formal system. Caucus members expect caucuses to be active at all stages of the policy process and to work both within and outside Congress.

During the 104th Congress (1995–96) there were 161 caucuses (Richardson 1996; *Congressional Yellow Book 1996*; author's data).[2] Twenty-five were inactive, 43 were newly established. (Ten that were active during the 103d Congress had disbanded.) Ninety one (57%) of the 104th Congress's 161 caucuses operated in the House only; these caucuses were often titled the "House Caucus on . . ." or the "Congressional . . . Caucus," to distinguish them from their Senate counterparts. Twenty-six (16%) were Senate caucuses. Often, parallel caucuses were established in both chambers: the House and Senate Steel Caucuses, for example, or the Senate and House Rural Health Caucuses. Forty-four caucuses (27%) were bicameral.

CAUCUS ORGANIZATION

During the 100th Congress, caucuses ranged from 3 members (the Territorial Caucus) to 325 members (the Environmental and Energy Study Conference).[3] Five caucuses—the Arts Caucus, the Competitiveness Caucus, the Democratic Study Group, the Coalition for Peace through Strength (renamed the National Security Caucus in 1988), and the Northeast-Midwest Congressional Coalition—each had 198 or more members. Eight caucuses had about 150 members. The larger caucuses were either House or bicameral ones. The smaller caucuses often included class clubs in the House, some regional caucuses (e.g., Border, Metropolitan Area), state delegations, and some industry-focused groups (e.g., Mushroom, Senate Wine).[4] In conjunction with caucus age, size determined to a degree its structure and the extent of its institutionalization.

The Democratic Study Group, one of the largest caucuses and the oldest in the contemporary era, had a well-differentiated leadership structure. It was one of the first caucuses to apply for legislative service organization status, which between 1979 and 1995 permitted a House or bicameral caucus to establish a caucus account for staff and office expenses and to be assigned office space in House buildings. The Arms Control and Foreign Policy Caucus, active until 1995, was similar. A large, long-established caucus, it developed a leadership structure to give representation to both chambers and both parties, and a task force structure, so that the bipartisan group could organize to work on policy issues with partisan leaders of the House and Senate. Smaller caucuses are less likely to have a well-differentiated leadership structure or to maintain ongoing research and information activities over a number of Congresses. Structural arrangements may include a chair with a number of officers, written bylaws or constitutions, executive or steering committees, ad hoc task forces, permanent committees, whip systems, and outside advisory bodies.

All caucuses have leaders. Most of those surveyed elected a single chair, but 17 percent had co-chairs, and 5 percent reported three or four chairs sharing leadership responsibilities. Co-chairs, typical of bicameral and bipartisan caucuses, are meant to give equal leadership representation to the two chambers or the two parties. Some caucuses (like joint committees) alternate chairs between the parties or the chambers, from one Congress to the next. Slightly more than half the caucuses surveyed also elected one or more vice-chairs; three caucuses reported six vice-chairs, and one reported seven. About 15 percent of the caucuses also reported other officers, such as a secretary or a treasurer. Larger caucuses with diverse memberships often establish a structure to give leadership representation to diverse groups—regional, ideological, or other. One-fifth of the caucuses—among them the DSG, the Arms Control and Foreign Policy Caucus, the Clearinghouse on the Future, and the Environmental and Energy Study Conference—reported an executive committee or a steering committee, which had varying responsibilities. House caucus leadership structures reflect the relative scarcity of leadership positions within the formal system; they give members additional leadership opportunities, albeit outside the formal system. No Senate caucuses have steering or executive committees, reflecting both the greater egalitarianism of the Senate and smaller caucus size.

Caucuses foster efficiency and specialization in the use of resources. Members pool resources by sharing staff aides to work on caucus matters or by designating aides to handle caucus issues. Aides often specialize in certain areas of caucus interest. Staffing reflects the informal nature of caucuses: more than two-thirds (70.7%) operated with only one staff member; another 11 percent operated with two staffers. These caucus aides were usually based in the offices of the group's leader and served as caucus coordinators. Staff aides in the office of each group member served as caucus contacts. Chief staff aides shifted when caucus officers changed.

However, 7 percent of the caucuses, the larger and longer-established ones, had from six to twenty-one staff members during the 100th Congress. Their staff structure was differentiated, with aides specializing in their duties and a chief of staff or executive director supervising the work of other aides. These staff members did not shift when caucus officers changed. The larger staffs reflect the caucuses' designation between 1979 and 1995 as legislative service organizations, which enabled them to acquire separate office space and central staff. After the rules changes at the start of the 104th Congress, all caucuses used the model of most 100th Congress caucuses, with the caucus chair's aide serving as caucus staff coordinator and caucus specialists or designated staff contacts being drawn from other members' offices.

Most caucuses operate from members' offices: three-quarters (74.4%) reported that caucus staff were based in members' personal offices. Eighteen caucuses (20%), however, had separate caucus offices, housed mostly in separate congressional space.[5] Three caucuses reported staff members based in committee offices: committee or subcommittee chairs served as caucus chairs, and committee staff handled caucus work. The caucus and the committee dealt with similar issues.[6]

PURPOSES AND ACTIVITIES

All caucuses exist to affect policy. Ninety-five percent reported that influencing policy was their primary purpose. Twelve percent sought to do so through information exchange. Others focused on the policy agenda, served as policy advocates for a region or an issue, or coordinated diverse ideological or geographical interests. One caucus had as its primary purpose the representation of constituency interests; another, re-election assistance. Two others, both class clubs, aimed primarily at the socialization and orientation of new members. Subsidiary purposes might include developing member expertise, seeking changes in party organization or operation, and serving as liaison with external groups or between members. Regardless of their principal purpose, caucuses serve as forums for the exchange of information on pending issues, legislation, and legislative procedure among members and with outside groups, executive branch officials, and on occasion, with the president (see table 2-1).

The data support a picture of caucuses as groups with strong policy interests and access to policy makers. House and bicameral caucuses were the most active and the most likely to meet with outside speakers and to hold meetings with congressional leaders and executive officials. House caucuses were also the most likely to hold meetings to set caucus positions and strategy. This may reflect the information exchange emphasis of many Senate and some bicameral caucuses. Twenty percent of the caucuses reported frequent meetings; most met occasionally (defined as once a month or less); few caucuses almost never met as a group. A majority of caucuses

Table 2-1.   Features of Caucus Meetings and Activities, by Chamber, 100th Congress (in percentages)

Feature	House (N=34)	Bicameral (N=30)	Senate (N=18)	All (N=82)
Meetings[a]				
With a speaker	52.9	43.3	16.7	41.5
	(18)	(13)	(3)	(34)
To exchange information	64.7	53.3	50.0	57.3
	(22)	(16)	(9)	(47)
With party leaders	32.4	16.7	0	19.5
	(11)	(5)		(16)
With committee leaders	38.2	13.3	5.6	22.0
	(13)	(4)	(1)	(18)
With White House officials	23.5	13.3	11.1	17.1
	(8)	(4)	(2)	(14)
With other executive officials	44.1	36.7	22.2	36.6
	(15)	(11)	(4)	(30)
With outside groups	55.9	33.3	27.8	41.5
	(19)	(10)	(5)	(34)
To set caucus position	47.1	26.7	27.8	35.4
	(16)	(8)	(5)	(29)
To set caucus strategy	47.1	30.0	22.2	35.4
	(16)	(9)	(4)	(29)
To set caucus committee strategy	47.1	20.0	16.7	30.5
	(16)	(6)	(3)	(25)
To set caucus floor strategy	41.2	16.7	16.7	26.8
	(14)	(5)	(3)	(22)
Preparing information				
Oral report	76.5	70.0	44.4	67.1
	(26)	(21)	(8)	(55)
Written report	76.5	56.7	50.0	63.4
	(26)	(17)	(9)	(52)
Preparing information, re committee				
Oral report	73.5	60.0	22.2	57.3
	(25)	(18)	(4)	(47)
Written report	61.8	36.7	16.7	42.7
	(21)	(11)	(3)	(35)
Preparing information, re floor				
Oral report	64.7	56.7	44.4	57.3
	(22)	(17)	(8)	(47)
Written report	55.9	43.3	27.8	45.1
	(19)	(13)	(5)	(37)

(Continued)

Table 2-1. *(Continued)*

Feature	House (N=34)	Bicameral (N=30)	Senate (N=18)	All (N=82)
Informal meetings[b]				
With cabinet officials	38.2	43.3	38.9	40.2
	(13)	(13)	(7)	(33)
With subcabinet officials	35.3	46.7	33.3	39.0
	(12)	(14)	(6)	(32)
With White House officials	29.4	30.0	38.9	31.7
	(10)	(7)	(9)	(26)
With president	14.7	20.0	16.7	17.1
	(5)	(6)	(3)	(14)
With bureaucrats	23.5	33.3	33.3	29.3
	(8)	(10)	(6)	(24)
Holding caucus hearings	11.8	23.3	11.1	15.9
	(4)	(7)	(2)	(13)
Testifying at hearings	35.3	26.7	16.7	28.0
	(12)	(8)	(3)	(23)
Testifying at House hearings	38.2	23.3		24.4
	(13)	(7)		(20)
Testifying at Senate hearings	5.9	20.0	27.8	15.9
	(2)	(6)	(5)	(13)
Drafting bills	41.2	30.0	16.7	31.7
	(14)	(9)	(3)	(26)
Drafting amendments	20.6	16.7	16.7	18.3
	(7)	(5)	(3)	(15)
Legislative work[b]				
With committee	26.5	23.3	11.1	22.0
	(9)	(7)	(2)	(18)
With committee chair	20.6	16.7	11.1	17.1
	(7)	(5)	(2)	(14)
With committee ranking minority member	14.7	10.0	16.7	13.4
	(5)	(3)	(3)	(11)
With subcommittee	29.4	26.7	11.1	24.4
	(10)	(8)	(2)	(20)
With subcommittee chair	26.5	20.0	11.1	20.7
	(9)	(6)	(2)	(17)
With subcommittee ranking minority member	17.6	13.3	16.7	15.9
	(6)	(4)	(3)	(13)

Note: Number of caucuses is given in parentheses.

[a]The question was, What was the meeting format: speaker; member information exchange; meeting with congressional party leaders; meeting with committee leaders; meet with White House officials; meet with other executive branch officials; meet with outside groups; decide caucus issue position; develop caucus issue strategy (in committee, on floor, other); other.

[b]This variable reports legislative work and meetings with officials and others on specific proposed actions or pending legislation.

met to exchange information. Nearly as many met on occasion with outside speakers or with outside groups. Some, however, made it a practice
never to meet with outside groups, preferring to keep the discussion
among colleagues or at least within the government. More than a third of
the caucuses met with executive branch officials. About a fifth of them met
with party or committee leaders to discuss caucus concerns. More than
half met to exchange information on issues of concern or pending legislation. Slightly more than a third met to establish caucus positions on issues or to determine caucus strategy in committee or before floor votes.

Caucus activities are designed to accomplish members' goals and caucus purposes. Through information and coordination activities, members
seek to overcome perceived deficiencies in the formal system. Institutional
goals—maintenance, legislative, and representational—are also served.
Some caucuses—the class clubs, for example—aid socialization; members
derive solidary benefits, such as tapping into friendship networks. Many
caucuses supply a leadership training function—for individual members
and for the institution as a whole. A number of caucuses are used by congressional leaders and executive officials to gain access to a group of members, to exchange information, and to build coalitions.

Most caucuses serve as a forum for information on issues or on pending legislation: 78 percent coordinate and exchange information, prepar-
ing research reports on policy issues or information on committee activities or pending floor legislation. Meetings held to establish positions on
issues or to determine caucus strategy serve also to coordinate a group of
members who are not all on the same committee and, at times, to aid work
on legislative proposals that fall under the jurisdiction of several committees. Caucuses also work with the executive branch on pending policy
matters of concern to caucus members and with groups outside Congress,
usually to obtain or exchange information and less frequently to map legislative strategy, to build coalitions on the floor or in committee, or to
draft legislation. Caucuses often work with each other, usually on committee and floor matters.

Caucuses are active at all stages of the legislative process. Although
there are no procedures for working within the formal structure, one caucus held hearings in conjunction with a House subcommittee. Caucuses
have testified at both House and Senate hearings, have helped draft legislation, and have worked with committee and party leaders on legislative
matters. Caucuses more frequently have sought to influence policy outcomes at critical stages by drafting bills or amendments than through tes-

Table 2-2.   Caucus Issues, 100th Congress

Issue	% of Caucuses Responding (N = 66)	
Social benefits	14	(9)
Resource and environment	8	(5)
Business, labor, economy (includes trade)	38	(25)
Defense and foreign policy	26	(17)
Functioning of government	4	(3)
Arts	3	(2)
Appropriations	6	(4)
Civil rights	2	(1)

Note: Number of caucuses responding is given in parentheses.

timony at hearings. Usually they have been active at the committee stage, although some report offering floor amendments. Caucuses operate primarily within Congress on potential or actual legislative issues (a very few are active at all stages of the policy process, including implementation, and some report working primarily with the executive branch).

Although their interests cover all policy areas, caucuses primarily respond to important national issues and constituency concerns. During the 100th Congress, caucuses most frequently acted on economic issues, especially trade. About a quarter of them focused on defense and foreign policy issues. Defense and foreign affairs, including international trade and immigration, dominated caucus-executive branch interaction: 20 percent worked on trade issues, 17 percent on national defense, and 13 percent on immigration, international human rights, and terrorism (see table 2-2). These figures may simply reflect the salient legislative issues of the 100th Congress—the immigration bill was passed and trade legislation was pending—or they may reflect the working style of caucuses concerned with those issues.

Decision makers and others in the policy process perceive caucuses as policy actors. Caucuses give congressional and executive leaders access to groups of members who can be useful for information and important to legislative strategy and coalition building. Twenty-three percent of the caucuses reported being contacted by party leaders for information, strategy support, or votes; 20 percent had been contacted by issue leaders in Congress; and 17 percent reported being contacted by the White House for information about an issue, strategy support, or votes. Bicameral caucuses, which are often very active in the House, are nearly as active as House caucuses on many of these measures. Much of the time, these groups act like House-only caucuses. But note that when activity in the Senate is measured (e.g., at Senate hearings), bicameral caucuses act more like Senate caucuses than like House caucuses.

HOUSE-SENATE DIFFERENCES

House and Senate caucuses are similar but not the same. Senate caucuses reflect the Senate's greater egalitarianism and individualism. The Senate has less need for coordinative mechanisms outside the party leadership and less demand for leadership opportunities outside the formal structure. Senators average more committee and subcommittee assignments than representatives, and most senators serve on at least one of the most important committees. Many chair or serve as ranking minority member of a committee or subcommittee. Many hold overlapping assignments—the Armed Services Committee and the Department of Defense Appropriations subcommittee, for example—that enable a senator to follow an issue from authorization through appropriation to oversight of implementation. For senators, the symbolic benefits of caucus leadership or membership are less than for their House counterparts, and the demands of their committees are more.

Caucuses developed later in the Senate than in the House. Three House, but no Senate, caucuses were established between 1959 and 1968. During the next five years (1969–74), the first three Senate and another seven House caucuses were founded. The pattern of caucus development in the Senate is similar to the House, however. The first Senate caucuses, focusing on a wide range of issues, were started by groups of members within a party who shared a similar ideology. These were followed by bipartisan caucuses, often with a narrower issue focus. There are fewer Senate caucuses (eighteen during the 100th Congress), and they are noticeably smaller.[7] They are generally less structured. One or two senators take the lead in calling meetings or in coordinating activity on an issue. There are not highly differentiated leadership structures or steering and executive committees. None has a large staff; all are located in senators' personal offices. One Senate caucus, the (Republican) Steering Committee, had separate office space in a Senate annex for several Congresses (it no longer does).

Senate caucus activities are less formal, and the caucuses are somewhat less active. House counterparts of Senate caucuses—Steel, Mining, Arts, and Human Rights, for example, in the 100th Congress—are typically more active at all stages of the legislative process, perhaps reflecting different coalition-building needs and styles. Senate caucuses also exhibit more organizational fluidity: caucus activity in the Senate varies from Congress to Congress more than in the House, and Senate caucuses more frequently die.

The relative informality of the Senate is reflected in the fact that Senate caucuses hold somewhat fewer formal meetings (17% for Senate caucuses, 29% for House caucuses). Like their House counterparts, a majority of Senate caucuses meet for discussion or to report on pending legislative matters or on policy issues. Senate caucuses have fewer formal meetings with outside speakers or groups and with executive branch officials, and they have none with party leaders (see table 2-1). Senate caucuses also hold meetings to establish caucus positions or strategy less frequently than their House counterparts: 28 percent of Senate caucuses, but 47 percent of those in the House, report meeting to establish a caucus position on issues. This does not mean, however, that Senate caucuses do not work on policy issues. Although they have fewer formal meetings, Senate caucuses report working with congressional, executive, and outside groups, often more extensively and at a higher level than House caucuses. Seventy-two percent, for example, talk with party leaders, compared with less than 47% in the House. The differences between the House and Senate are evident also in interaction with other policy actors: a higher percentage of Senate than House caucuses, for example, are contacted frequently by the executive branch and the White House.

These differences reflect the chambers' characteristics. In the House, with more members and where seniority means more, most legislative work by caucuses is done through the formal committee and party systems. More House caucuses provide information on research or on pending legislative issues for their members. And House caucuses are more likely to develop legislation and to work as caucuses on pending committee or floor matters.

A Typology

Although all caucuses have policy goals and seek to affect policy through similar techniques (research and information, influencing governmental agendas, developing legislation, or building coalitions), caucuses also differ. Although current theories of congressional organization do not account for the development of the caucus system, they can help explain parts of it.

Some caucuses (thirty-five during the 104th Congress) focus on issues of interest to a particular industry: beef, steel, biotechnology, or textiles, for example. These caucuses often seek industry-specific remedies from the executive branch or through legislation. Their concerns and actions are analogous to those of distributive committees, although they do not, of course, have formal authority. Their members hold intense preferences on issues of concern to the caucus. Industry-focused caucuses offer an alternative means of pursuing these interests. This is particularly important for junior members and for those who do not serve on the relevant committees. By joining an industry-focused caucus, they can indicate to their constituents that they care. They can also take substantive action by seeking policies to assist the industry. Caucus membership also provides election and policy benefits, and group support can help a committee member leverage power.

The same argument can be made about caucuses that focus on regional issues and, to a lesser degree, about those that work on state/district issues. Although the questions with which these caucuses are concerned are broader than those of industry-focused caucuses, their actions have often been similar. They have sought and achieved programmatic formulas and legislative provisions to assist the region, sometimes at the expense of other regions. State/district-focused caucuses also seek remedies for problems of those constituencies.

Caucuses that represent the interests of women, blacks, Hispanics, or Vietnam veterans have broad concerns that fall under the jurisdiction of numerous committees, so the distributive perspective fits less well as an explanation for their development. Some caucus concerns—civil rights, for example—have wide support and would appear to be general benefit issues, rather than the particular benefit issues of distributive groups.

Partisan theories may explain to some degree caucuses that are formed by intraparty groups. If electing Democrats, for example, helps all the Democrats in the House, members of party-based caucuses will seek to better their re-election chances, thus helping to bring about (or to continue) their party's control of the House. Appropriate committee assignments and legislation that caucus members can vote for (both activities that party caucuses undertake) help re-election bids. Because members of party caucuses seek to work within their party, they are operating as would be expected in an era of conditional party leadership (Rohde 1991).

For caucuses that are not explained by either of these theories, the informative theory may assist in understanding their actions. Caucuses such as the Arms Control and Foreign Policy Caucus, the Environmental and Energy Study Conference, and the Constitutional Liberty Caucus are neither party nor constituency based. Members join them for information and to pursue policy. As with policy committees such as International Relations, constituency interest may be minimal (Fenno 1973). But members who join become better informed and, on occasion, specialists. And in this group of caucuses, those that go beyond information and education activities have been successful in achieving policy goals, due in part to specialization.

If caucuses are grouped by the reasons for which members join and the range of issues on which a caucus works, six types can be distinguished. The caucuses within each group are alike because of a similar range-of-issue focus and because members have a common characteristic, such as party and ideology, representation of constituency interests, or personal interest in an issue.

Party Caucuses

Most party caucuses are formed to articulate and advance the policy views of an intraparty group. Members of a party caucus generally share both party and ideology. The Conservative Democratic Forum (CDF), known as the Boll Weevils, are conservative-to-moderate Democrats who are at times at odds with a more liberal party leadership and, in the early 1980s, were an important element in the coalition that achieved passage of Reagan budget and economic legislation. The members of the House Wednesday Group are moderate and liberal Republicans. The Republican Study Committee members were more conservative Republicans. Similar party groups, although fewer in number, exist in the Senate.

Party caucuses describe themselves as intraparty groups differentiated within the party by ideology. The Senate Wednesday Group "provides liberal to moderate Republican senators with a forum for informal discussion on subjects of common interest" (*Congressional Yellow Book 1996*, VI-50). The Democratic Study Group "is a legislative research and policy organization of . . . liberal and moderate Democratic members of the House" (*Congressional Yellow Book 1986*, VI-21).[8] "The Conservative Action Team (also known as CATs) is an organized group of Republican

House Members who are both fiscally and socially conservative" (*Congressional Yellow Book 1996*, VI-28). The mean conservative coalition scores for the Ninety-seventh Congress intraparty groups indicate the ideological differentiation among them.[9]

Party Caucus	Mean Conservative Coalition Support Score
Democratic Study Group	42
United Democrats of Congress	55
House Wednesday Group	66
Democratic Research Organization	73
Republican Study Committee	84
Conservative Democratic Forum	86

Class clubs, established in the House by freshmen members of each party (e.g., the 100th New Members Caucus [Democrats]), are a small subset of the party caucus category. In recent years, class clubs have been active for several congresses, but as members become more involved in committee work and climb the seniority ladder, they disband.

Personal-Interest Caucuses

The common characteristic for members of personal-interest caucuses is interest in an issue—for example, foreign policy, the arts, or families and children. Although many of these caucuses focus on one concern—such as children, the environment, or pro-life—the question itself is broad and encompasses numerous parts (in the case of children, these can be economic, family, health, social benefits, or education), or it is an issue (such as pro-life) that falls under the jurisdiction of various committees. Caucus activities are not directly linked to representation of constituent interests. Many personal-interest caucuses focus on agendas or information because their large memberships agree on the importance of an issue but not on specific programs. Personal-interest caucuses are generally bipartisan and often bicameral, like the Arms Control and Foreign Policy Caucus. Caucus size varies, from large and diverse (340 members of the Environmental and Energy Study Conference in the 103d Congress) to quite small (6 in the Senate Pro-Life Action Task Force for Women, Children, and the Unborn; figures from Richardson 1993, 1995). The Congressional Arts Caucus "is a bipartisan group . . . who share a concern for the future role of the arts in America" (*Congressional Yellow Book 1996*, VI-45). The Arms Control and Foreign Policy Caucus was open to any member of Congress who "subscribes to its general purposes of co-ordinating congressional concern for world peace into specific action for the development of international cooperation, a strengthened United Nations, and arms control and disarmament" (*Congressional Yellow Book 1992*, VI-37). The Congressional Caucus for Science and Technology wants "better understanding throughout Congress of issues that affect or are affected by science and technology" (VI-29).

National Constituency Caucuses

The four other types of caucuses are constituency based and bipartisan. Members of national constituency caucuses are perceived, and perceive themselves, as representing groups nationwide, outside and within their congressional districts or states: blacks, women, Hispanics, Vietnam-era veterans. They work on a range of issues. The Congressional Black Caucus "responds to [a] national and worldwide constituency" (*Congressional Yellow Book 1996*, VI-26); the Congressional Caucus on Women's Issues "works to advance the economic equity of women and their families" (VI-43); the Vietnam Era Veterans in Congress "act as legislative advocates for veterans of the war in Vietnam" (VI-43). Caucus concerns are diverse, and the focus is on a wide range of issues. The size is self-limiting, since caucus members share the characteristics of the groups they represent. Some of these caucuses have in recent years sought to broaden their membership base: non-Hispanics may become associate members of the Hispanic Caucus; between 1981 and 1995 men joined the Congressional Caucus on Women's Issues, although only women members served on the caucus executive committee.[10]

Regional Caucuses

Regional caucuses work on issues of particular concern to a geographic region, the Sunbelt or western states, for example. Caucus members come from contiguous states or districts that share common problems or a common perspective on an issue. The Western States Coalition, for example, is "an informal, bipartisan group of members of Congress who collaborate on issues of interest to members from western states" (*Congressional Yellow Book 1996*, VI-36). The issues of concern to a regional caucus transcend party lines and are perceived as requiring cooperation or federal action to address.

Regional caucuses vary in size, although many are quite large: virtually all members of eighteen state House delegations belong to the Northeast-Midwest Congressional Coalition; the Sunbelt Caucus, which had 158 members in the 104th Congress, draws most of the representatives and senators from the southern and western states. In contrast, there were seven members of the Long Island Congressional Caucus in 1996.

State/District Caucuses

Members of state/district caucuses work on matters affecting individuals and groups throughout members' states or districts. The locally rooted concerns of caucuses like the Rural Caucus, the Family Farm Task Forces, the Urban Caucus, and ethnic caucuses (e.g., the Caucus on India and Indian-Americans) are widespread, diffused throughout the member's district or state, and may have a normative, as well as economic or other, basis (e.g., the value to America of family farms). The Senate Rural Health Caucus "is a bipartisan group of . . . senators from rural states . . . who share a concern for maintaining quality health care for rural Americans" (*Congressional Yellow Book 1996*, VI-53). The Older Americans Caucus helps "develop legislative responses to aging issues . . . serve[s] as a clearinghouse for aging information and help[s] members form a consensus about . . . legislation" (VI-37). These caucuses focus on issues that transcend party lines and typically cut across committee jurisdictions. Caucus size varies from 140 members of the Rural Caucus to only a handful in the High Altitude Caucus, which was made up of representatives from districts with areas over 2,000 feet high.

Industry Caucuses

Industry caucuses work on problems of a specific industry within the state or district. The caucuses are narrowly focused in their concerns, representing a small (sometimes a very small) portion of the constituency. Caucuses are explicit about this focus: the Boating Caucus is "concerned with issues affecting boating, recreation, and the marine industry" (*Congressional Yellow Book 1996*, VI-35); Congressional Mining Caucus members "represent districts with mining interests" (VI-30); the Medical Technology Caucus is "concerned with the obstacles the health care industry faces" (VI-33). Many of these caucuses are quite large: the Congressional Steel Caucus had 100 members during the 104th Congress; the Travel and

Tourism Caucus, 301; the Beef Caucus, 76. These caucuses have close ties to a subsystem, and the issues cut across party lines, although they may also bring about alliances between business and labor, which usually oppose one another.

SUMMARY

Organization theory explains the development of the caucus system, but other theories suggest explanations for differences among caucuses. These theories offer explanations for the development of different groups of caucuses based on the collective purpose of caucus members, groups that seek to affect policy by working within the party, by pursuing non-constituency-based issues that cut across committee jurisdictions, or by representing broadly based constituency groups or narrowly defined constituency interests. Grouping caucuses in this way also permits the development and examination of alternative explanations for observed differences and a fuller understanding of the caucus system.

3/ WHY CAUCUSES ARE ESTABLISHED

Since the early days of the Republic, groups of senators and representatives have worked informally together to affect policy. Although the legislative arena in which caucuses now operate is more complex and although contemporary caucuses differ in significant ways from the earlier groupings of members, their lineage goes back to much earlier precursors.[1]

Temporary groupings of members within the emerging political parties characterized the early Congresses. Most were shifting groups with little stability. Coalitions formed around policy issues, state delegations, and regional blocs, all of which were component elements in the formation of political parties (R. Bell 1973; Cunningham 1981; Henderson 1974; Ryan 1971; Young 1966). According to Young, the boardinghouse groups of members of Congress operated as voting blocs, devising strategy and influencing vote outcomes, although current studies indicate that party was a more significant factor than boardinghouse groups in congressional decision making (Bogue and Maclaire 1975; Cooper 1975).

By the early nineteenth century, informally organized blocs of members sought to influence congressional action. The War Hawks, described as "catalysts" and the "main agents" of the decision to go to war in 1812, were a Republican war faction organized and sustained in the pursuit of a specific policy issue (Hatzenbuehler 1972, 1976; Horsman 1964; Perkins 1961; Risjord 1961). The Invisibles, also called the Smith faction because it was led by (militia) General Samuel Smith of Baltimore, senator from Maryland, was a bipartisan informal anti-Madison group also considered important in moving toward war (Pancake 1955). The South Carolina congressional delegation also strongly supported and worked for the war decision (Latimer 1955; Pancake 1955).

Speaker Henry Clay (R-Ky.) appointed members of the War Hawks to strategic committees, with War Hawk freshmen disproportionately obtaining seats on standing committees and on the prestigious Foreign Affairs Committee. War Hawk members on Foreign Affairs and Ways and Means Committees coordinated information and strategy on aspects of

36

the issue, including the early war measure, the embargo, and war taxes. More informally, John Calhoun (War Democrat–S.C.), as a member of Clay's boardinghouse mess, was able to represent the War Hawk view in that milieu (Hatzenbuehler 1976, 9–14). Similarly, members of contemporary caucuses now seek equitable representation on committees from party leaders and coordinate information and strategy on policy issues.

Like that of recent years, the legislative environment of the nineteenth century was conducive to the development of alternative forums to pursue policy goals. There was, for example, a lack of standing committee positions for many representatives in the Congresses of the nineteenth century. Existing procedures were also hostile to certain ideas and initiatives. In 1841 a group of abolitionist members hired a staff aide to assist them in fighting the notorious gag rule, which prevented consideration of petitions and legislation opposing slavery. Since 1836 the House had maintained rules barring debate on such petitions. In a letter, Theodore Weld describes the purpose of the nascent caucus and the invitation to serve as its aide:

> A number of Abolition Members of Congress . . . during the session . . . have resolved to bring in bills and introduce resolutions of inquiry, etc., etc., which will open the whole field for discussion in a shape in which *the gag* or any gag which it is possible for Congress to pass cannot touch them. . . . As they are pressed with multiplied duties in the House on Committees, etc., etc., and have little leisure for gathering materials they request me to spend the winter there and aid them in the matter. . . .
>
> . . . *not one of these men has been able fully to investigate the question of Slavery or any of the points upon which they propose to speak.* The subjects are out of the range of ordinary congressional investigations and debates, the men are all lawyers in large practice and have had no time for *thorough* looking at such matters; besides, nothing that can help them on those points can be found in print, except in our Anti-slavery publications, and on *most* of those subjects we have either published nothing *at all* or nothing much to the point. On the whole the more I look at the subject the more I feel as though I *dare* not assume the responsibility of refusing to comply with such a request. (Barnes and Dumond 1934, 880–81)

Weld accepted the offer and acted as an early predecessor of the informal caucus staffs hired by members to conduct research on multifaceted issues. The focus on a complex issue, falling out of the range of usual congressional activity and the public relations and media aspects of the group's proposed activity, is also characteristic. The Abolitionist Group had an impact, and their antislavery speeches on the floor, delivered at every opportunity, "were widely reported in the press and distributed throughout the country under the franking privilege" (Dillon 1974, 103).

In 1842 members reorganized an earlier group and established the Congressional Temperance Society. Focusing on "abstinence from all intoxicating drinks," the group sought geographic diversity with nine vice presidents from different states (Barnes and Dumond 1934, 915n). This organizational structure is not unlike that of some contemporary caucuses. Although the group did not work on legislative issues, it apparently served other individual and institutional goals. Weld describes a meeting of the society that served as an opportunity for slavery supporter Henry Wise (Whig-Va.) to express unusual cordiality toward abolitionist member, Seth Gates (Free-Soil Whig–N.Y.), an early instance of an informal caucus serving to enhance the comity of the institution (ibid.). A few years later an ad hoc group of antiwar Whig members, led by Joshua Giddings (Anti-slavery Whig–Ohio), opposed the Mexican War because it feared the war was being pursued to add more slave territory to the United States. The group operated in 1846 and 1847 through such tactics as making floor speeches and offering amendments to appropriations bills (Stewart 1970, 124–26).

Geographic groups have sought to influence legislative behavior since the First Congress. In the 1790s, "New England was the most cohesive region of the nation; it ordered priorities and achieved its goals with greater success than did the relatively divided southern and middle states" (R. Bell 1973, 31). During the pre–Civil War period, the gag rule was the result of southern representatives' meetings. At the turn of the twentieth century, groups of western senators from silver-producing states formed informal groups that were both regional and single-issue. The predominately Republican silver senators were joined by several populists in their efforts to affect public policy. They were perhaps most prominent and cohesive in the protracted struggle over repeal of the purchase clause of the Sherman Silver Act. The Treasury Note Act of 1890 had directed that treasury notes be issued on silver bullion; the price the United States would pay for silver was set lower than producer states wished. Although the clause was ultimately defeated, during 1893 the "guerrillas" sustained a five-month filibuster in favor of repeal of the clause (Timberlake 1978, 39).

In this same era, freshman Republicans, led by Robert Nevin (R-Ohio), founded the Tantalus Club after the chair of the Post Office Committee, Eugene Loud (R-Calif.), snubbed Nevin during a floor debate. A forerunner of contemporary freshman class clubs, which provide orientation, information, and strategy support to newly elected members, the Tantalus Club sought to support members and to work on legislation. The origin of the group's name echoes some of the frustrations of more recent freshmen: "The new member of Congress was very much in the situation of Tantalus; everything that he wanted was just out of reach" (MacNeil 1963, 295–96). Two decades later, during the agricultural depression of 1920, Lester Dickinson (R-Iowa) brought together a bipartisan farm group of midwestern Republicans and southern Democrats. He was encouraged and assisted by the American Farm Bureau. During the 1920s the representatives were influential and successful, achieving, for example, legislation to control grain exchanges and federal assistance for farm financing and crop exports (Capper 1922; MacNeil 1963, 289; Rice 1924, 20, 32). Today, this pattern continues. Agricultural issues are still important to caucuses, outside interest groups encourage and assist caucus formation, and accomplishment of legislative goals is sought by contemporary caucuses.

The conservative coalition (Republicans and southern Democrats), which emerged as a voting bloc in the 1930s, also serves as a prototype for recent informal caucuses. Although never formally organized (and therefore not technically a caucus), the coalition's successes in affecting voting outcomes made formally organized policy groupings attractive options for members.

THE CONTEMPORARY ERA

The contemporary caucus system differs significantly from the scattered, ad hoc, informal groups of earlier eras. Caucuses now are persistent, highly organized, and active. They are accepted by members and recognized by the institution as ongoing, legitimate actors in the policy process.

If the caucus system is an adaptation to changes in the external environment and resultant demands that cannot be handled by the formal congressional structure, newly established caucuses are likely to reflect these external changes and internal deficiencies. New caucuses can be expected to focus on emerging or newly salient issues or issues that are not being handled by the formal committee and party systems. It is likely that more caucuses will form to address issues that fall under the jurisdiction of multiple committees rather than under a single major committee.

Are structural issues important to caucus formation? We might expect that party control of the White House affects caucus establishment and that caucuses form to oppose presidential policies with which caucus members disagree. It is likely that this is the motivation for caucuses of opposition party members, although bipartisan groups or groups of members who disagree with their president's party might also form caucuses. Does party control of the Senate or the House matter? We might expect more intraparty caucuses (party caucuses) to be established by majority party members; majority parties need to hold their members together, and intraparty groups view caucuses as a way to work within the party and, at the same time, a way to advance both individual and collective (party) interests. Caucuses increase the leverage of outlier groups within a majority party and of party groups with preferences close to those of members of the other party (e.g., moderate Republicans and conservative Democrats). If the formal system has failed members, intraparty groups of either party that feel neglected by party leaders can also be expected to form caucuses.

In a formal system that lacks sufficient coordinating mechanisms, caucuses arise to fill that gap. There are several kinds of coordination. One is coordination of issues that fall under the jurisdiction of multiple committees, such as children or trade. Another is coordination of concerns that are shared by a number of districts or states. A third is coordination of members of Congress who share a strong issue interest but are not on the relevant committees or who share a common constituency interest but are separated as committee members and nonmembers. A fourth is coordination of adversaries or of interested parties from diverse constituencies or representing different constituency perspectives, such as producers and consumers or business and labor.

Party caucuses are more likely to develop if a party is in the majority or if a group within a party is being ignored by the party leadership (the formal party system fails them). Distributive caucuses will be formed when issues shift, for example, when regional concerns become salient or trade issues affect an industry. Party control of a chamber does not influence the formation of distributive caucuses nor does party control of the White House, unless a president's specific policies affect a region or industry.

Factors influencing the formation of informational caucuses, which reflect members' personal interests, are less clear. These groups can also be expected to form in response to salient, emerging, or neglected issues.

Chamber control as a factor in caucus formation may matter indirectly through the committee system. If committees ignore, or do not have, or seek jurisdiction over issues of interest to these caucuses, more informational caucuses are likely to form. White House control may affect caucus formation in the same way.

Striking aspects of the caucus phenomenon in recent years are the increasingly rapid rate at which groups have been established, a shift in the range of interests caucuses pursue, the later development of a Senate system like that of the House, and the development and predominance of bipartisan caucuses. For six years, from 1959 through 1964, the only informal group of members that was not either a social club or a state or city delegation was the Democratic Study Group. In the succeeding five years, 1965–69, only two more groups were established: the Wednesday Group (moderate to liberal Republicans in the House) and the bipartisan, bicameral Members of Congress for Peace through Law (later renamed the Arms Control and Foreign Policy Caucus). From 1970 to 1974, ten more groups were started; three were in the Senate, a new development, and about half were bipartisan.

Caucus formation exploded in the late 1970s; by 1977–78 it had more than doubled from four years earlier, and by 1979–80 it had more than tripled. After this period, the number of new caucuses formed each Congress was fairly stable, until the large increases in 1989–90 (thirty-one) and 1995–96 (forty-three). The rate of caucus formation accelerated from less than one each Congress in the 1959–70 period, to seven per Congress in the early and mid-1970s, to nineteen each Congress in the late 1970s. By the late 1980s, caucus formation increased to twenty-five each Congress. In the early and mid-1990s, it remained high (see tables 3-1 and 3-2).

Several changes occurred as the rate of caucus formation accelerated. First, Senate caucuses were not established until after 1970; the Senate lags the House by about five years in the rate of caucus establishment. The period 1971–76 in the Senate, for example, was more like the period 1959–69 in the House, when few groups were established and, of those established, most were partisan. (Caucuses in the Senate also differ from those in the House in a number of other ways.) Second, groups formed during later periods were more likely to be bipartisan. After 1970 in the House and since 1975 in the Senate, most newly established caucuses have been bipartisan. Third, caucuses established earlier engage in a broad range of issues, while most of the more recently established groups focus more narrowly on a single issue or industry.

Table 3-1.   Caucus Establishment, by Chamber, 1959–1996

Time Period	House	Senate	Bicameral
1959–70	3	0	1
1971–76	9	5	6
1977–80	22	7	9
1981–86	28	16	20
1987–90	32	9	9
1991–96	54	6	16
Total	148	43	61

Source: Compiled from Congressional Research Service, *Informal Congressional Groups and Member Organizations,* various years; Congressional Research Service, *Caucuses and Legislative Service Organizations,* various years; Richardson 1993, 1996; *Congressional Yellow Book,* various years; author's data.

Note: Class clubs are not included. If the 22 class clubs established in 1975–76 are included, the number of House caucuses established is 170 and the total number of caucuses established is 274. Two House class clubs were established in 1969–74 (the clubs of the Ninety-fourth Congress), four in 1977–80, six in 1981–86, four in 1987–90, and six in 1991–96. Note also that some parallel caucuses exist in both Senate and House. Typically, they focus on the same industry: beef, coal, footwear, mushrooms, steel, textiles, trucking. Less frequently, they focus on the same issue area: children or North American trade, for example.

Table 3-2.   Caucus Establishment, by Caucus Type, 1959–1996

	Caucus Type						
Time Period	Party	Personal Interest	National Constituency	Regional	State/ District	Industry	Total
1959–70	2	1	0	1	0	0	4
1971–76	5	6	2	5	1	1	20
1977–80	1	5	3	5	9	15	38
1981–86	6	25	0	7	10	16	64
1987–90	2	17	0	7	8	16	50
1991–96	7	21	1	9	21	17	76
Total	23	75	6	34	49	65	252

Source: Congressional Research Service, *Formal and Informal Congressional Groups,* various years; Congressional Research Service, *Informal Congressional Groups and Member Organizations,* various years; Congressional Research Service, *Caucuses and Legislative Service Organizations,* various years; *Congressional Yellow Book,* various years; Richardson 1993, 1996; author's data.

Note: Class clubs are not included. Two freshmen class clubs (one Republican, one Democratic) have been organized in every Congress, starting with the Ninety-fourth (1975–76). If class clubs are included, the number of party caucuses increases to 45 and the number of caucuses to 274.

Several factors help explain these patterns. The mid-1970s changes in the House gave members more resources, such as staff, and distributed these more equitably. There were some changes in the committee and party systems as well. Subcommittee leaders received more resources, and limits on the number of committee leadership positions that a member could hold at any one time spread participation opportunities. But compared with increased demands from the external environment, these were not enough for the rank and file. At the same time, the coordination needs of Congress became particularly severe as it sought to deal with increasingly complex, complicated issues in the domain of multiple committees (see Cooper and Collie 1981). Jurisdiction poaching (King 1994; Baumgartner and Jones 1993), controlled by committee system leaders, was not sufficient to handle these demands. Members perceived that new, highly visible issues, as well as comprehensive subjects touching numerous committees, were not being addressed. A "separated" presidency (C. Jones 1994) did not bring easy cooperation with the White House, even though the same party controlled both branches of government; some major legislation was achieved (on energy, for example) but only after agonizing delay and negotiation. By the late 1970s, too, there were successful caucuses to serve as models; the Democratic Study Group had been instrumental in achieving the changes of the mid-1970s. Together, these factors can explain the tremendous increase in the number of caucuses that occurred in the late 1970s and the shift from a variety of unrelated caucuses to a caucus system.

Newly formed caucuses reflect important and emerging issues. The earliest caucuses of the contemporary era were established to enable a group of members to focus on arms control (1966), on black Americans (1971), and on the emerging economic issues of the Great Lakes, New England, the Midwest, and rural America. In the mid and late 1970s, caucuses formed around issues relating to women, the environment (the Environmental and Energy Study Conference, the High Altitude Caucus, the Solar Coalition), and some foreign policy areas (National Security, South Africa Monitoring). Some caucus formation occurred around regional issues, and starting in 1975–76, around industry issues. By the 1980s, members had learned how useful caucuses could be to them for information and for affecting policy outcomes. New caucuses, and some name changes of existing caucuses, continued to reflect issue changes in the external environment. Caucuses of the Reagan years reflect the importance of budget and deficit reduction concerns (Balanced Budget), trade (Export; Competitiveness), new foreign policy issues (terrorism), and emerging social issues (family and crime). Some industry caucuses arose as a response to efforts to cut back the scope of government (Depot, B-2 Stealth, and Senate Air and Space). New 1990s caucuses reflect the continuing importance of trade (Jobs and Fair Trade Caucus and the Task Force to End the Arab

Boycott), more specific environmental issues (regional ecosystems), health issues (Health Care Reform Caucus), and efforts to cut back government (Constitutional Liberty, Debt Limit, and Porkbusters caucuses). New caucuses also were a response to changed economic conditions (Small Business Survival Caucus). Particularly in the 104th Congress, several emphasized the prevailing conservative philosophy. Many of these new caucuses operated as informational groups, focusing on the education of members and the development of expertise.

Partisan theories seem to account for party caucuses in the House in the 1990s. Prior to the 1995 shift in party control, more caucuses were formed by House Democrats than by Republicans. But during the Republican-controlled 104th Congress, more Republican groups established caucuses (four new Republican groups and only two new Democratic groups; seven Republican and five Democratic groups, not including the class clubs, operated in the House during that Congress). In the House, more party caucuses form within the party controlling the chamber because potential benefits are greater for majority party members. Senate party caucus formation is not as easily explained. Only four intraparty groups have formed Senate caucuses. Three, one Democratic and two Republican (the latter two still active), were formed before 1981, during Democratic control, and the fourth, Republican, was formed in 1990, also during Democratic control. During the 104th Congress, three groups, all Republican, operated in the Republican-controlled Senate (Richardson 1995, 19; Richardson 1996, 21). The partisan theory of organization does not seem to fit. It is likely that Senate rules and norms of behavior and senators' more immediate access to party leaders make party caucuses less effective for getting the attention of party leaders.

Informational caucuses are established when members want information, expertise, and the benefits of specialization. In the 1990s numerous informational caucuses formed around health care issues. Distributive caucuses have been formed throughout much of the contemporary period, primarily in response to economic issues affecting regions and industries. In the 1990s new industry caucuses took account of emerging technologies (e.g., High Technology, Ferroalloy, and Biomedical Research).

CATALYSTS FOR CAUCUS FORMATION

A large proportion of caucuses attribute their existence to new or changed issues and policy or coordination needs (see table 3-3).[2] The differ-

Table 3-3. Primary Reason for Establishing Caucuses, by Caucus Type

		Caucus Type					
Reason	Party	Personal Interest	National Constituency	Regional	State/ District	Industry	Total (%)
Policy	8	15	0	5	1	2	20
Coordination	1	10	5	8	7	5	23
Issue	0	14	0	5	16	25	38
Leader or party failure	9	1	1	1	2	0	8
Other	0	2	0	6	4	3	10

Note: Class clubs are not included.

ences among caucuses offer support for the theoretical arguments about the development of the caucus system and the establishment of certain types of caucus. Party caucuses overwhelmingly cite failure of the formal party system, in conjunction with policy concerns, as a catalyst for their establishment. Non-party-based caucuses mention this only occasionally.

For personal-interest (informational) caucuses, new or changed issues, policy concerns, or coordination needs were the major reasons for formation. National and regional constituency caucuses primarily were a response to coordination needs. And state/district and industry caucuses were largely formed to react to new or changed issues. All of these constituency caucuses can be considered distributive, although national constituency caucuses are somewhat different, in part because their constituencies are nationwide and they work on general benefit issues rather than narrow, special interest issues. Interview data describe in more detail the factors that precipitate caucus formation. Members and staff tell of concerns about emerging issues, economic crises, and coordination needs among constituencies or within Congress. They also describe the entrepreneurial aspect of caucuses. To start a caucus with focus and staying power requires determination and dedication. As would be expected in a system that is not a permanent feature of formal organization in either chamber, caucuses are started by entrepreneurial members interested in issues or, less frequently, in latching onto an issue to use it symbolically.

External Events

Twenty (12.5%) of the caucuses established between 1959 and 1988 were begun as a response to new or newly salient issues. The Environmental Study Conference was formed in 1975 to keep environmental issues on governmental agendas, even though these issues appeared to be peaking. A name change to the Environmental and Energy Study Conference in 1981 indicates the increasing importance of energy impact on the environment. The Congressional Black Caucus (1971) and the Caucus on Women's Issues (1977) were congressional responses to the civil rights and women's movements. The Competitiveness Caucus, established in 1986, borrowed the current buzzword and incorporated the global interconnections of economic and political issues. The increasing importance of social issues to the electorate also influenced the establishment of caucuses during the 1980s; for example, the Pro-Life Caucus and the Congressional Coalition for Adoption.

Thirty caucuses, almost one-quarter of the total, were started in direct response to crises in the external environment. Reflecting economic problems within constituencies, 70 percent of these focused on industry concerns and 20 percent on state/district issues. The closing of several major steel plants, with the loss of hundreds of jobs, precipitated the creation of the Congressional (House) and Senate Steel Caucuses. Founders thought that a congressional group, working in conjunction with labor and industry, would be able to dramatize the plight of the nation's steel industry and, more important, to keep the issue from losing its prominence on the highly competitive congressional agenda. "It was [begun] to save the American steel industry and the jobs it provides," according to one observer. Similar circumstances, the closing of the ARCO-Anaconda smelter and refinery in Montana, precipitated the establishment of the Senate Copper Caucus. New York City's fiscal crisis in the 1970s prompted the New York state delegation, in spite of its ideological diversity, to develop a formal organizational structure and hire staff. The decision was a reaction to the perceived complexity of a long-term situation. The gasoline shortage of 1977 prompted the founding of the Congressional Travel and Tourism Caucus and the Congressional Alcohol Fuel Caucus, both formed in response to constituent demands.

Other caucuses are a result of less dramatic changes in the external environment. Ten percent, all representing regional, state/district, or industry constituencies, were started because of economic decline. The Northeast-Midwest Congressional Coalition and the New England Congressional Caucus sought to alleviate the problems and decline of urban centers in these regions. Long-term problems, such as foreign imports, environmental regulations, and the rise in gold prices, precipitated the jewelry industry's plea to its congressional representatives for assistance, resulting in the Congressional Jewelry Manufacturing Coalition.

The importance of ideology is reflected in some of the 1990s caucuses, such as the Constitutional Caucus, the Constitutional Liberty Caucus, and Republican party groups like the Conservative Action Team, the Mainstream Conservative Alliance and the New Federalist Group.

The Internal Environment

Internal factors also serve as catalysts for caucus establishment. Caucuses permit coordination in nontraditional ways, allow attention to issues that cut across the jurisdictions of existing committees, and permit a large number of members to work together on a specific issue. Congressional actors often explain the establishment of caucuses in these terms.

Members see caucuses as a response to a decline in the strength of party leadership within Congress and to leaders' failure to adapt congressional structures to handle the increasingly complex and crosscutting issues facing the institution. For 10 percent of the caucuses, the weakness or failure of party leaders was the primary factor in caucus formation; 40 percent mentioned it as an important contributing factor. A typical view is presented by Representative Robert Edgar (D-Pa.), chair of the Northeast-Midwest Congressional Coalition in the Ninety-seventh Congress: "Chief among the reasons [for caucus formation] were such factors as failure of the . . . leadership structure to adjust to an era in which more educated, better informed Members are requiring better leadership on increasingly complex public policy problems" (U.S. House of Representatives 1982, 57; see also U. S. House of Representatives 1987). A similar argument is made by a former caucus director, who says that caucuses were established because of "the new independence of congressional members from the traditional formal leadership of the House, which, in its thus weakened state, allowed ad hoc groups to arise and fill the vacuum" (Feulner 1983, 2). Another caucus staff director noted that "the breakdown of [party] leadership, and also the breakdown of committee leadership, has probably helped to create all the special interest and special purpose caucuses."

The failure of party leaders to respond to members' specific policy concerns was also important. For example, liberal Democrats established the Democratic Study Group to counteract the party leadership, including committee chairs (Ferber 1971; Stevens, Miller, and Mann 1974). The Hispanic Caucus was established to overcome "the inaccessibility of the leadership." A factor in the formation of the Republican Study Committee was that "party leadership staff is not available to rank and file members for assistance on their legislative agendas" (Feulner 1983, 24). For the more recently established bipartisan caucuses, which focus on a single concern (rural Americans) or an industry (steel, textiles), failure of party and party leaders to address major crosscutting interests of members and constituents were important elements in caucus formation.

Members' concerns continued even after leaders responded by expanding the whip systems and establishing mechanisms such as leadership task forces. Caucuses benefited from this more inclusive leadership style, with caucus representatives appointed to party committees and caucus experts serving on leadership task forces. But success in achieving inclusion encouraged caucus formation. As House speakers became more involved in setting House agendas and in working on issues before committee consideration (see, e.g., Barry 1989), caucuses formed because issues were not on the leaders' agenda, and members saw caucuses as an effective means for changing that.

More than a quarter of the caucuses were started to coordinate information, members, or issues. Issues may be under a committee's jurisdiction but not on a committee agenda, or they may be so fragmented that they are neglected by all committees. A senior aide said, "Caucuses give you a chance to gather information and get visibility on issues where you may not otherwise have comprehensive enough jurisdiction—or any jurisdiction—to address issues." The Congressional Caucus on Children, Youth, and Families reported that it brings together "members spread across many committees and organizations in order to create a focused effort to address the many problems of children and families" (*Congressional Yellow Book 1996*, VI-37).

Other caucuses began because members wanted a vehicle for bringing together different perspectives of members or of constituent and sometimes of adversarial groups outside Congress. The Pacific Northwest Trade Task Force sought a unified approach to trade issues: "We saw that we were dealing with basically one river system and had within the region's delegation three distinct positions on port user fee legislation. For example, two senators supported a specific port-by-port cost recovery system. . . . We had some in favor of a national unified user fee. And then there were others who didn't favor any kind of an additional user fee." A participant reported that the Agricultural Forum, for example, was started "to bring together some of those factions that simply refused in the past to discuss agricultural issues with each other."

Other Structural Factors

Other factors internal to Congress include members not being on relevant committees and junior members wanting to influence policy making. A caucus staff director explained: "Caucuses have been successful in being able to focus attention on certain issues and promote some sort of action. . . . This [starting and chairing a caucus] is an opportunity to participate in an issue that he feels strongly about. It's a vehicle . . . for some sort of participation." For 5 percent of caucuses, ease of establishment was a major factor in their establishment. A respondent described this:

> Of course, the problems of establishing a Senate committee are very complicated, and it wouldn't make sense to have a committee on North American trade or even a subcommittee; it's just too complicated a process and too specialized an interest. So we asked around, and the general conclusion was that the best vehicle would probably be a caucus, because it doesn't take any Senate rule; any group of senators can come together and form a caucus . . . and then if you get a good cross-section of senators—such as, from different committees—then you form your own little group of senators who are interested in that particular subject and who, when the occasion arises, might be willing to take it up within their committees, if it's referred to their committees.

Caucuses are also started because other caucuses are successful. The Senate Steering Committee, a party caucus, was modeled on a House caucus: "Senator Curtis, who was one of the founding senators, used the House Republican Study Committee as a prototype," according to a former caucus aide. The Wood Energy Caucus was modeled on the Solar Coalition. Members considered early industry caucuses as successful models of congressional response to constituent concerns and copied them for new industry problems. Occasionally, models exist in the formal system. Senators founded the Senate Children's Caucus to match the House Select Committee on Children when they wanted to work on comparable issues.[3]

Caucuses are also started to respond to, and often to oppose, established groups. The success of the Democratic Study Group, particularly in affecting the 1970s reforms in the House of Representatives, spurred other intraparty groups, both Democratic and Republican, to organize. And the work of the Northeast-Midwest Congressional Coalition influenced the formation of other regional caucuses, such as the Northeast-Midwest Senate Coalition and the Sunbelt Caucus.

Established caucuses were also copied by dissatisfied factions within them. The Conservative Democratic Forum (the Boll Weevils) broke away from the Democratic Research Organization because "there was a lot of disgruntlement with the DRO," and members who shared a "common philosophy" wanted a smaller unit for "ideological cohesiveness." Michael Harrington (D-Mass.), disappointed with the inactivity of the New England Congressional Caucus after he was "shoved out" as a caucus leader, started the Northeast-Midwest Congressional Coalition. In 1995, during the first months of the 104th Congress, this fluidity continued. The Coalition, or Blue Dogs—a group of conservative Democrats—spun off from the Conservative Democratic Forum as a smaller group designed to develop and negotiate acceptable centrist legislation. And the GOP Conservative Action Team organized to counteract the moderate Republican Tuesday Lunch Bunch.

Some caucuses are started to represent the have-nots, including intraparty groups that see inequities in committee assignments, regions that were not getting a fair share of federal funds, or groups that felt neglected by the federal government. A former staff director of the Senate Northeast-Midwest Coalition described how the group began: "There was the flight of industry and people from the northeastern and midwestern states to the Sunbelt. The Frostbelt started to suffer more of a tax burden, and there was less and less income to fill state coffers. As a result of that, they were losing out in terms of formulas for federal programs and losing out on tax revenue and losing out in terms of growth of industry."

The Vietnam Era Veterans in Congress Caucus was started "mainly because Vietnam veterans seemed to be getting short shrift both within the Veteran's Administration and in the Congress. . . . Committee leaders were older . . . out of touch with the younger vets' problems and concerns, and hadn't really done much of anything to really handle those problems. . . . There needed to be some forum for ideas and a source of information and ways to solve these problems outside of the Veterans' Affairs Committee." And a caucus was "easy to form."

POLICY GOALS

For more than one-quarter of the caucuses, achieving policy goals was the primary motivating factor in establishing the caucus, although changing issues or deficiencies of congressional structure were the catalysts. The Solar Coalition was founded as an "informal, almost ad hoc, group with legislative interest." The Auto Task Force "grew out of the Chrysler loan guarantee legislation. . . . We realized there was an industrywide problem." Founders of many party caucuses felt isolated or not able to influence policy within the party. Conservative Democratic Forum founders wanted to pursue "fiscal responsibility, strong defense, and revitalizing free enterprise." Others, primarily regional caucuses, sought policy successes similar to those of caucuses representing competitor regions. A few were organized in reaction to a president's policies. These include the Northeast-Midwest Democratic Senators, the Nuclear Non-Proliferation Task Force, and the Northeast-Midwest Republican Coalition (the Gypsy Moths).

Caucuses conduct basic research, delineate the parameters of a problem, develop legislative or administrative remedies, exchange information on legislative and executive branch activities, and build policy coalitions. They also focus the attention of Congress, the administration, and the public on one or more issues. The Congressional Black Caucus, for example, is successful at increasing the visibility of various policy matters of particular concern to African Americans.

SUMMARY

When members and staff reflect on the development of the caucus system, they describe policy information, education, and coordination as benefits of caucus formation and activity. One respondent summed up this way: "Caucuses form because there really is a need for them. . . . It relates both to gaps in legislative personal staff and in committee staff and to the need for sources of information. With so many personal staff hired with relatively little experience . . . there is really no expertise in certain issue areas. The caucuses can offer expert information gathering and analysis and serve as an extension of the member. . . . In addition, members can trust the information because they know who is giving it to them, and . . . what the biases are." Another respondent pointed out benefits when caucuses focus on issues that are bipartisan and cut across traditional divisions: "The [Space] Caucus and the interests of the caucus cut across party lines, they cut across territorial boundaries and rabid ideology, if you will. We range from rabidly conservative Republicans to wildly liberal Democrats. The geographic distribution is widely varied. They are able to work and function together as a unit because of their shared interest."

A staff director of the Senate Family Caucus said: "We're pretty fractionalized here in Congress. . . . Basically, the caucus started because no one is looking at how government policies affect the family, what things affect the stability or instability of the family. Welfare falls under the Agriculture Committee with AFDC, child nutrition is under Finance or Ways and Means, and job training and some issues like that under Labor. So the issues are all spread out." Participants also argue that policy and coordination benefits result from an in-depth focus on one issue. Nearly two-thirds of the caucuses established since 1984 were established to work on issues that fall under the jurisdiction of multiple committees. The remaining one-third, many of them industry caucuses, are concerned with issues that are dealt with by two committees—the relevant authorizing and appropriations committees.

Few caucuses form explicitly to oppose a president's policies, but two of the three that did form are intraparty groups that established a caucus to oppose policies of a president of the opposite party. Control of the White House does not affect the formation of other types of caucuses. Party control of a chamber, particularly the House, matters for party caucuses, although not for other types of caucuses. A possible alternative explanation attributing the development of the caucus system to an increasingly decentralized congressional structure is not supportable. Decentralization during the 1970s may have contributed to the initial ease of caucus formation; certainly during a period of "czar rule," creation of a caucus system is unlikely. Nevertheless, caucuses have continued, and new ones have continued to form in the House in a period of greatly increased centralization, as evidenced by caucus activity during the command and control operation of Speaker Newt Gingrich in 1995–96.

Members view the caucus system as a logical adaptive response to organizational stress. They perceive caucuses as assisting them in accomplishing individual goals and as contributing to much-needed structural coordination and policy outcomes. Caucuses are easy to establish and can be maintained with little effort, ready to be reactivated if events and inclination so dictate. Caucuses are also efficient for members: they pool resources to work on group concerns and reduce duplication at the individual member level. External shifts in demand and internal organizational attributes, in conjunction with members' goals, have resulted in the development of the congressional caucus system.

4/ THE LIFE CYCLE OF CAUCUSES

All congressional caucuses have been started by one member or a small group of members to address an issue or a group of issues (see table 4-1).[1] Caucuses institutionalize, adapt, and change in response to changes in the external context or to a shift in members' goals. Their flexibility allows them to reorganize without reference to either chamber rules or the formal congressional structure and to become inactive for a period until circumstances spur members to reactivation. Or, they can disband.

Most founding entrepreneurs are driven by policy goals. The liberal, junior Democrats who founded the Democratic Study Group sought to increase the likelihood that their positions would prevail. Members of the Rhode Island delegation, responding to pleas from their jewelry manufacturing constituents, established the Jewelry Manufacturing Coalition to address the immediate crisis of rising gold prices as well as long-term trade and regulation issues. Other entrepreneurs seek re-election or power in the Congress. The Northeast-Midwest Congressional Coalition, for example, originally seemed to be a publicity and intra-House leadership vehicle for its founder, Michael Harrington (D-Mass.). The symbolism of founding or joining a caucus in response to constituent concerns drives some members. John Jenrette (D-S.C.) is reported to have founded the Travel and Tourism Caucus to achieve publicity and re-election. A founding entrepreneur appears to be critical to initial organization and the shift to a continuing, organized group.

BUILDING AND MAINTAINING CAUCUSES

For many caucuses, the first year or two is devoted to inviting colleagues to join, coordinating members' interests, and identifying the parameters of concern. Outside interests sometimes recruit members for industry-focused caucuses, urging senators and representatives to join the new congressional group and, in some instances, lobbying them heavily. Although Travel and Tourism Caucus staff say that the caucus was estab-

Table 4-1.   A Partial List of Caucuses and Caucus Founders

Caucus	Founder
Arms Control and Foreign Policy Caucus (formerly, Members of Congress for Peace through Law)	Sen. Joseph Clark, Rep. Brad Morse
Congressional Arts Caucus	Rep. Fred Richmond
House Border Caucus	Rep. Thomas Coleman
House Coal Caucus	Rep. Nick Rahall
Conservative Democratic Forum	Rep. Charles Stenholm
Conservative Opportunity Society	Reps. Newt Gingrich, Vin Weber
Task Force on Devaluation of the Peso	Reps. Morris Udall, Duncan Hunter, Richard White
Democratic Study Group	Reps. Eugene McCarthy, Lee Metcalf, Frank Thompson, Chet Holifield, John Blatnik
Senate Drug Enforcement Caucus	Sen. Paula Hawkins
Export Task Force (House)	Reps. William Alexander, Don Bonker
Senate Caucus on the Family	Sen. Jeremiah Denton
Congressional Fire Services Caucus	Rep. Curt Weld
Senate Footwear Caucus	Sen. William Cohen
Congressional Human Rights Caucus	Reps. Tom Lantos and John Porter
Senate Jewelry Manufacturing Coalition	Sen. John Chafee
Mainstream Forum	Rep. David McCurdy
Military Reform Caucus	Sen. Gary Hart, Rep. George Whitehurst
New England Congressional Caucus	Rep. Michael Harrington
Northeast-Midwest Congressional Coalition	Rep. Michael Harrington
Northeast-Midwest Senate Coalition	Sen. John Chafee
Congressional Port Caucus	Rep. Walter Jones
Congressional Social Security Caucus	Rep. C. W. (Bill) Young
Senate Rail Caucus	Sen. David Durenberger
Senate Steering Committee	Sen. Carl Curtis
Congressional Travel and Tourism Caucus	Rep. John Jenrette
Wood Energy Caucus	Rep. James Jeffords

lished a number of months before the industry expressed interest in a caucus, members also report that industry strongly urged them to join the caucus, and some believe that there was too much pressure from industry.

During the first Congress in which it operated, the Senate Family Farm Task Force focused on identifying the problems of family-owned and

-operated farms, gathering information, and formalizing relationships with outside interest groups and the Department of Agriculture, which was conducting its own study of family farming. Structurally, the caucus was designed to develop relationships within the Senate among members and between members and committees, to coordinate House and Senate activities and concerns, and to establish staff relationships and tasks. Members expected that the first two years would lay the basis for activity and influence in shaping the Omnibus Agriculture Bill during the succeeding Congress. One congressional respondent described the process of building caucus credibility to ensure permanence: "There are a couple of things you have to do. One, you have to put out regular presence pieces, which indicate you're there and doing work in a given area. You sort of capture the market in a given area. . . . Secondly, you put out substantive pieces—these kinds of things build credibility so that members trust you. Maybe you can keep a caucus going by having a meeting every three months or something, but if you're really going to have something going on a regular basis . . . you have to show that presence and you have to have credibility."

Some caucuses have sought to maintain themselves as ongoing organizations by expanding membership or offering information and coordination to a wider group. Research by the Northeast-Midwest Congressional Coalition provided data for founding members to expand membership. By the mid-1980s all representatives from the northeastern and midwestern states belonged to the Coalition. A typical information and membership benefit was the 1990 report on the contributions of member states to the federal budget and federal expenditures in member states. This report detailed the burden on the Northeast and the Midwest in the savings and loan bailout and became a factor in the FY1991 budget negotiations.

For some caucuses, the organization and goals developed in the establishment phase persist. The Environmental and Energy Study Conference, for example, maintained its initial focus to provide only information. Many caucuses, however, adapt goals and structures to respond to changes in the external environment or to better assist members in achieving their goals.

Adapting to Change

As caucuses mature, many undergo change as issues shift or as caucuses seek the most appropriate membership and staff structure to meet members' goals. Structural adaptation and goal modification or displacement may take place (Selznick 1949). Their experiences illustrate both the challenge and the opportunities of the caucus system.

Shifts in Goals and Structure

The New England Congressional Caucus gradually shifted its agenda by broadening its focus from oil imports to a range of concerns, including energy, population change, and industry assistance. The move from a narrow issue to broader concerns resulted in hiring additional staff, further formalizing relationships with outside interests (both private sector and government groups), and arranging the establishment of an affiliate, the New England Institute.[2]

The Democratic Study Group went through similar change. Its early organizational phase was characterized by the relative informality of meetings and structure, and the focus was on the exchange of legislative information and coalition building. In the late 1960s, the DSG changed the thrust of the information it disseminated to members about issues and pending legislation and shifted from advocacy to the presentation of more background information and balanced summaries of issues and bills. The DSG also changed its emphasis from substantive policy to changing Democratic caucus and House rules and structure to achieve policy goals.

The DSG's growing credibility, enhanced by the success of its informational and structural reform activities and by the influx into the House of new Democrats (giving the party increasingly large majorities), resulted in a rapid increase in DSG membership. The demographics of caucus membership changed. Traditionally, DSG members were liberal Democrats; they could reach agreement on policy goals and legislative issues as Congress processed civil rights and Great Society legislation. However, by the Ninety-fifth Congress (1977–78) DSG membership was diverse. Even conservative southern Democrats joined the DSG to receive its legislative information. The Young Turks of the early DSG years had become congressional leaders of the late 1970s, and DSG members were in positions of party or House leadership. Issues, too, had shifted; many did not divide House members along traditional party or ideological lines. The result of the issue and membership changes was further adaptation. DSG leaders continued to be activist and liberal Democrats, but it became increasingly difficult for the group to agree and to act effectively on divisive legislative issues.

By the mid-1980s, the DSG's information on legislative issues served an important function for the House Democratic party. After DSG leaders declined the invitation to become a formal group within the caucus of all House Democrats, the group continued to take the lead, often behind the scenes, on substantive legislative issues. The group also continued to advocate organizational and procedural Democratic caucus and House reforms designed to facilitate its own policy goals. Both internal and external factors led to this very successful caucus adaptation, in which a group increased its influence on—and its contributions to—the work of Congress while retaining its basic character.

After September 1995, when the DSG joined forces with the caucus of all House Democrats, the group's goals were no longer clear. With an even more diverse membership, achieving agreement on legislation or strategy was more difficult. Nevertheless, the DSG considered itself unlike such groups as party task forces: although "accountable to the Democratic caucus," because the caucus now elected the DSG chair and executive board, "the DSG is not controlled by the leadership," and it expected to continue to be an independent actor in the policy process.

The Midwest Conference of Democratic Senators also illustrates the interaction of structural change and caucus goals. After expanding membership to include senators from certain mountain states contiguous to the Midwest, the conference could no longer reach agreement on the agricultural policy issues that had initially brought the group together. The caucus continued but floundered as members searched to recapture its purpose.

Some caucuses expand or shift their goals without structural change. For caucuses such as the Travel and Tourism Caucus, the Automotive Caucus, and the Senate and House Steel Caucuses, all of which were founded in response to crises in the external environment, adaptation and goal displacement became necessary for survival after the immediate crises were resolved. Some caucuses expanded their agendas and focused on longer-term and broader economic issues. The Automotive Caucus, for example, which was founded in 1981 as the Auto Industry Task Force in response to the Chrysler Corporation funding crisis, broadened its focus to the economic problems of the whole auto industry.

Caucus goals also change. The Budget Study Group, for example, began as an informational caucus. As it matured organizationally, it attracted additional, nonfreshman, representatives to its meetings. Subsequently, the caucus broadened its membership and revised its priorities from information exchange to influencing legislation. Some argue that the House Wednesday Group altered its focus in the opposite direction, from working on specific issues in its early years to general information exchange in the 1970s. The Congressional Clearing House on the Future went from education on "futures issues" to the more specific goal of legislative foresight work by committees. Other caucuses, particularly those focusing on one industry, after achieving the initial goal of placing an issue on the congressional agenda, have adapted to that success by changing their goal to maintaining agenda salience for the issue.

Changing Strategies

For some caucuses, goals remain the same but strategies to achieve those goals vary. The Democratic Study Group is a prime example, with its switch to a focus on changing Democratic caucus and House rules in order to gain the policy goals it had been unable to achieve through floor votes on the issues. Other caucuses have moved to a different policy arena. The Textile Caucus, formed in 1978, initially sought to affect executive branch decisions. With the introduction of H. Res. 1562, the Textile and Apparel Trade Enforcement Act of 1985 by caucus chair Ed Jenkins (D-Ga.), the group adopted a congressional strategy and began to work in an arena in which caucus members were leading players. The Textile Caucus also increased its activity significantly in the late 1980s in response to pending trade negotiations by seeking allies among other industry caucuses and making use of caucus members' service on relevant committees and in the House leadership.

The situation of individual members also brings strategic change. Newly elected members of Congress form class clubs to compensate for not being assimilated into congressional group and policy processes. Typically, the class clubs of freshman members are most active during the first two years. The Ninety-eighth Democratic Members Caucus, for example, was very active in the Ninety-eighth Congress, particularly on deficit reduction and jobs. The group was the foundation for new members to develop expertise, but by the end of the Ninety-ninth Congress it was much quieter.

Control of institutional sources of influence—White House, congressional party, and committee leadership positions—may change, and cause a caucus to alter its strategies. With Richard Nixon's election in 1968, DSG leaders knew that they could no longer depend on the executive branch as a source of information or liberal policy leadership. This was a major reason for their new emphasis on changing party and House rules and procedures. Similarly, the election of a Democratic administration in 1976 lessened the desire for an active Midwest Conference of Democratic Senators, founded during the Nixon administration to create and mobilize support for a Democratic-oriented farm program.

The Congressional Crime Caucus was more active when Republicans controlled the Senate than after 1987, when Democrats regained control. As their members gained seniority and positions of party and committee power, both the Democratic Study Group and the Congressional Black Caucus followed insider strategies, working closely with the formal power structure to achieve policy goals. This contrasts with the Conservative Democratic Forum (the Boll Weevils), which continues to offer amendments and to support those positions that differ from party leaders (although Boll Weevils, too, occupy powerful strategic positions within the Democratic party).

Changing Structure

Some caucuses spin off from another caucus to pursue broader goals. The Science and Technology Caucus started as a task force of the Congressional Black Caucus to improve science and math education and minority participation in these fields. It became a separate caucus when goals changed to focus on educating members of Congress on science and technology issues, causing task force members to seek a broader membership. The Conservative Democratic Forum is a similar spin-off from the more moderate Democratic Research Organization, although until the DRO disbanded some members belonged to both caucuses. The Coalition (the Blue Dogs) spun off from the Conservative Democratic Forum during the 104th Congress to form a small group designed to allow "every member" to be "committed and active," according to a participant.

Some caucuses metamorphose into successor caucuses. When the House Northeast-Midwest Republicans (the Gypsy Moths) became inactive, members moved to the newly established '92 Group, which continued the policy goals of the predecessor caucus but also focused on a new goal, a House Republican majority by the 1992 election. But the goal was not met in the 1992 congressional elections, and in the 103d Congress (1993–94), the '92 Group became the Tuesday Lunch Bunch. During the 104th Congress, after Republicans took control of the House, the Lunch

Bunch met regularly with Speaker Gingrich and effected changes in legislation as party leaders sought Lunch Bunch votes.

Some caucuses serve as successor caucuses after leaders or members of existing caucuses move to another caucus. Typically, the goals of the successor caucus include, and go beyond, the goals of the predecessor caucus. Structural change thus accompanies a shift in goals. Also typically, the predecessor caucus becomes inactive. The Senate Caucus on North American Trade was encompassed by the Senate Competitiveness Caucus, and the Peaceful Uses of Space Caucus, which focused on the ABM Treaty, was succeeded by the more broadly focused Space Caucus.

Other Change Factors

Changes in issues, personnel, and institutional control bring about caucus change. For both the Democratic Study Group and the Midwest Conference of Democratic Senators, a change in party control of the White House affected goals and strategies. Entrepreneurial leaders are important not only for founding caucuses but also for sustaining a caucus presence and caucus activities. When caucus leaders change, particularly in recently established and less institutionalized caucuses, policy and operational consequences that affect group maintenance may result. Leadership change can be dramatic, as through electoral defeat, or gradual, as through generational change. The leaders of both Senate and House Family Farm Task Forces left Congress after the 1980 elections. In the succeeding Congress, the task forces organized but were virtually inactive.

Caucus leaders' situations within Congress may also change and thus affect caucus operations. The Senate Caucus on North American Trade became inactive when caucus chair Max Baucus (D-Mont.) became more involved in the Competitiveness Caucus. The Senate Children's Caucus went through two changes. When Christopher Dodd (D-Conn.) succeeded Paula Hawkins (R-Fla.) as chair, the focus of caucus activity shifted from drug and alcohol abuse to child care and parental leave issues. After Dodd assumed the chair of the Senate Subcommittee on Children, Families, Drugs, and Alcoholism, the caucus became inactive. The Coalition for the Peaceful Uses of Space became inactive when the chair of the caucus became co-chair of a broader-based group, the Congressional Space Caucus. Activities were then carried on jointly by the two caucuses, with the Peaceful Uses of Space caucus in effect merging with the Space Caucus.

Member goals also bring about caucus change, as when caucus leaders or members find that the costs of caucus activity begin to outweigh the benefits or when they seize opportunities to pursue their goals through other caucuses or through committee and party activity. If success is achieved on one front, expanded goals may become the group focus (e.g., the Automotive Caucus). If efforts are less successful, a caucus may develop intermediate goals or new strategies, as occurred when the Democratic Study Group began to emphasize organizational change in rules and procedures to achieve continuing policy goals. Caucus structure may also alter.

Unchanging Caucuses

Some caucuses persist without changing their goals or organizational structures. The Arms Control and Foreign Policy Caucus, for example, maintained its focus on arms control, defense, and foreign policy although the specific issues on which it worked were different. The Congressional Caucus on Women's Issues continues its central purpose but, in recent years, has shifted its strategies to attain its goals. Class clubs usually continue to emphasize socialization, although recent freshmen groups pushed congressional reform in the 103d and 104th Congresses, and freshman Republicans pushed the "Contract with America" in the 104th. Many caucuses that are based on members' personal interest rather than on constituency concerns, such as the Arts Caucus, maintain a focus on specific aspects of issues, although the level of activity may vary over time.

The Conservative Democratic Forum and the House Steel Caucus have continually operated from the chairs' offices, with staff contacts in the offices of other members. All Senate caucuses—except the Steering Committee, which briefly had a separate office and staff—continue to operate through staff based in members' offices and to be coordinated by a senior aide to the caucus chair.

Caucus Mortality

Caucuses in Congress disband more easily and at a higher rate than in more hierarchical and bureaucratic organizations and more easily and at a much higher rate than the subcommittees, committees, and party organizations of the formal system.[3] The same fluidity of structure that supports the easy establishment of caucuses makes it easy for these groups to disappear when the policy context changes and issues fade, when leaders' goals alter or the caucus no longer serves to achieve those goals, or when the internal structure changes to affect how members achieve their goals—as when a committee co-opts caucus activity on an issue. Many groups simply operate in a quiescent state for a time, with only minimal maintenance activities until conditions change and they are reactivated. This has been the case with a number of industry groups: their fortunes rise and fall in reaction to the concerns and crises of the industry. Caucuses tied closely to a congressional entrepreneur who loses interest or groups that focus on a policy issue that becomes less salient may remain organized but inactive.

Some groups, however, simply fail or disband. Others accomplish their goals and, rather than find new ones, celebrate their victory and cease operations, like the Freshman Senators Group. Caucuses also end because the function of the group may no longer be necessary. All class clubs eventually disband, but many now continue during the sophomore term, albeit with gradually diminishing activity, and some continue thereafter. The Ninety-fourth New Members Caucus (Democrats) continued through the Ninety-fifth, Ninety-sixth, and into the Ninety-seventh Congresses. Its agenda even expanded as members found themselves sharing common policy and congressional reform goals. During the 104th Congress (1995–96), freshman caucuses of earlier Congresses (Republicans of the 100th and 103d, Democrats of the 101st and 103d) were still active. Class clubs that are diverse in ideology or on issues are more likely to disband immediately after the freshman Congress.

If leaders leave Congress, groups may die. Although the continuance of the more highly institutionalized groups is not tied to leaders, the more informally organized, less structured groups tend to be dependent on the original leadership. The Blue Collar Caucus folded when Edward Beard (R-R.I.) was defeated. Although the Family Farm Task Forces limped along into the next Congress (the Ninety-seventh) after founders Senator Donald Stewart (D-Ala.) and Representative Richard Nolan (D-Minn.) left the Congress, neither caucus was organized in the Ninety-eighth Congress.

The number of caucuses abolished each Congress has remained relatively stable since the mid-1980s (see table 4-2). We would expect that caucuses based on personal interest or on a constituency with narrow issue concerns are more likely to be abolished. If an issue becomes settled or loses urgency, caucuses without a broad range of issue concerns have

Table 4-2. Number of Caucuses Abolished, by Caucus Type and Congress

Congress	Party	Personal Interest	National Constituency	Regional	State/ District	Industry
Before 98th	1	3	1	0	3	2
98th	0	0	0	0	4	0
99th	4	0	0	1	3	2
100th	0	1	0	1[a]	1	1
101st	0	2	0	2	3	1
102d	0	5	0	2[b]	0	3
103d	0	6	0	2	3	4
104th	1[c]	3	0	1	1	4
(% abolished)	(26)	(30)	(17)	(30)	(44)	(29)

Source: Congressional Research Service, *Informal Congressional Groups and Member Organizations,* various years; Congressional Research Service, *Caucuses and Legislative Service Organizations,* various years; Richardson 1993, 1996; *Congressional Yellow Book,* various years; author's data.

Note: Caucuses that merged are not included; class clubs are not included. Caucuses that were abolished for successor caucuses are included. Total caucuses established, 252; including class clubs, 274. Percentage of total caucuses abolished, 28%; including class clubs, 32%.

[a]Disbanded at end of Ninety-ninth Congress. Reorganized and reactivated in 103d Congress.

[b]Conference of Great Lakes Congressmen was abolished as an independent caucus and taken over by the Northeast-Midwest Congressional Coalition. In the 104th Congress (1995–96), it was reestablished and registered as a congressional member organization.

[c]Republican Study Committee taken over by Republican Conference (of all House Republicans) and Republican leadership; ended as a caucus.

fewer reasons than other types of caucus to expand or shift goals—and turf (see King 1994; Baumgartner and Jones 1993). And as table 4-2 shows, there is a high level of caucus demise among personal-interest, state/district, and industry caucuses. The last two groups have the narrowest issue focus, and personal-interest issues are often linked to specific bills, which do not necessitate attention over a long period. In contrast, national constituency caucuses and party caucuses, many of which were established early in the caucus era, are the most permanent.

Just as members respond to changes in issues and constituent demands by establishing caucuses, they disband caucuses for similar reasons. The Social Security and Notch Caucuses were established and active when those issues were hot, but when the issues were no longer salient they were abolished. Regional caucuses that focused on the environment and water were active in the 102d and 103d Congresses, when the renewal of the 1974 Clean Water Act was on the congressional agenda, but by the end of the 103d Congress most of these caucuses (e.g., the Hudson River Caucus, the Chesapeake Bay Congressional Coalition, the Congressional

Coalition for Clean Water) had been abolished. A few caucuses exist for only one or two Congresses: the Fairness Network (of members interested in military base closures) was established in the 101st Congress, active through the 103d Congress, and abolished at the start of the 104th Congress after the Military Base Closure Commission reported its recommendations.

An important element in caucus mortality appears to be that there are multiple avenues to individual goal accomplishment. If a group disbands, other means of pursing goals are readily at hand. In fact, members often merely shift attention to a different caucus or to another subunit of which they are already members. Thus, although not many groups have in fact disbanded, the occurrence is more frequent and the impact less severe on either members or the institution than in more hierarchical organizations.

Summary

As informal organizations within the formal congressional structure, caucuses are easy to establish and can vary their level of activity according to issue salience, caucus leadership, and member desire. They can react to contextual changes in the policy environment and can respond to members' individual interests and goals through goal adaptation and displacement, structural change, and strategic shift. They may remain quiet for a time but resume activity when issues or members' individual agendas demand it. Some disband. Caucus maintenance and life cycles are linked to contextual factors and member goals and are framed by the parameters of a legislative institution and the opportunities for organizational adaptation.

5/ CAUCUS MEMBERSHIP

By the Ninety-seventh Congress (1981–82), much like other recent Congresses, all representatives and nearly all senators belonged to at least one caucus. On average, House members joined nine caucuses. Four representatives were members of only one caucus; one representative belonged to twenty-two caucuses. Democrats, on average, belonged to more caucuses. Party leaders are less likely than their House colleagues to join caucuses. Committee and subcommittee leadership also reduces caucus membership, although less so than for party leaders.

FACTORS INFLUENCING MEMBERSHIP

The more senior a member, the less likely he or she is to be a caucus member (see table 5-1).[1] During the Ninety-seventh Congress, 31 percent of junior and middle-level seniority members belonged to one to six caucuses; about 40 percent were members of ten to twenty-two caucuses. In contrast, 57 percent of the most-senior representatives (eight or more terms) joined one to six caucuses, and only 23 percent of the most senior representatives joined ten or more caucuses (see table 5-1). Increased seniority reduces caucus memberships more for Democrats than for Republicans, perhaps because senior Democrats held important committee assignments until 1995, when they became the minority party. For each additional term of seniority, Democrats join 0.3 fewer caucuses; for each additional term, Republicans belong to 0.2 fewer caucuses.[2]

Ideology also affects caucus membership. The more conservative a member, the fewer caucuses the member joins.[3] Although conservatism is a significant variable for both Democrats and Republicans, it constrains Republicans more. That both the most liberal and the most conservative members join caucuses may reflect a perception that some issues of particular interest to them do not receive institutional attention through the committee system. Legislation is, after all, generally the result of compromise, and a caucus can take a more extreme view than a committee or

Table 5-1.   Caucus Membership in the Ninety-seventh Congress, by Seniority (in percentages)

Seniority (in terms)	1–6 Caucuses	7–9 Caucuses	10–22 Caucuses
Junior (1–3)	31	30	40
Middle (4–7)	31	30	39
Senior (8 or more)	57	19	23

Note: N = 434.

the House as a whole. Representatives from marginal districts are slightly more likely than their colleagues from safer districts to become caucus members, suggesting the benefits of caucus membership—especially because some of those benefits can be gained within months rather than years.[4] Regionally, on average, representatives from the Northeast join more caucuses than representatives from the South, the Midwest, and the West. Overall, the number of caucus memberships increases for more liberal members, more junior members, Democrats, those who are not party or committee leaders, and representatives from the Northeast.

Between 1976 and 1981–82, House caucus membership grew substantially.[5] In 1976, 60 percent of the House belonged to caucuses; in 1981–82, 100 percent did. In 1976, no representative joined as many as six caucuses; only two representatives belonged to five. By 1981, just over 20 percent of the House held membership in five or six caucuses, and nearly 66 percent were members of seven or more. In 1976, 26 percent of the representatives joined only one caucus; by 1981, the percentage had dropped to 0.9 (four members). In 1976, representatives were members of slightly less than two caucuses, on average. By 1981, that figure more than quadrupled, to nine caucuses. Senators, too, joined more caucuses in the late 1970s and early 1980s (but they were still fewer than for House members). In 1976, only 45 percent of the Senate belonged to any caucus, and no senator had more than two memberships. By 1984, 98 percent were members of at least one caucus, 24 percent were members of one or two, and 74 percent were members of three or more; the average was between four and five caucuses.

The differences between the parties are evident over time. In 1976, House Democrats joined an average of 2.07 caucuses, House Republicans, 1.5. In 1981, the average for House Democrats was 10.04 caucuses, for Republicans, 8.01. Although there were party differences in the Senate, the differences were not as great: in 1976, Democrats belonged to an average of 1.1 caucuses, Republicans belonged to 1. By 1984, the average for Democratic senators was 4.57 caucuses, while the average for Republican senators was 4.27.

As caucuses became institutionalized and the number increased, House committee and subcommittee chairs and ranking minority members became caucus joiners. They were members, on average, of 0.66 caucuses in 1976 and 8.95 in 1981. Committee leaders, however, continued to join fewer caucuses than the rank and file (an average of 9.38). Similarly, party leaders belonged to fewer caucuses (7.12 on average) than other representatives (an average of 9.22 caucuses). Leaders are busy with official duties and also do not need caucuses as much. In fact, on occasion, leaders have actively opposed the formation and operation of caucuses. In 1976, the average number of caucus memberships generally decreased as seniority increased. In 1981–82, the pattern was similar. However, by 1984 the highest number of caucus memberships was held by representatives with midlevel seniority: an average of 4.31 memberships for first-term representatives; often 5 or more for members in their third to seventh terms; 2.65 memberships, on average, for representatives with twenty-one or more years seniority (Congressional Research Service 1984). The pattern likely reflects the leadership needs and opportunities of maturing caucuses as well as the manifold allegiances and relationships that a midlevel member will have established.

In contrast to the House, Senate committee chairs and ranking minority members belonged to more caucuses (0.47 in 1976; 4.19 in 1984) than did freshman members (0.45 in 1976; 2.33 in 1984; see Congressional Research Service 1984). The greater difference in 1984 may be due to the small number of freshmen that year. Informal Senate leaders emerge when issues that cannot be neatly compartmentalized divide members in new ways (see Smith 1990). And in the egalitarian and smaller Senate, issue leaders can arise and be effective without the institutional base of a caucus (see Hammond 1990). The increase in senators' caucus memberships supports these findings.

A senior representative from a western state described typical decisions about joining caucuses. The Rural Caucus provided information and education on an issue: "I got into it because one of the areas I don't know a lot about is the farm issue, and it was interesting to listen to them." He later dropped his membership because "there are only so many hours in a day, and representing [my district] is all I can justify." He joined another caucus to serve as a link between the caucus and a committee task force he chaired on the same issue. He joined two other caucuses to work on constituency issues and problems and there pursued both representation and policy goals. He was also instrumental in establishing a national constituency caucus, because the caucus's issues "tend to be ignored here. Everybody's for them, but they never get to them." He concluded, "Congress deals with very complex legislation, and it's always hard to figure out how it affects everybody. [Caucuses help] people make sure they don't get rolled" and "get information from a reliable source."

For a northeastern Republican, caucus memberships primarily help achieve policy and representation goals, and different caucuses yield different benefits. Some are important for information related to policy: "the research of the House Wednesday Group [is] helpful . . . but the information exchange is really the most useful." The Environmental and Energy Study Conference offered him a weekly newsletter, meetings, and briefings, often with a speaker, about each stage of an issue. A regional caucus provided representation opportunities through its geographic focus and has obtained committee assignments for its members and legislation with provisions, formulas, and funding helpful to the region. This representative joined an industry caucus, and expected to become more active in it, because groups in his district "wanted me to be a member, and I agree. . . . It's a major industry in the district and very important." He described his own personal calculation this way: "In joining a caucus, I need to assess two things: how much am I willing to commit funds [that could otherwise be used for personal staff] and how much am I willing to commit my own time?"

Concern about a particular piece of legislation can prompt caucus membership. A representative described taking part in the High Altitude Caucus: "One of the biggest problems that we have at our altitude is, when they pass all these clean air things, they tend to do it for sea level, and it often doesn't work at high altitudes. For example, if you set a carburetor on a car for sea level, and you bring it to a mile high, it doesn't work, [but] it's a federal crime to tamper with it. You . . . have to crank that in." The caucus was successful in having the law amended on this issue, in part by this member's "telling them I'm an environmentalist, too, and I'm not doing this because I want dirty air . . . [but] what you've done for clean air at sea level makes dirty air at [high] altitudes." The caucus's symbolism was also important: "when you call a group a High Altitude Caucus, people realize there are differences . . . and then you explain it. . . . That was the only way I knew to get their attention."

A freshman Republican liked the solidarity and informational benefits of the class club, which provides information on emerging issues and a broad context for events going on in Congress. A not incidental benefit is the contact it provides with other Republican members. This member's primary purpose in joining other caucuses was policy information, to "get someone else's opinion and viewpoint on the issues. . . . [Caucus information] helps me do my job better." A freshman Democrat also emphasized access to policy information as being among his chief reasons for joining caucuses: "The DSG's regular research material and information on issues is most helpful. . . . The materials outline the content of legislation and the major issues on both sides, and they're reasonably objective. . . . I'm a member of the Environmental caucus for their research materials—they're used by my staff. . . . I attend Environmental Conference meetings to hear guest speakers on a particular subject . . . and meetings of the class club when people from the administration—cabinet secretaries—speak. . . . It's the most direct contact that you'll have with cabinet officers and a chance to ask questions and to get some sort of real feeling for the person's views."

This representative joined other caucuses "because of wanting to work on a particular problem and being able to work with people who represent districts where those problems are important. [For example] the Suburban Caucus has been working on some legislation regarding the current federal regulations which require federal offices to be located in center city areas and moved out of suburbs, and I represent both the center city and the suburbs in my district, as do many people, and we've been working for some changes in those regulations." A more senior representative emphasized caucus membership as a means of achieving policy goals important to him. Although a subcommittee leader, he joined and worked for a state/district caucus as a way to get around both party and committee leaders in pursuing his policy goals.

One member summed up and echoed his colleagues' views on why members join caucuses: "The problems are complex and members have a need and a desire to deal with a particular problem that affects their districts . . . in an in-depth way. The best way to do that is for members having common interests to get together and work" in a caucus. A freshman representative said, "Being able to focus my attention on a problem and feel that I have a way of addressing some problems . . . is helpful," and pointed out that caucuses cut across committee jurisdictions and, unlike the formal committee system, welcome freshmen participation.

Data on membership in the six types of caucus confirm these comments (see table 5-2). Caucus membership was analyzed in two ways. First, the variables that affected the number of caucuses of each type that a member joined were assessed using regression analysis. Second, logit was used to examine the factors that affected whether a member joined any caucus within a category; here, the dependent variable was whether the member joined an industry or a regional caucus, for example, but not the number of caucuses joined in the category. Ideology (conservatism), party, seniority, leadership, and constituency variables were included in each equation.

Seniority and conservatism are both significant variables affecting memberships in party caucuses, for both Democrats and Republicans. Party leaders are more likely to join more party caucuses than their colleagues. Committee leaders are less likely to join any party caucus. Increasing conservatism decreases membership in party caucuses for Democrats. However, increasing conservatism increases membership in party caucuses for Republicans. Interviews confirmed that Republican caucuses have been important in providing information and developing legislation that offered alternative perspectives in the House before 1995 and in the Senate when the Republicans were the minority party.

Membership in personal-interest caucuses is also affected by ideology and seniority. The more conservative or the more senior the representative, the fewer are the caucus memberships. Party and ideology significantly affect whether a representative joins any personal-interest caucus. The data confirm that joining personal-interest caucuses is affected primarily by personal interest and inclination. Selected constituency characteristics related to caucus issues are significant variables for membership in national constituency caucuses. As expected, members of the Congressional Black Caucus and the Hispanic Caucus have districts with a high proportion of blacks and Hispanics, respectively. Congressional Black Caucus members come from districts that are 47 percent black, on average, in contrast to 9 percent black constituents for representatives who are not Congressional Black Caucus members. Hispanic Caucus members represent districts that are 49 percent Hispanic, compared to 4 percent Hispanic constituents for colleagues who have not joined the caucus. Seniority and degree of conservatism or liberalism are also significant for these caucuses—and also for the Women's Caucus.[6]

Ideology and party drive membership in regional caucuses. Rural characteristics, the percentage of foreign-born, and levels of agriculture and manufacturing in the region are also significant. Members whose dis-

Table 5-2. Variables Affecting Caucus Membership, by Caucus Type, Ninety-seventh Congress

Caucus Type	Party	Ideology (Conservatism)	Terms (Seniority)	Party Leader	Committee Leader	Prestige Committee Member	% of Workforce in Agriculture	% Rural Constituency	% Workforce in Manufacturing	% Foreign-born Constituents
Personal interest										
Number of caucuses joined	.1161	-.0243*	-.0332***	.0142	-.1622	-.1177				
Whether member is in any caucus	.5106***	-.0315*	-.0483	.0797	-.1288	-.4152				
National constituency[a]										
Whether member is in caucus	-1.42***	-.039*	-.055	-.912	-6.936	-.247				
Regional										
Number of caucuses joined	-.6787*	-.0138*	-.0126	.0672	-.0191	-.0392	-3.30**	1.263*	3.134*	2.958*
Whether member is in any caucus	-1.10*	-.0425*	.0117	.3662	-.0684	-.1635	-8.296**	3.064*	8.933*	4.640*
State/district										
Number of caucuses joined	.2688	-.006***	-.0666*	.0127	.0231	-.242	.159	.4438	-.0144	2.355*
Whether member is in any caucus	.8659**	-.011	-.1065*	-.4139	-.0685	-.3023	-5.359	2.998*	-1.607	5.408*

Industry

Number of caucuses joined	.2782**	−.0025	−.0302	.1836	.0342	.1059	−8.565*	1.961*	1.003	1.683**
Whether member is in any caucus	.227	−.0078	−.0722	.4947	.2969	−.1177	−11.94**	3.319*	.3471	1.587

Party[b]

Number of caucuses joined	.8339*	.0109*	−.006	.1649***	−.1483	.0750
Whether member is in any caucus	1.106*	.0078*	−.0140	.8222	−.8826***	.1643

Democratic Party

Number of caucuses joined	.095*	−.0177	.3133*	−.2182	.1649
Whether member is in any caucus	−.0397	.0728***	.4532	−.6974	.3034

Republican Party

Number of caucuses joined	.0134*	−.0627*	−.0475	−.0699	−.1549***
Whether member is in any caucus	.0540*	−.1142*	−.1440	−.1397	−.1382

Note: Number of caucuses (of a type) joined: OLS runs; report unstandardized coefficients and significance levels (based on *t*-statistics). Whether member is in any caucus of that type: logit runs; report unstandardized coefficients and significance levels (based on Wald Statistic).

[a]Because most national constituency caucuses (e.g., Congressional Black Caucus, Vietnam Era Veterans in Congress Caucus) are joined by all eligible members, only membership in the Congressional Caucus on Women's Issues, which is not joined by all women representatives, is analyzed here.

[b]Class clubs not included.

* = *p* < .005

** = *p* < .01

*** = *p* < .05

tricts are primarily rural or have a high percentage of foreign-born constituents join state/district caucuses that focus on concerns related to these
state- or districtwide characteristics. Constituency characteristics significantly affect whether members join industry caucuses and the number of
these caucuses joined. A higher percentage of rural and of foreign-born
constituents increase the number of industry caucuses that members join.
Higher levels of agricultural employment decrease, and of rural constituents increase, the chance that any caucus in this category is joined.
The percentage of the workforce employed in manufacturing is not a
significant variable, although it may be that agricultural employment
captures industrial interests.

Ideology and seniority are significant caucus membership variables,
overall. When membership in the different types of caucuses is analyzed,
there are varied patterns. Ideology and seniority continue to be significant for membership in party and personal interest caucuses. However,
constituency variables affect membership in constituency caucuses, with
ideology and seniority significant only for some types.

THE BENEFITS OF MEMBERSHIP

Caucuses provide opportunities to be a leader and to learn leadership
skills. Identification as a future leader is also important, particularly for
members who hope to gain influence and power within the chamber.
Leading a caucus is one route. The chair of a freshman class club said that
"being the leader of the class club has given me an entree to the leadership, not only on Capitol Hill but also at the White House. It's also allowed me to personally visit, talk with, and get information from people
whom, as an individual, I would not have had the opportunity to come
in contact with."

Informal leadership—that is, leadership outside the formal structure—
is likely to be created around new issues, established issues that divide
the membership in new ways, and issues "that do not fall neatly within
a single committee's jurisdiction" (Smith 1990, 79). And caucuses make
informal leaders into "leaders with portfolio" because, like committee
and party leaders, they have an organizational base and, thus, influence
(Hammond 1990). Newt Gingrich (R-Ga.), elected speaker in the 104th
Congress, became identified as a rising star through his leadership of the
Conservative Opportunity Society. Charles Stenholm (D-Tex.) enhanced
his influence in the House through his leadership of the Conservative

Democratic Forum and his work with the Agricultural Forum. He continued as a major and influential issue leader in the 104th Congress through his leadership of the Coalition and his continuing work as chair of the Conservative Democratic Forum.

In 1987 freshman Curt Weldon (R-Pa.) became known within the House after he identified an issue, established a caucus, and served as its chair. Weldon's interest in fire safety and emergency services stemmed from his academic training in fire protection and emergency preparedness and his experience as a firefighter and businessman (Shaiko 1992). He soon determined that there was no organizational locus in Congress for these issues and no way to deal with them systematically. In late 1987, Weldon organized the Congressional Fire Services Caucus to focus on fire safety and emergency services. In the first six months, 100 senators and representatives joined. In May 1988 a fire occurred in Speaker Jim Wright's office, which was down the hall from Weldon's. The system in place to handle fires was inadequate, and the response to this fire was badly bungled. Weldon put the fire out—and the relevance of the issue of firefighting increased enormously. Weldon became recognized as its chief spokesman and expert. Membership in the Fire Services Caucus grew dramatically— to 380 by 1992—becoming the largest caucus in Congress (and including, in its 1988 membership, Speaker Wright). The caucus has a legislative agenda that includes firefighting, disaster preparedness, emergency medical services, rural fire services, disposition of hazardous materials, health and safety issues, and industry regulation (ibid., 8). Caucus members represent these concerns on the relevant committees, which in 1992 included more than eighteen House committees and subcommittees.

Calls for congressional reform were the rallying point during the 102d Congress for seven freshman Republican representatives who organized as the Gang of Seven. The members gained experience and identification as leaders, and they significantly increased the visibility in Congress and in the constituencies of congressional reform issues. They developed federal budget data bases on computer disk and made them available to members of Congress and constituents. (The data included appropriation and expenditure information by line item and an assessment of the cost or savings of each bill, and all bills together, sponsored or cosponsored by each member of Congress. The data were used by both political parties in the 1992 congressional election races. It can be argued that data on individual members is only one element, and likely a skewed one, of a member's record.) Six of the Gang of Seven were re-elected in 1992. Identified by colleagues as issue leaders and perhaps future formal leaders, they continued their work and focus in subsequent Congresses.[7]

Gradually, as it became evident that caucuses offer opportunities for achieving personal as well as collective goals, caucuses gained legitimacy and became institutionalized. Senate caucuses are more informal than House caucuses; most operate out of senators' offices with the administrative assistant or a legislative assistant assuming duties as caucus staff director or coordinator. Bicameral caucuses active in the House are subject to House caucus provisions and regulations.

Some caucuses are represented on party committees either through tradition or informal rule. In this way, caucus members gain direct access to party leaders, are identified as future leaders within the formal structure, and have the opportunity to influence policy and strategy. Democratic speakers appointed members of several caucuses—the freshman class clubs, the Black and Hispanic Caucuses, the Congressional Caucus on Women's Issues, and the Boll Weevils—to the party's Steering and Policy Committee (since 1995, the Steering Committee and the Policy Committee). Similarly, appointments to the Democratic Caucus's Party Effectiveness Committee ensured representation for various congressional caucuses. Republican class clubs elected representatives to party committees and their whip organization.

By the 103d Congress (1993–94), the roles and activities of the freshman clubs were institutionalized, and freshmen in the 103d had increased their clout. At the start of the Congress, freshman Democrats and Republicans both organized early, electing interim chairs in early December, when party organizing meetings were held, and choosing congressional chairs shortly thereafter. The House freshman groups were large (sixty-four Democrats, forty-six Republicans). They were also vocal: they were covered by journalists and were carefully watched and encouraged by party leaders. Many of the freshmen had called for congressional reform during their campaigns; virtually all the Republicans, for example, had endorsed term limits for members of Congress. Freshman Republicans were important in the election of Richard Armey (R-Tex.) as chair of the Republican Conference and in the conference vote to limit the terms of committee ranking minority members to six years.

Both Democratic and Republican freshmen negotiated with party leaders and obtained seats on two major committees, Appropriations and Ways and Means. Democrats also obtained an additional seat on the Democratic Steering and Policy Committee. They agreed to support the rules changes developed by the Democrats' Task Force on Organization, Study, and Review in the organizing meetings of all Democrats, but they negotiated an agreement with party leaders that, after a sixty-day period, amendments to those rules could be offered by freshmen. In 1995, freshman continued to represent caucus groups on party committees. Freshman Republicans received important committee assignments, and they became a significant force in the election of Republican leaders and in supporting the "Contract with America" during committee and floor consideration.

The institutionalization of caucuses provides a structure, outside of the formal system, that permits participation by junior members, offers accessible leadership positions, and enables members to develop expertise and become recognized informal leaders. Junior members frequently establish, and disproportionately chair, caucuses. A high proportion of freshmen who have served as caucus leaders are later appointed to major committees or junior positions in the party. By the Ninety-ninth Congress, 66 percent of the Ninety-seventh freshman Democrats who had been caucus leaders were serving on an exclusive committee or were in a party leadership position (usually as part of the whip organization). Only 31 percent of non-caucus-leader freshmen held these positions.

Caucus leadership often precedes attractive committee or party positions and gives freshman members substantive expertise and leadership visibility. During her first term in the House, Barbara Boxer (D-Calif.) was president of the New Members Caucus and a member of the '82 Freshman Budget Group, which began meeting to exchange information but which became a significant force on budget issues. (It also expanded beyond the freshmen, as senior Democrats and party leaders began attending caucus meetings.) Boxer decided, as class president, to attend whip meetings and, on occasion, participated in those meetings, although she was not a member of the whip organization (*Politics in America* 1986). In the Ninety-ninth Congress, she was appointed an at-large whip and won a seat on the Budget Committee. Both she and Mel Levine (D-Calif.) developed acknowledged expertise on military procurement issues as a result of their work with the '82 Freshman Budget Group. Levine later co-chaired the Military Reform Caucus, and Boxer was appointed to the Armed Services Committee. In 1992, Boxer was elected to the U.S. Senate.

For junior members or members who do not serve on a relevant committee, caucuses provide an opportunity to gain expertise and develop issues that may be placed on the formal agenda and given attention by congressional leaders. Caucus members with subject expertise may be included in leadership task forces and strategy meetings. Buddy MacKay (D-Fla.) was active on budget issues after leading the Budget Study Group of the class caucus during his freshman term. Jim Courter's (R-N.J.) activities on defense procurement during the 100th Congress stemmed "from his co-chairmanship in '83–'84 of the Military Reform Caucus." In 1983, when George Miller (D-Calif.), a fifth-term representative, was appointed chair of the Arms Control and Foreign Policy Caucus's Task Force on Central America, he did not serve on any relevant committee. The caucus, led by the task force he chaired, went on to develop and obtain passage of an amendment to the FY1985 Department of Defense authorization bill that prohibited sending U.S. combat troops to Central America. A leadership aide confirmed the role of caucuses in developing issue expertise and a route to leadership: "Especially for junior members, caucuses are an alternate committee structure. . . . The '82 Budget Group probably spent as much time on budget issues as [Budget] committee members did. . . . Caucus members can be as conversant with an issue as someone on the committee." Through caucus activity, a junior member may become identified as a leader and rising star, and chairing one of the long-established congressional caucuses may legitimize leadership within the broader environment of the House. Because the alternate structure intersects the formal structure of the House, caucus training has become a legitimate route to formal positions of power.

Members must, however, be aware of possible negative consequences. Serving as a caucus leader may tag the member as too ambitious, too adversarial, or too closely tied to an issue position, which can later work against attaining leadership positions. However, the potential risks do not deter members from joining and leading caucuses.

SUMMARY

Members join caucuses to pursue representation and policy goals, and almost all members of Congress belong to them. Those joining fewer caucuses than their colleagues include Republicans, more senior or more conservative members, and party or committee leaders. Constituency factors affecting membership are, for industry caucuses, the presence or absence of industry; for state/district caucuses, district characteristics such as rural or foreign-born constituents; and for national constituency caucuses, proportion of black or Hispanic constituents.

Caucuses offer the opportunity to pursue and achieve individual goals (which are not necessarily in conflict with institutional goals). Members represent their constituents through caucus work, because caucus concerns are often explicitly linked to constituencies. Even if representatives and senators are not active in a caucus, their membership, alone, sends a message to constituents that the member shares their concerns. Members also achieve power in Congress through caucus work: caucuses identify and train future leaders of Congress and are one route to House leadership positions. Not least, caucuses help members achieve their policy goals through information sharing, coalition building, and legislation.

In reflecting on their personal calculations in joining caucuses or in describing why an increasing number of caucuses have been established, congressional members cite the growing complexity of issues and the need for coordination by like-minded colleagues on issues not typically handled by the formal structure. The achievement of policy, power, re-election, and most immediately, publicity entice members to join caucuses.

6/ CAUCUSES AND THE NATIONAL AGENDA

Congress's organization defines the opportunities for caucuses to affect the national agenda. There are numerous access points for individuals, groups, and institutions outside of Congress: a decentralized and sequential decision process, a wide distribution of resources, and congressional norms of full participation in legislative development. All these encourage caucus members to influence the agenda-setting process, most often through problem identification and policy formulation.

Caucuses serve as agenda entrepreneurs and are well positioned to recognize and to capitalize on a policy window (Kingdon 1995). Further, caucuses contribute to issue definition and help shift attention to new issues or new perspectives (Riker 1982; Kingdon 1995; Baumgartner and Jones 1991, 1993; Jones 1994). They also fit the approach that emphasizes macrosocietal factors and expert groups that dominate the agenda stage of the policy-making process (Weaver 1996). Caucuses use strategic flexibility (a key attribute for affecting agendas) to their advantage: they can work easily at all levels of government and the private sector and are constantly in touch with district and state constituencies. Because group members are high-level decision makers, they have access to others like them and can draw attention to caucus issues. All of these characteristics give caucuses the ability to respond rapidly and meaningfully to external change and policy opportunities.

Caucuses and agendas can be assessed by examining the following questions: Is caucus activity directed to some agendas but not to others (e.g., a congressional but not an administrative agenda)? Is caucus activity directed to certain types of issues but not to others (e.g., discretionary but not nondiscretionary; see Walker 1977)? Is there systematic variation among different types of caucus in setting or maintaining agendas? What factors affect caucus agenda activity?

The following analysis focuses on two types of agenda: the *public* (or systemic) *agenda* and the *governmental* (or formal or institutional) *agenda*

(Cobb, Ross, and Ross 1976; Cobb and Elder 1983). The public agenda "consists of issues which have achieved a high level of public interest and visibility" (Cobb, Ross, and Ross 1976, 126). The governmental agenda "is the list of items which decisionmakers have formally accepted for serious consideration" (127). Its focus is the congressional agenda—those issues that are the subject of debate, hearings, or legislation (bills and resolutions) in the Congress—and the administrative agenda—those issues that are given attention by the president or executive branch and by independent agency personnel. It may also include "pseudo-agenda issues—matters placed on agendas for symbolic reasons" (ibid.).

Caucuses may affect these agendas either by agenda setting or by agenda maintenance. Agenda setting occurs when caucuses change agendas by placing items on them or keeping items off them. Caucuses perform agenda maintenance when they keep issues on agendas. For administrative agendas, caucuses are likely to engage primarily in agenda maintenance because of the difficulty of establishing (in contrast to reacting to) these agendas. For congressional agendas, caucuses may pursue both agenda setting and agenda maintenance because of members' ability to participate directly in congressional decision making. Caucuses' attention to the public agenda might vary, although it seems likely that members will maintain rather than set agendas, given the greater investment of time and energy required for the latter. Because caucuses and caucus members are interested in policy outcomes, caucuses place a high priority on agenda activities. These activities are likely to vary systematically among caucus types.

AGENDA ACTIVITIES

A major and probably the foremost role that caucuses play in national policy making is agenda setting. The majority of congressional caucuses (80%) are active in both establishing and maintaining governmental and public agendas.[1] Agenda setting and the impact of this activity result from the work of the caucus and sometimes group leaders or group staff working with group leaders, rather than from caucus members' other positions. Caucuses serve a precommittee function in policy making within Congress: they may provide the initial contact between Congress and the external environment; they raise issues to the level of discussion and policy formulation; and they identify emerging problems, define their parameters, and develop legislative solutions before the issue appears on any committee's agenda.

On the administrative agenda, caucuses have achieved organizational change (e.g., the U.S. Travel and Tourism Administration, headed by the undersecretary for travel and tourism), have put program proposals on administrative agendas, and have influenced agendas by helping agencies formulate proposals sent to Congress. More indirectly, a few have affected administrative agendas through proposing and achieving specific personnel appointments. They can even keep issues off governmental agendas by keeping open communications between themselves and departmental secretaries and the White House.

Some caucuses, most particularly those representing national constituencies and those based on personal interest, devote a portion of their resources to expanding issues to the public agenda. Most, however, devote their major resources to placing items on governmental agendas. As elected officials, caucus members have ready access to governmental decision makers and, in many cases, are themselves able to place issues on a governmental agenda.

Seventy-six (94%) of the caucuses report that their primary purpose is to shape policy and that influencing policy agendas is only one of many strategies. Sixteen (20%) state explicitly that affecting agendas is a primary goal (as distinct from purpose) and work primarily to influence agendas. Twenty-nine (35%) meet for the purpose of establishing a caucus position on an issue. Thirteen (16%) hold hearings on issues or bills. Twenty-six (33%) report drafting legislation; 20 percent of these do so frequently. Sixteen caucuses (20%) offer floor amendments; eight of these do so several times a session. Forty (nearly 50%) work with party leaders, 33 percent on legislative issues and another 11 percent seeking to influence their members' committee assignments.

These data, however, do not capture the full range of agenda activities. Research affects agendas and, in fact, is often undertaken explicitly to do so. The House Wednesday Group of moderate to liberal Republicans focuses the attention of government policy makers through research reports, which increase the salience of certain issues. Caucus reports help place issues on the public and congressional agendas and are important in shaping the parameters of subsequent debate. Wednesday Group reports in the 1970s on U.S. policy toward China and on the volunteer army, for example, bore directly on those policy debates. More recently, the caucus affected U.S. policy toward Japan (see House Wednesday Group 1992a, 1992b) and environmental policy (see House Wednesday Group 1994). The 1994 report assessed and maintained on the environmental policy agenda an approach first developed for the Clean Air Act Amendments of 1990, giving industry permission to buy and sell emissions allowances. Caucus research can make a point and drive it home: one purpose of the Congressional Black Caucus's alternate budgets, for example, is to get the attention of colleagues on issues of government spending priorities.

Caucuses also affect agendas by meeting with high-level executive officials. Fourteen (17%) reported meetings with White House officials during the 100th Congress. Thirty (37%) met with other executive officials, and eighteen (22%) met with committee leaders (either the chairs or ranking minority members of committees or subcommittees). One-fifth met with party leaders. Although not all meetings are explicitly devoted to agendas, these offer opportunities for influencing agendas. During the Reagan presidency, for example, the Western Coalition met with cabinet members, White House staff, and the vice president to keep proposals for a merger of the Interior and Energy Departments off the governmental agenda. The Congressional Black Caucus (CBC) has met with several presidents to discuss and seek support for its agenda issues, including programs and funding levels. Regular access to the White House can also be a more low-key, routine affair: both the Senate Steering Committee and the Senate Wednesday Group regularly held luncheon meetings with Vice President Quayle during the Bush years. And according to an observer, the Tuesday Lunch Bunch had a "special in" at the Clinton White House.

There are, of course, constraints on caucus agenda activity at the individual, subunit, and institutional levels. At the individual member level, a senator's or representative's goals and perceptions of caucuses set the parameters for involvement. At the subunit, or caucus, level, limited resources such as staff or funds for research or publication may constrain agenda activity. A membership with diverse views on an issue constrains caucuses from seeking to affect agendas, although some caucuses influence agendas by disseminating information on issues rather than by developing a particular viewpoint. The informal nature of the caucus system can impede success, yet this does not generally appear to be a constraint. Members accept the use of informal procedures and are sensitive to the need for interaction with the formal party and committee systems. The relationship with congressional committees is particularly important, whether it is cooperative, as with the Port Caucus, or so antagonistic that it results in the demise of a caucus, as was the case with the Senior Citizens Caucus.

Table 6-1.   Agenda Priorities of Congressional Caucuses (in percentages)

		Administrative		Administrative and Congressional (equal focus)	Congressional	
Caucus Type	Public	Primary Focus	Partial Focus		Primary Focus	Only Focus
Party (N = 14)	36 (5)			7 (1)	57 (8)	36 (5)
Personal interest (N = 14)	50 (7)		14 (2)	14 (2)	57 (8)	28 (4)
National constituency (N = 4)	100 (4)			75 (3)	25 (1)	
Regional (N = 11)	45 (5)	9 (1)		45 (5)	36 (4)	
State/district (N = 8)	13 (1)	0		63 (5)		38 (3)
Industry (N = 18)	0		33 (6)	44 (8)	17 (3)	6 (1)

Source: Based on author interviews. N differs from telephone survey N.
Note: The table reports the agenda priorities of those caucuses active in agenda building. The N varies due to missing data; the percentages may add to more than 100 due to multiple coding. Number of caucuses is given in parentheses. Differences on public agenda setting and attention to the congressional or administrative agendas are significant at the .001 level, using the Pearson chi-square.

ACTIVITIES BY CAUCUS TYPE

There is systematic variation among the different categories of caucus (see table 6-1). Party caucuses, the only type of caucus seeking to influence national party agendas, work primarily on congressional agendas. Caucuses based on personal interest also work primarily on congressional agendas, although a small percentage focus on administrative agendas. Caucuses representing constituency interests show a systematic pattern in locus of agenda activity, with all national constituency caucuses wanting to influence the public agenda. Few regional, fewer state/district, and no industry caucuses seek this. A similar pattern is evident regarding governmental agendas: national constituency caucuses work on both congressional and administrative agendas, while industry caucuses devote most of their attention to administrative agendas.[2]

Caucuses also differ in their attention to discretionary and nondiscretionary issues (see table 6-2).[3] More than three-quarters of all caucuses work on discretionary issues. All constituency caucuses (including industry caucuses) that seek to affect agendas work on discretionary issues, while a high proportion of party and personal-interest caucuses do so. Industry caucuses differ from other types of caucus regarding agendas because, unlike the others, they focus primarily on administrative agendas and only on discretionary issues. State/district caucuses are most like in-

Table 6-2. Agenda Setting, by Caucus Type, Discretionary or Nondiscretionary Issues (in percentages)

Caucus	Discretionary Issues		Nondiscretionary Issues	
Party (N = 14)	93	(13)	86	(12)
Personal interest (N = 14)	78	(11)	50	(7)
National constituency (N = 4)	100	(4)	100	(4)
Regional (N = 11)	100	(11)	82	(9)
State/district (N = 8)	100	(8)	25	(2)
Industry (N = 19)	100	(19)	0	

Note: Includes both congressional and administrative agenda. Number of caucuses is given in parentheses.

dustry caucuses in that many give attention to administrative as well as congressional agendas and focus primarily on discretionary issues. The focus of constituency caucuses on nondiscretionary issues, however, does not follow this pattern: all national constituency caucuses work on these issues, while few regional caucuses, still fewer state/district caucuses, and no industry caucuses do. Most party caucuses and half of the personal-interest caucuses also work on nondiscretionary issues.

Further differences among types of caucus are revealed when the data on caucus work on agendas are disaggregated (see table 6-3). Caucuses use an array of activities and strategies to affect agendas. Variation on agenda activity and meetings with executive officials and party leaders are affected by the relationship of caucuses to party leaders, the constituencies being represented, and control of the White House.

Party caucuses are more active than other types of caucus on most agenda activities. Although they rarely hold public hearings, they work more with party leaders on issues. They also seek to affect agendas through their role as party insiders, working, for example, with party leaders on committee assignments. Nearly three-quarters of personal-interest caucuses work with the executive branch, and about half work with party leaders, particularly on issues before committees. National constituency caucuses more than other caucuses pursue activities designed to influence the public and congressional agendas. Regional caucus activity is high and is directed toward both congressional and executive branch agendas. State/district caucuses focus primarily on activities that affect executive agendas. Industry caucuses focus on administrative agendas and, on occasion, use insider activities to affect congressional

Table 6-3. Caucus Agenda Activities and Meetings, by Caucus Type, 100th Congress (in percentages)

Activity or Meeting	Party	Personal Interest	National Constituency	Regional	State/ District	Industry
Meeting to set caucus position	38 (5)	17 (4)	80 (4)	67 (8)	10 (1)	39 (7)
Meeting to set caucus strategy	54 (7)	21 (5)	80 (4)	75 (9)	0	17 (3)
Holding hearings	8 (1)	17 (4)	40 (2)	42 (5)	0	6 (1)
Testifying at hearings	38 (5)	17 (4)	40 (2)	50 (6)	0	33 (6)
Drafting bills	38 (5)	33 (8)	40 (2)	42 (5)	30 (3)	17 (3)
Drafting amendments	31 (4)	17 (4)	20 (1)	25 (3)	0	22 (4)
Working with party leaders	62 (8)	54 (13)	20 (1)	58 (7)	10 (1)	56 (10)
Working with party leaders: legislative issues	46 (6)	21 (5)	40 (2)	17 (2)	0	44 (8)
Working with party leaders: committee assignments	38 (5)	8 (2)	20 (1)	0	0	6 (1)
Working with party leaders: committee activity	31 (4)	25 (6)	40 (2)	17 (2)	10 (1)	28 (5)
Working with executive branch	38 (5)	71 (17)	40 (2)	75 (9)	60 (6)	67 (12)
Working with national party	38 (5)	8 (2)	20 (1)	17 (2)	0	11 (2)
Meeting with White House officials	38 (5)	17 (4)	20 (1)	25 (3)	0	6 (1)
Meeting with other executive branch officials	38 (5)	33 (8)	60 (3)	42 (5)	30 (3)	33 (6)
Meeting with Speaker of the House	46 (6)	37 (9)	60 (3)	58 (7)	60 (6)	20 (3)
Meeting with committee leaders	31 (4)	8 (2)	40 (2)	50 (6)	10 (1)	20 (3)
Activity with cabinet officials	46 (6)	37 (9)	20 (1)	58 (7)	30 (3)	39 (7)
Activity with sub- cabinet officials	46 (6)	42 (10)	40 (2)	42 (5)	0	50 (9)
Activity with president	31 (4)	8 (2)	40 (2)	25 (3)	0	17 (3)

Note: Number of caucuses is given in parentheses.

agendas. This may reflect caucus-committee overlap. For example, Ed Jenkins (D-Ga.), chair of the Textile Caucus, was also a senior member of the Ways and Means Subcommittee on Trade, which handles legislation affecting the textile industry. This overlap is typical of industry caucuses and reflects the fact that these caucuses deal with issues usually handled through subsystem politics.

Agenda activities are also affected by type of issue, with industry caucuses working primarily on those handled by the executive branch. These caucuses therefore seek to influence administrative agendas and discretionary issues. They do not use a public agenda strategy or engage in activities that may bring publicity, such as holding hearings or press conferences or testifying at congressional hearings.

In sum, types of caucus differ on agenda work, although not in the same way on every dimension. We turn now to a more detailed discussion of the agenda activities of the various types of caucuses.

Party Caucuses

All caucuses, but especially party caucuses, work on congressional agendas. The Democratic Study Group, for example, regularly worked with the Democratic leadership of the House to structure rules changes at the start of a Congress. Agenda setting can also be a way for new or unnoticed caucuses to raise their profiles. In the early 1980s, the Conservative Opportunity Society sought a more confrontational role for House Republicans through changes in restrictive rules of floor debate and by calling for roll call votes on usually routine actions, such as adoption of the preceding day's journal. The COS also pushed the Republican House leadership to bring the disputed 1984 election results in Indiana's Eighth District to the House floor for a vote; Newt Gingrich (R-Ga.) first raised the issue and was strongly supported by his colleagues in the COS. Although the election of Democrat Frank McCloskey was confirmed, so was COS's ability to affect the chamber's agenda by allying itself with the party's leadership.

Party caucuses work on a wide range of issues. Caucus interests are both substantive and procedural, and party groups have been important factors in agenda setting in both these areas. Most party caucuses (e.g., the Democratic Study Group, the House and Senate Wednesday Groups) represent a point of view within the party, and these groups have used procedural change as a major strategy to facilitate passage of their issue positions.

Above all, party caucuses are concerned with the congressional agenda.

Thirteen of the fourteen party caucuses that are active in agenda setting focus primarily or totally on Congress. Five also seek to affect the public agenda (see table 6-1). Their activity includes both discretionary and non-discretionary issues (table 6-2). Class clubs form a subset of party groups and may be ideologically diverse. While agreement on issue positions is problematic, agreement on procedural changes—regarding, for example, staffing or loosening the seniority system—is possible and can assist both group and individual goals. As a result, class clubs have been important in suggesting and supporting structure and rules changes.

The freshman class clubs of the 103d Congress (1993–94) are typical. These freshmen did not put reform on the congressional agenda—that had been done by their seniors and predecessors in the 102d Congress, who responded to constituency concerns and their own frustrations. The freshmen did, however, put specific reforms on the agenda for consideration and achieved some success. Both class clubs of the 103d established task forces to propose changes and reached final agreement on proposals in full caucus meetings.

The Democratic freshmen proposed limiting their party members to one committee or subcommittee chair and reducing legislative branch appropriations by a very large 25 percent. Although neither was approved as proposed, some reduction in appropriations occurred. Divided freshman Democrats could not agree on the more controversial items, such as term limits. The class divided along lines determined by constituency: freshmen from marginal districts endorsed institutional reforms, freshmen from economically troubled districts wanted to focus on economic issues, freshmen from safe districts, and often with (realistic) ambitions for moving up in the House, sought to work within the system and supported party leaders rather than radical reform. A split in the class was encouraged by party leaders, and the class did not work as a bloc (Donovan 1993, 807–10).

The Republican freshman proposal to limit the terms of committees' ranking minority members was adopted by the Republican conference, but the proposal to cut committee funding and staff by 25 percent was not. Both freshman groups also changed the scheduling of agenda items. They obtained a promise from party leaders during consideration of the FY 1994 budget that the leadership would schedule voting on deficit reduction before voting on an economic stimulus package. The freshmen reflected constituent concerns about cutting spending before increasing it and achieved a major change in the scheduling of House business.

Other party groups, including the Democratic Study Group, have also achieved procedural change in pursuit of their policy goals. In the late 1960s, the DSG placed on the congressional agenda the reform of some party (and House) rules and procedures and succeeded in effecting changes that democratized the selection of committee leaders, dispersed decision-making power among members, and otherwise made it easier for the views of rank-and-file party members to receive attention. DSG leaders intended to increase the likelihood that relatively liberal issue positions could prevail in party and committee.

In subsequent Congresses, the DSG continued to lead in putting specific reforms on the agenda. During the 103d Congress, in June 1994, after the Joint Committee on the Organization of Congress had made recommendations, and as the House and Senate prepared to take up those recommendations in floor debate, the DSG released a report on the increased use of the filibuster in the Senate. The study reported that there were more than twice as many filibusters in the 102d Congress (1991–92) as in the entire nineteenth century and that the increase had a detrimental impact on the passage of legislation and on policy making. The DSG sought a change in Senate Rule XXII to eliminate the supermajority requirement (sixty members) for ending a filibuster. This action maintained an agenda item, in that several House members of the Joint Committee had proposed this rule change as a committee recommendation. The caucus also explicitly acted to put the issue on the public agenda as a way of putting it on the Senate agenda. The DSG chair, Mike Synar (D-Okla.), expected the DSG report "to pique public interest in the filibuster, and force Congress to include [the elimination of the supermajority requirement] in its upcoming internal reform packages. . . . The use of the filibuster clearly shows it's going to take outside pressure to show the Senate what democracy ought to be" (Foerstel 1994). The use of a public agenda strategy by a party caucus is unusual, as is the attack on Senate rules by House members, but the focus on rules changes to obtain policy goals is quite typical of party caucuses.

Procedural issues in Congress tend to be discretionary. They are not regularly recurring issues, such as appropriations or authorizations, nor are they a response to a crisis. Procedural issues must therefore be established and maintained on an agenda by an entrepreneurial group or individual member. Because procedural issues often involve change, it is unlikely that Senate or House leaders or formally constituted subunits will provide the entrepreneurial impetus. Party caucuses, operating outside the formal structure, are the obvious subunits to do so.

Substantive issues of concern to party caucuses are both discretionary and nondiscretionary. On nondiscretionary issues, party caucuses have developed and proposed different solutions (new agenda items) to existing congressional agenda matters, as the Populist Caucus did in the Ninetieth Congress. This caucus's Task Force on Agriculture called attention to a provision of the Farm Credit Relief Act that would have adversely affected small farmers by raising loan limits at a time when the Farmers Home Administration's funds were in short supply. Through caucus efforts, including "Dear Colleague" letters, floor speeches, and the mobilization of outside interest groups to encourage their members to contact their representatives about the issue, the House amended the provision during floor debate.

On discretionary issues, party caucuses also successfully influence the congressional agenda, as the Wednesday Group did as a result of its research and information-sharing activities on issues such as foreign investment in the United States, U.S.-China trade, the volunteer army, and market-oriented environmental policies. All were timely, but none was systematically pursued on the policy agenda of Congress. In the 102d and 103d Congresses, the Conservative Democratic Forum (the Boll Weevils), led by Charles Stenholm (D-Tex.), was instrumental in placing the Balanced Budget Amendment on the House floor agenda. In succeeding Congresses, Stenholm continued as a leader on this issue, and in 1995 his version of the Balanced Budget Amendment was the one approved by the House, after a version supported by Republican leaders was defeated.

Party caucuses serve as information-exchange networks, which are critical to agenda building. They distribute material on legislation (the Democratic Study Group), or their research (the Wednesday Group), or "Dear Colleague" letters. They hold briefings and informal meetings at staff and member levels that influence agendas, both by adding items to them and keeping items off them. They draft and introduce legislation and offer amendments in committee and on the floor. Interview data confirm that these caucuses very actively seek to shape governmental agendas but that they prefer to work behind the scenes rather than to go public with their efforts.

A typical example is the DSG's role in developing legislation on the issue of reflagging tankers during the Persian Gulf crisis in 1987. DSG staff, at the direction of the executive committee of the caucus and in consultation with party leaders, drafted legislation, developed strategy, and sought to build a majority in favor of stopping the reflagging of foreign tankers under the U.S. flag, in opposition to the president's position. Mike Lowry (D-Wash.), chair of the caucus, with Dick Conlon, the highly respected staff director of the DSG, sought language acceptable to a broad array of House members in order to bring the legislation to a floor vote. Lowry billed his proposal—to delay implementation of the administration's reflagging plan—as the moderate course (other bills prohibited reflagging or only required notice to Congress before providing naval escort to reflagged tankers). Opposition to the tanker reflagging raised a number of issues, among them the role of Congress under the War Powers Resolution, the importance of Congress in foreign policy decision making, the best ways to ensure inclusion of Congress in foreign policy decision making, and how to proceed if Congress opposed a president's policy. On July 8, 1987, the House approved the DSG option as an amendment to H. Res. 2342, the Coast Guard Authorization Bill. The press did not report DSG's activity, although Lowry (according to *Congressional Quarterly Almanac 1987*, 258) was identified as coordinating the effort to delay implementation of the reflagging plan.[4]

Another example of caucus agenda activity occurred in 1993 during Budget Committee negotiations on the budget package for FY1994. Charles Stenholm, leader of the Conservative Democratic Forum (the Boll Weevils), worked to achieve proposed changes (new agenda items) for less stimulus expenditure and more budget cuts. Although he talked with the press about the group's perspective, the negotiations were closed to the public, and Budget Committee Democrats sought to come to an agreement in bargaining sessions. Members pushed colleagues for changes, but they needed a package that would be approved by the full House. Stenholm and the Boll Weevils achieved some success: the provisions of the bill that emerged from these negotiations were more in line with the group's views than the initial package had been.

Party caucuses can also influence the administrative agenda through off-the-record meetings with cabinet members and White House staff (see table 6-3). Note that nearly half the party caucuses, a higher percentage than any other type of caucus, report meeting with White House officials, and these are the only caucuses to report that they go to the White House frequently. Which party controls the presidency is important to whether or not party caucuses will seek to affect administrative agendas. During the Carter presidency, the United Democrats of Congress met with officials to discuss existing and emerging issues. Members of the Republican Steering Committee in the Senate met informally with President Reagan, and as a result a number of issues of concern to the senators subsequently appeared on the administrative agenda. At the start of his administration, President Clinton met with Democratic freshmen to discuss pending issues and noted that both he and they were the "new kids on the block sent to Washington to get things done" (Fessler 1992, 3789). Party caucuses are likely to be concerned with broad issues on the administrative agenda, rather than with issues directly related to matters of their constituency (although both the Boll Weevils and the Gypsy Moths have placed constituency-related matters on the administrative agenda).

Unlike other caucuses, some party caucuses work to build national party agendas, thus influencing the public agenda and subsequent governmental agendas. The Populist Caucus, for example, established a network of outside advisers to draft economic planks for the 1984 Democratic Convention. The caucus reported "working on . . . setting the political agenda for the [late] 1980s." The United Democrats of Congress were active in Democratic party platform discussions, arguing for a "moderate" approach on a number of issues, an approach congenial to the group's philosophy and also, in its view, the correct strategy to ensure election wins for the largest number of congressional Democrats.

Party caucuses' agenda building differs from that of other caucuses in several important ways. First, agenda setting or maintenance may occur with respect to a particular ideological point of view; this is the focus of the agenda activities of most of the nonclass party groups. Second, party caucuses engage in intraparty politics and seek to affect party agendas both within Congress and at the level of the national party. Third, the agenda role of class caucuses has been recognized and institutionalized; in the House in recent years, at least one seat on the Democrats' Steering and Policy Committee had been held by a freshman member elected by the freshman class caucus.[5] In 1993, at the start of the 103d Congress, Democratic freshmen elected three of their class to an expanded number of freshmen seats on the Steering and Policy Committee, and Republicans named three freshmen to their Committee on Committees. Since the 103d Congress, freshmen have continued to serve on party committees. Representation of intraparty interests is important to party leaders. As a consequence, these caucuses work primarily on the congressional agenda and also primarily within the party structure to achieve policy goals.

Personal-Interest Caucuses

Many personal-interest caucuses were established specifically to affect agendas. Although arms control and environmental issues have been on both public and governmental agendas, many topics of interest to these caucuses—for example, military reform and funding for space technology or for the arts—reach such agendas only through the efforts of attentive and responsive citizens or governmental decision makers. Like party caucuses, personal-interest caucuses focus primarily on the congressional agenda. Unlike party groups, though, some personal-interest caucuses also work on the administrative agenda. Half seek to affect the public agenda.

Personal-interest caucuses work on both discretionary and nondiscretionary agenda issues (see table 6-2). For instance, the Congressional Clearinghouse on the Future was established to raise the level of awareness within Congress on the study of trends, with the hope that such awareness would improve the quality of long-range policy making. Other caucuses were established in response to fears that particular issues, like human rights and industrial innovation, were becoming less important on the congressional or administrative agendas. Personal-interest caucuses also work extensively on nondiscretionary issues. A few caucuses—the Military Reform Caucus, the Arms Control and Foreign Policy Caucus, and the Coalition for Peace through Strength—have emphasized a particular perspective on a perennial issue, proposing new solutions (and therefore new agenda items) to a recurring agenda matter.

Personal-interest caucuses meet less frequently than other types of caucus to establish a position or to set caucus strategy but are more active than most in trying to influence the legislative agenda. Because caucuses in this group are bipartisan and often have a large and diverse membership, they typically establish task forces or an executive committee to determine caucus strategy on issues. Members of subgroups then work with their party leaders on caucus issues.

Personal-interest caucuses with a large and diverse membership often find it difficult to agree on a particular policy proposal and, therefore, often do not take positions on issues. They do, however, seek to maintain an issue on a governmental agenda through informational activities. The bipartisan Environmental and Energy Study Conference, with more than three hundred members during the 103d Congress, is typical. According to a senior aide, it was founded because of a belief "that environmental concern had peaked on the Hill and was on the wane, becoming just another issue." The founders "felt a collective need to keep environmental questions—the environmental implications of decisions—before the Congress at large." The caucus's founders rejected advocacy as an approach and chose instead to emphasize educational activities: "We reach out, educate, get the environmental point of view across to people who may vote right one out of ten times. Thus the thrust is on . . . keeping the air pollution issue before the Congress but not keeping the clean-air point of view. It's different."

Until the 104th Congress, when it restructured, the caucus distributed information through regular publications, which described relevant events inside and outside Congress. It also held meetings, briefings, and workshops, which were believed to be effective in agenda maintenance and, occasionally, in agenda setting. For instance, having decided that the "Global 2000 Report," a long-range look at resource trends and their impact on the country, was "a legitimate issue for Congress to deal with," the group "invited the secretary of state and the head of the Environmental Protection Agency to a members-only breakfast. Forty to fifty members sat down for an hour and got talked to about this. We're serving as a catalyst . . . to raise an issue here on the Hill (and perhaps in the executive) that hasn't previously been raised."

The Congressional Space Caucus is an example of a personal-interest caucus created to stimulate congressional response to the decline of an issue on the administrative agenda. Some scientists and members of Congress perceived President Reagan's FY1982 budget allocation for space science as a "shutdown budget." The relevant portion of the scientific community was in no position to react effectively: "Scientists have traditionally believed that the program was funded because of its 'stellar virtue' . . . and, therefore, there has never been any large lobbying effort by scientists on the Hill. And therefore the awareness of members of Congress was very low. . . . The caucus tried to create a high-level profile for space and space-related technologies [in Congress], to point out that an investment in space is one of the soundest economic investments that we can make." The caucus focused its efforts on "making noise on Capitol Hill" and encouraging scientists to lobby. It sponsored briefings; issued reports, information kits, and brochures; sent out "probably fifty" "Dear Colleague" letters during a session; and organized one-minute floor speeches. In 1993 the caucus continued this approach by circulating a report on public attitudes toward the space program (there was more support than many expected) and holding a briefing on the NASA budget, which was "attended by 150–200 members and staff."

Some personal-interest caucuses bring up new issues or new solutions to continuing issues. The Congressional Clearinghouse on the Future has been successful in including studies of future trends on the ongoing institutional agenda of Congress. Due largely to the efforts of its members, the House changed its rules in 1974 to require House committees to estimate the long-range impacts of their policy recommendations (H. Res. 988, The Committee Reform Amendments of 1974). The Clearinghouse can assist committees in carrying out this responsibility.

The Pro-Life Caucus, established in 1981 to keep attention on the abortion issue, introduces and organizes support for pro-life bills and amendments to authorization and appropriation bills. Commenting on the caucus's successful record on amendments to eliminate abortion funding from federal programs, a spokesman said that Democratic House leaders, who were then leaders of the majority party, "know that we've won on the funding bills." The Hyde Amendment and its variations continue to be an agenda issue. In 1993 a majority of House members supported a less-restrictive amendment, which prohibited the use of federal funds for abortions but permitted abortions in federal medical facilities if paid for by private funds. Also in 1993 the House passed a less-restrictive Hyde Amendment, which permitted federal funds for abortions not only to save the life of the mother (as in previous amendments) but also in cases of rape and incest. The Congressional Caucus on Women's Issues led, but lost, the fight for an even more liberal amendment. During 1995–96, more-restrictive Pro-Life Caucus amendments were again approved.

Half of the personal-interest caucuses generate support for their positions by expanding issues to the public agenda. On some issues, caucus success depends more on increasing the number of participants among attentive, and even mass, publics and expanding the issue arena than on parliamentary strategy or persuading decision makers directly. For example, faced with the recurring failure of attempts to have Congress pass a balanced budget constitutional amendment, Congress and Leaders United for a Balanced Budget Caucus organized to persuade targeted state legislatures to call for a constitutional convention to amend the constitution (thirty-two of the required thirty-four states had done so by the end of 1985). After 1985, the focus again shifted to Congress and deficit reduction measures.

Like national constituency caucuses but unlike other types of caucus, personal-interest caucuses devote a major part of their activities to agenda setting. They focus on issue identification, interest aggregation, and affecting the parameters of public and government discussion. Like party caucuses, they work primarily on the congressional agenda, although there is considerable interest in the public agenda also. Most work on discretionary issues, but unlike most other groups of caucuses, only half are active on nondiscretionary issues.

National Constituency Caucuses

All national constituency caucuses seek to influence both the public agenda and the governmental agenda (table 6-1). All work on both discretionary and nondiscretionary issues (table 6-2). And all follow the agenda-building strategy of mobilizing the public as well as decision makers. The profile of national constituency caucuses, therefore, differs from other caucus types and is likely based on the nationwide constituencies of these caucuses and their members.

These caucuses generally are involved in a large number—and a wide range—of issues. Some are discretionary agenda items. During the Ninety-seventh Congress, the Congressional Caucus on Women's Issues sought to include provisions for retraining older women in the legislation reauthorizing the Vocational Rehabilitation Act, and in the 102d (1991–92) and 103d (1993–94) Congresses, the Family Leave Act was a priority issue. Other concerns are nondiscretionary, such as funding levels for programs affecting women and children. The caucus continues to seek higher funding levels, but the issue itself is nondiscretionary.

Like the Congressional Caucus on Women's Issues, the Congressional Black Caucus works especially on civil rights and economic issues. The Hispanic Caucus has concentrated on government personnel issues, economic issues, the Simpson-Mazzoli Immigration Bill (in the Ninety-eighth Congress), and (in succeeding Congresses) U.S. treatment of undocumented aliens and other immigration-related matters. The Vietnam Era Veterans in Congress Caucus has focused primarily on health issues and Department of Veterans Affairs (formerly, Veterans Administration) treatment of Vietnam veterans.

The formation of caucuses of blacks, Hispanics, women, and veterans provides opportunities for caucus members to call attention to their concerns within Congress, to use their committee memberships to obtain information, to examine existing programs and proposed legislation for impact on those concerns, and to formulate a coordinated legislative program or agenda. As caucus members gain seniority, positions of power in the committee system provide new opportunities to influence the status and the content of legislation of interest to the caucus. In 1993, at the start of the 103d Congress, the political context also changed for several of these groups with the election of a Democratic president and a large increase in the number of women and black members of Congress, especially in the House. There were sixteen new black representatives, five of whom were women, and the first black woman senator. The number of blacks in the House increased from twenty-five in the 102d Congress to thirty-eight in the 103d. With the 1992 election, the number of women senators went from two to six; a seventh woman, Kay Bailey Hutchinson (R-Tex.), was elected in a special election in June. The number of women in the House rose from twenty-eight to forty-eight. The CBC talked of organizing a voting bloc of women and blacks; both caucuses emphasized the power of cohesive bloc voting and discussed coordinating legislative strategy. The 1994 elections, when Republicans gained control of both the Senate and the House, changed the political landscape considerably, but the number of women and blacks remained about the same.

Each of these caucuses has developed an agenda of issues to pursue and publicizes them at the start of each congressional session. The CBC makes a practice of placing its legislative agenda in the *Congressional Record* and, in recent years, has presented its own federal budget for consideration during the congressional budget process. The caucus's aspiration to a major role was highlighted (as was its public agenda strategy) when a July 1993 caucus meeting with President Clinton and a series of caucus rebuffs to the president on scheduling the meeting were extensively covered by the media, all of which helped bring the caucus's issues to public attention.

Unlike other types of caucus, national constituency caucuses work to place issues on the public agenda and thus to influence governmental and congressional agendas. Also unlike other types of caucus, a high proportion of national constituency caucuses engage in a wide range of agenda-setting activities (see table 6-3). Within Congress they testify at hearings, draft bills and amendments, and work with party leaders on committee issues. There is no clear pattern to the activity of these caucuses in setting administrative agendas; they choose their strategies according to the issue and their estimate of success. They generally do not carry on continuing dialogues with specific bureaus, but they have been successful in placing items on the administrative agenda when that has been the chosen strategy. The CBC has maintained long-term, albeit sporadic, dialogues directly with several presidents, and more recently, the Congressional Caucus on Women's Issues and the Hispanic Caucus have held similar meetings. The ease of access to high-level decision makers increased for the Vietnam Era Veterans in Congress Caucus when former member Albert Gore (D-Tenn.) became vice president.

The Congressional Caucus on Women's Issues has achieved some success in influencing the Department of Health and Human Services and the National Institutes of Health to give greater attention to women's health issues. On the administrative agenda, the caucus fought for including women in clinical trials and health studies and for more funding for research on diseases, such as breast cancer, specific to women. Through letters, meetings with administration officials, and occasionally the threat of legislation, the caucus achieved success. Their issues began as equity issues, but as health care, particularly the cost of illnesses and the focus on prevention, became important on the national agenda, the issues became broader economic and family issues.

Frequently, the Congressional Caucus on Women's Issues has succeeded in placing items on administrative and congressional agendas simultaneously. Caucus members testified on health care issues and drafted amendments to earmark monies for breast cancer research in appropriations bills at the same time that the caucus was pressing the executive branch to change the National Institutes of Health budget. The caucus has also brought together congressional committee, federal agency, and private sector groups to exchange information and to devise strategy on such issues as pensions for wives, widows, and divorcees and federal assistance to battered wives and abused children.

The Congressional Hispanic Caucus, like other national constituency caucuses, has worked to increase saliency among the mass and attentive publics and among congressional and administrative decision makers. A senior staff aide said that the group has "two goals simultaneously. One [is] to impact on government; the other [is] to impact on the constituency—let them know what is going on." The process, particularly that of influencing administrative agendas, is "not highly structured," according to one respondent; nevertheless, the caucus can point to a number of successes. The process is described as follows: "Relationships with . . . the agencies are not formal. . . . There is a great deal of cooperative give-and-take, both at the social level [it is a community that knows each other] and at the professional level. . . . The caucus has been able to make a good contribution, getting all the agencies off the taco and guitar track into what we hope are substantive things." The caucus has promoted the appointment of Hispanics to federal agencies (resulting in more than two hundred during the Carter administration) and has maintained contact with these officials on issues of concern to the community.

National constituency caucuses regularly monitor administrative actions. The Congressional Caucus on Women's Issues, for example, successfully objected to the proposal to abolish the National Cancer Institute's Central Task Force on Breast Cancer, and most caucus members signed a letter opposing the 1982 Health and Human Services proposal to require family planning clinics to inform parents when their teenage daughters were given contraceptives. Women members of the caucus later opposed the imposition and continuation of the gag rule on abortion counselling, "as a restriction of the free speech rights of medical personnel at family planning clinics" (Thompson 1993, 37).

The Vietnam Era Veterans in Congress Caucus has been active in monitoring the actions and agenda of the Veterans Administration and the Department of Veterans Affairs regarding the herbicide Agent Orange. The caucus was a significant player in putting the issue on the governmental agenda—and in keeping it there. During the Bush administration, the caucus achieved major successes with Veterans Affairs Department rulings that Vietnam veterans with diseases linked to the use of Agent Orange in Vietnam would be eligible for medical care at Veterans Administration facilities. The 1993 decision by the department to increase the number of illnesses for which veterans could receive disability benefits based on exposure to Agent Orange in Vietnam is considered an important accomplishment by the caucus.

The work of the CBC exemplifies the public-agenda-setting activity of national constituency caucuses. The caucus draws its brain trust of advisers from the entire country. Through its "action alert communication network," members of more than 150 black grassroots organizations can be mobilized to speak out to the general public or to lobby members of Congress. Congressional, presidential, and public attention are drawn to CBC issues through wide press coverage of its activities. Meetings with the president, for example, and the Black Caucus Weekend each autumn, which draws blacks from across the nation for a weekend of issue seminars, dinners, and fund-raising events, increase the salience of and gain public support for issues of concern to the caucus. Twenty-three thousand attendees, including President Clinton (who spoke at the Black Caucus Foundation dinner), attended the September 1993 weekend. The acceptance of caucus members as spokespersons for the national black community is essential to caucus success in placing matters on the public agenda—and high-profile events contribute to such acceptance.

Members of these national caucuses and their constituencies strongly share the media's perception. The staff director of the Hispanic Caucus, for example, said that "the main purpose of the caucus is really to represent the Hispanic constituency at the federal level of government. Obviously, this group of Hispanics [in Congress] has the highest level of visibility in the country, serves a broader constituency than their own districts, and have banded together to service that constituency at the federal level." Part of that service is to put issues on the public agenda, to activate their grassroots constituency, and thus to affect the governmental agenda. Governmental officials outside of Congress consider national constituency caucus members representatives of their group; for example, in 1993 the governor of Puerto Rico met with two Hispanic Caucus members from New York regarding statehood for Puerto Rico, because the representatives had a large number of Puerto Rican constituents.

In contrast to other caucuses, national constituency caucuses simultaneously mobilize the public and put issues on governmental and public agendas. During congressional consideration of the federal budget, for example, the CBC Budget Task Force works with its network of black organizations and the National Black Leadership Roundtable, as well as with committee and personal staff, to develop an alternative budget. It seeks and receives widespread media coverage to draw public attention to issues and to obtain public support for its proposals. The Congressional Caucus on Women's Issues operates in a similar fashion, bringing representatives of outside groups together and obtaining media coverage of their legislative and administrative efforts on issues that affect women, such as pensions for women, credit opportunities for women business owners, and women's health issues.

Regional Caucuses

Regional caucuses are among the most active in seeking to influence the national agenda. Most use all available strategies to achieve their goals. All undertake agenda activities within Congress and work on discretionary issues. Nearly half devote as much attention to administrative agendas as to congressional ones, and nearly half seek to influence the public agenda. Almost all also work on nondiscretionary issues. Two of the most active have been the Northeast-Midwest Congressional Coalition and the New England Congressional Caucus, which invest much effort in developing agenda items and legislative initiatives on a wide range of issues. These issues are diverse on the surface yet have deep regional implications. Some are clearly discretionary.

The New England Caucus reached a peak of activity during Thomas P. (Tip) O'Neill's tenure as majority leader and speaker. It subsequently disbanded in the 100th Congress, reorganized, and became active again in 1993, during the 103d Congress. The caucus, in cooperation with Tufts University, sponsored the New England Energy Congress in 1978 and 1979. Its work resulted in a detailed report, which provided the ideas for a package of twenty-two bills introduced by caucus members. Several of these bills were enacted into law. Similarly, the Northeast-Midwest and New England Caucuses joined with other northeastern organizations to sponsor a Nova Institute study of the region's water needs and problems. Out of that study grew a successful coalition effort to include in the 1980 Water Resources Development Bill language permitting the Army Corps of Engineers to take part in repair and rehabilitation projects for urban water systems.

During the 100th Congress, the Northeast-Midwest Coalition provided background research for the development of legislation on hazardous waste disposal. In the 1990s, alerted by the state demographer of Indiana, the caucus was "instrumental in getting congressional hearings and energizing the political community" on the Census Bureau's proposed adjustment of 1990 census figures used to allocate federal funds. The Northeast and the Midwest would have lost funding, because the head count undercounted urban industrial centers in comparison with other areas. In the hearings, "significant problems with the adjusted figures came out—[adjusted] numbers were accurate for the national level, but when you're distributing money, you need accurate state and local numbers." (Eventually, the Census Bureau announced it would use head count numbers, a procedure subsequently confirmed by a federal court ruling.)

A large number of issues that receive the attention of regional caucuses involve authorizations or appropriations for existing programs and, hence, are nondiscretionary—that is, the issues recur regularly on the congressional calendar because reauthorizing or appropriations legislation is required in order to continue a program. (The level of funding, or the program guidelines, are discretionary, but the calendaring of consideration is nondiscretionary.) As has been the case with national constituency caucuses, regional caucuses, by using their data to point out "inequities" in the formula by which federal funds are allocated, have performed an agenda function by redefining the terms of legislative debate. The politics of distribution have been replaced in some cases by the politics of redistribution, as members have become increasingly aware of how the interests of their constituents have fared relative to those of constituents from other regions. The Northeast-Midwest Congressional Coalition, the New England Congressional Caucus, and the Congressional Sunbelt Caucus have been particularly active in raising questions of equity in the distribution of federal funds (see, e.g., Dilger 1982).

Regional caucuses put issues on committee agendas by introducing legislation and offering amendments during committee markup of bills. They propose amendments during debate, and they affect the floor agenda. These caucuses also strive to affect development and administration of a wide range of federal programs within the administrative structure. The Conference of Great Lakes Congressmen, for example, worked extensively with the Departments of Transportation and State to modify proposals for increasing St. Lawrence Seaway tolls. Regional caucuses work with executive agencies as tax and energy proposals have been developed. And caucus members and staff meet with departmental and Office of Management and Budget officials in efforts to affect formulas for grants.

The Congressional Border Caucus affected Reagan administration agendas. Its members were consulted and were asked to testify at hearings held by the President's Task Force on Border Concerns throughout the Southwest. The Northeast-Midwest Coalition advanced its agenda during the Reagan presidency when Republicans in the caucus discussed budget priorities with the White House. They also obtained support for a one-year extension of the Maybank Amendment repeal (to help depressed industries of the Northeast and the Midwest), for an agreement to reevaluate federal program formulas, and for the establishment of a Northeast-Midwest economic advisory group within the White House. An observer summarized the activity: "The coalition's agenda was being forced on the administration by the Northeast-Midwest Republicans. And they were working as Republicans with Republicans but pushing what had been the coalition's agenda—and being somewhat successful."

Regional caucuses also perform a negative agenda function, as the Western States Coalition did by convincing the White House, during the Carter administration, to drop its proposal for a Department of Natural Resources. Many issues of concern to regional groups are dealt with in the relevant subsystem: the Border Caucus and the Task Force on Devaluation of the Peso, for example, brought national attention to the economic impact of Mexico's fiscal crisis in the 1980s. Expansion to the public agenda may activate opposition groups, but on issues with broad regional appeal (e.g., oil imports in New England) it is a useful strategy.

Regional caucuses typically seek to work with officials and groups in their regions to place issues on governmental agendas. Communication with attentive publics is regular and, occasionally, institutionalized (e.g., through panels of regional advisers). The general public, usually, has not been a part of regional caucus activity.

State/District Caucuses

State/district caucuses seek to influence both congressional and governmental agendas; only one caucus, the Rural Caucus, also works to place items on the public agenda. All of these caucuses work on discretionary issues; one-fourth work also on nondiscretionary matters. As with regional and industry caucuses, work with subsystem actors is most typical. State/district caucuses are among the least active in agenda setting and other activities, perhaps because of the diffuse nature of the issues they address.

The concerns of state/district caucuses are broad and include rural issues, the interests of small cities, and the benefits of stimulating imports. Often, different aspects of a problem are under the jurisdiction of several congressional committees or executive agencies, and these caucuses serve an integrative function in placing the broad issue on the governmental or public agenda.

The Family Farm Task Forces, for example, were established "principally to take a look at what was happening in agriculture regarding the disappearance of the family farm. There hadn't been enough specific focus on that one issue, and it was serious enough that it was due. . . . Maybe if you generated enough interest among members (via a caucus), you might get that focus." In Congress, no one committee looks at the full range of issues affecting family farms, such as taxes, land prices, price supports, and production expenses. The task forces, by taking into account the interrelations of a number of subissues, hoped to raise the question of family farms to governmental agenda status. These broad, crosscutting issues are discretionary when viewed as a single issue but are often tied to nondiscretionary matters, such as the reauthorization of programs.

Caucuses that address specific foreign policy concerns held by sets of citizens in members' electoral constituencies—the Soviet Jewry caucuses, the Irish caucuses—seek to place discretionary issues on U.S. governmental agendas and to influence the activities of other countries.

The activities of the Congressional Rural Caucus are typical of caucuses that seek to influence agendas by identifying problems, defining their parameters, and developing legislative solutions. During the Ninety-sixth Congress, this caucus worked on the Rural Development Act, gathering information, coordinating private sector groups, helping draft legislation, and following the legislation. In 1994 a caucus-initiated report on the increase in poverty among rural children sought to raise this issue to formal agenda status (U.S. House of Representatives 1994). The caucus articulates and lobbies for the interests of small cities and rural areas at the Budget Committee, authorization, appropriation, and Rules Committee stages of the legislative process.

An amendment that would have prohibited the sale of U.S. weapons to Great Britain for use in Northern Ireland was offered to an appropriations bill by the chair of the Ad Hoc Committee on Irish Affairs. It was described by its author, Mario Biaggi (D-N.Y.), as leading "to a first-time discussion on the House floor of the Irish question. For approximately one hour . . . myself and fifteen of my colleagues spoke. . . . The amendment led to a commitment by the House Foreign Affairs Committee chairman that a full investigation and hearing would be held in the matter. This was done some two weeks later" (*Congressional Record*, June 10, 1980, E2848) The Department of State then reversed its previous decision to approve such arms sales. When President Reagan assumed office, caucus leaders wrote him to urge that the embargo be maintained, and they were assured by the White House that this would be the case. In speaking of this and other efforts, the caucus chair emphasized the importance of agenda setting: "The Ad Hoc Committee exists and will continue to exist to ensure that the Irish question is addressed in an adequate fashion by the Congress and the Administration" (ibid.).

The congressional agenda has been viewed in part as a means of attracting administrative attention. For instance, before the breakup of the Soviet Union the Ad Hoc Monitoring Committee on the Baltic States and the Ukraine regularly obtained special orders for making floor speeches to commemorate events such as Lithuanian Independence Day. Members of the Ad Hoc Committee on Irish Affairs frequently use the *Congressional Record* to publicize caucus activities as well as their own views and the views of U.S. and Irish political leaders on conditions in Northern Ireland: "The significance of this exercise should be understood," remarked the caucus chair. "In addition to the 535 senators and representatives and the thousands of Executive Branch personnel who read the *Record* daily, it is also read by each foreign embassy in the United States. This includes the Embassy of Great Britain, which is very sensitive about its international image. Negative publicity about the situation in Northern Ireland presents a great embarrassment" (*Congressional Record*, August 18, 1980, E3803).

Like many other caucuses, the Congressional Rural Caucus maintains a dialogue with a number of departments and agencies, for instance, with the Environmental Protection Agency about sewage treatment programs, the Community Services Administration about low-income programs, the Department of Labor about employment and training programs, the Department of Housing and Urban Development about matters related to small cities and rural areas, and the Farmers Home Administration. Unlike most other caucuses, the Rural Caucus has gone to court over issues of concern to it. During the Nixon administration, the caucus sued the Office of Management and Budget for the release of $4.5 billion in impounded funds for sewage treatment programs. When Gerald Ford assumed the presidency, the suit was withdrawn without prejudice, and much of the money was released by the new administration.

Industry Caucuses

Almost all these caucuses formed to publicize, consider, and find solutions for the problems of particular industries. They try especially to affect administrative agendas and to work on discretionary issues; they are involved in subsystem politics.

Few of the discretionary matters of concern to industry caucuses are dealt with in major programs that routinely come up for reauthorization. This has given these caucuses considerable flexibility in choosing the timing, setting, and political vehicle by which to achieve their goals. However, on some issues, such as trade (particularly with regard to modes of relief such as import quotas or tariffs) industry caucuses lack this flexibility. Unless they wish to alter existing trade legislation, on which they would likely encounter significant opposition, industry caucuses must influence the agenda of the U.S. trade representative or persuade both chambers of Congress to reverse a presidential decision against providing the relief recommended by the International Tariff Commission. Industry caucuses rarely try to affect the public agenda; the issues with which these caucuses are concerned are more typically handled by subsystem politics.

Several industry caucuses seek to create an industry identity in order to encourage placing concerns on governmental agendas. One example is the Congressional Travel and Tourism Caucus. According to a senior caucus staffer, "Travel and tourism was not appropriately understood or appreciated because it is such a diverse, diffuse industry. No one really understood it was an industry. . . . [There is the] little gift shop, the hotel, the motel, and the bus on the street, but you never see it as an industry. . . . With a caucus, we could pool our information and our energies and exchange information and advice to further [industry] needs to ensure fair and equitable treatment."

Because the issues of primary interest to these caucuses in most cases directly affect only a minority of constituents in a minority of districts or states, caucus leaders call attention to their problems within Congress and the administrative structure. For industries with continuing problems, caucuses shift from agenda setting to agenda maintenance. The Congressional Automotive Caucus, which was formed to help the Chrysler Corporation obtain a federal loan, has more recently seen its primary function as keeping "the problems of the domestic auto industry on the front burner in Congress."

More than any other type of caucus, industry groups try to influence the administrative agenda, a reflection of their concerns over imports and exports and administrative regulations. In the 1980s several caucuses shifted some attention to the congressional agenda, hoping to attract the attention of administrative officials through legislation or hearings. Groups are in contact with executive personnel mostly at bureau levels or with Executive Office of the President agencies, such as the U.S. trade representative. On occasion, these caucuses also meet with high-level political appointees. But their ties to government bureaus permit them to maintain items on agendas, to monitor program implementation, to identify issues they want placed on administrative agendas, and to influence agenda priorities through information exchange.

The Mushroom Caucus, for example, influenced the executive branch into putting a three-year limitation on the importation of canned mushrooms. The group had suggested putting the issue on the congressional agenda, but industry leaders preferred to focus on the administrative structure. Working primarily with the U.S. trade representative, the caucus drew attention to the industry's plight and, subsequently, claimed to be instrumental in obtaining the trade agreement. The caucus then monitored the agreement. The Travel and Tourism Caucus had similar success in keeping issues related to tourism on administration agendas. During the Carter presidency, the caucus regularly sought a separate agency for tourism, opposing the president's proposal to incorporate tourism programs into the Commerce Department's International Trade Administration. In December 1980, President Carter pocket vetoed a caucus-sponsored bill, S. 1097, which would have established a quasi-public corporation to implement tourism policy. In 1981, caucus members introduced H. Res. 1311, which proposed creating an undersecretary for travel and tourism in the Commerce Department, to oversee an upgraded existing bureau on tourism, and the annual development of a comprehensive national tourism marketing plan. The bill was supported by the industry and, reluctantly, by the Reagan administration. The legislation was approved in October 1981. During the 104th Congress (1995–96), the caucus fought, but lost, a downgrading of this function within the Commerce Department.

More than any other caucus category, industry caucuses participate in subsystem politics. In comparison with other types of caucus, industry caucuses work disproportionately on the administrative agenda. Although these caucuses exhibit the typical tactical flexibility of congressional informal groups, moving among governmental levels or shifting from executive branch to congressional branch, caucus members rarely seek to expand arenas or to increase the number of participants in agenda setting.

These caucuses generally have routinized means of receiving input from industry and other local leaders. The Congressional Automotive Caucus has held public meetings in House districts to hear testimony from mayors, state officials, and management and labor spokespersons, the speeches being inserted in the *Congressional Record* as one means of alerting the Washington community to the industry's problems. The Senate Steel Caucus has heard off-the-record testimony from company and labor leaders, hearings to which the trade press were invited. More typically, these caucuses schedule fairly regular meetings between caucus and private sector leaders, as the Senate Steel Caucus does, or informational meetings with representatives from industry, labor, and consumers, as the Senate Rail Caucus does. Some caucuses, active on issues around which outside interests are not well coordinated, have established advisory boards composed of corporate and interest group leaders to provide input to caucus agendas.

SUMMARY

A majority of caucuses seek to influence agendas, and many do so successfully. Caucuses play an important precommittee role, which is critical for successful agenda setting. This role fits with caucus members' views of the caucus system as supplemental to, but not supplanting, the formal committee and party systems. In conducting research, exchanging information, drafting bills and amendments, and working with the executive branch and within Congress, caucuses carry out activities that are essential to influencing agendas. As expected, they work to establish and maintain issues on the congressional and public agendas. But contrary to expectation, they put issues on administrative agendas as well as maintain them there. Their agenda influence with the executive is broad and appears to reflect that caucus members are also elected officials with constituencies and that caucuses establish ongoing, stable relationships with executive personnel.

As expected, there is variation among types of caucus in agenda focus and activities. The type of caucus (party, constituency, or personal interest) and the issues of interest to the caucuses are determining factors. Party caucuses work within the party, as partisan theories of congressional organization would predict. Because these caucuses, and party leaders, seek to settle concerns within the party, the groups focus primarily on congressional agendas. However, if a president is of the same party as the caucus, it will also meet with the president, White House staff, and on occasion, high-level bureaucrats. Much less frequently, party groups that are possible swing voting blocs meet with opposition party presidents or aides.

Constituency caucuses vary in their agenda focus and strategies according to the type of constituency represented, which determines the issues of interest to the caucus and the place within the government where the issue is handled. As the constituency base and the issues of concern narrow, the proportion of constituency caucuses seeking to affect the public agenda drops sharply. National constituency caucuses, more than any other group, pursue a public-agenda-setting strategy. These caucuses serve as representatives of a broad and dispersed national constituency that can be mobilized through media reports, grassroots organizations, and the caucuses' networking systems. In addition, the caucus's perspective on various issues is shared not only by the national constituency but also by a broad group of the public. Regional caucus issues are of more localized interest. If these caucuses seek to put issues on a public agenda, they do so to activate the region, not the nation. These groups work on both congressional and administrative agendas. On a specific issue, the agenda effort is determined by the locus of responsibility for the issue within government and by the stage of the policy process. For instance, is legislation being developed by the executive or by Congress? And if by Congress, is it in committee or on the floor? Two types of constituency caucus, notably state/district and industry, focus more on administrative agendas than on congressional agendas. The issues on which they work are narrower, and decision responsibility is often in the executive branch. Particularly for industry caucuses, subsystem actors may agree on an approach but proposing congressional action may activate opposition. No industry caucus seeks to influence the public agenda.

The explanation for the focus of personal-interest caucuses on the congressional agenda, on some public agendas, and very occasionally on administrative agendas appears to be issue driven. It depends on whether or not the issue is of broad concern in the polity and whether governmental responsibility is lodged with the executive or with the Congress. These same factors explain the agenda activities of the various types of caucus. Party, state/district, and industry caucuses, since they undertake fewer public activities, such as holding hearings and testifying at hearings, than other caucus groups, are typical of insiders and subsystems. Constituency caucuses with broader issue concerns and a wider base of support undertake both the visible and the less visible agenda activities. Personal-interest caucuses present a mixed activity pattern.

Possible alternative explanations are not supported. If caucus size affected agenda setting, we might expect that larger caucuses would be more likely to use public-agenda-setting strategies. But caucus size does not distinguish between caucuses that work on different agendas. Nor does homogeneity of membership: members of a caucus will hold the same viewpoint on an issue even though on other indicators (party, ideology) they are not the same. Members of industry caucuses, for example, agree on the plight or the problem of their constituent industries. Members of regional caucuses, drawn from both parties and with differing ideologies, concur on the needs of their region. Overall, the agenda activity of caucuses confirms the role of the caucus system as an alternative to the formal congressional systems of party and committee.

7/ CAUCUSES AND PARTY LEADERS

Congressional leaders operate in a context shaped by the external environment and the internal organizational structure of Congress (see, e.g., Cooper and Brady 1981; C. O Jones 1981; Mackaman 1981; Sinclair 1989, 1995). In the contemporary era, that context has been characterized by the decline of party influence in the electorate and by the increasingly complicated and crosscutting issues on governmental agendas. Congress has become more decentralized and more egalitarian.

At the same time, leaders have been given more tools with which to manage the legislative process. Changing norms and more opportunity for active participation by individual members have increased expectations that leaders will respond to demands of individuals and groups within the institution (see, e.g., Bullock and Loomis 1985; Deering and Smith 1985; Ornstein, Peabody, and Rohde 1985; Sinclair 1981, 1983, 1995). In the highly individualistic Senate there has been less need for leaders to accommodate caucuses, and party leaders continue to build coalitions by working with individual senators. But the relationship of House caucuses to party leaders is quite different. To understand this relationship, we need to raise the following questions: What is the relationship between the work of party leaders and caucus formation? What are the links between party leaders and the caucus system? What factors affect the interaction of the two systems? How do caucuses affect the work of leaders in managing the House and the legislative process? What are the lessons of the leader-caucus relationship in the contemporary Congress?

As the data presented below reveal, caucuses are represented on party committees and perform leadership socialization functions. They work with party leaders on legislative issues, primarily at the point of floor consideration. The various caucus types work differently with party leaders, and there are major contrasts between party caucuses and other caucus types in their relationship with congressional leaders.

CAUCUS FORMATION AND FORMALIZATION

Among the factors creating the conditions for an accelerated rate of caucus formation in recent years, deficiency of party leadership is one of the most significant. As detailed in chapter 3, leaders' failure to adapt congressional structures to handle contemporary problems or to address members' policy concerns were important in caucus establishment. Rank-and-file members were not given staff assistance to work on these issues, and leaders had increasing difficulty coordinating a decentralized and even fragmented institution.

Initially, party leaders felt threatened by the new and uncontrolled congressional subunits—caucuses—that arose to handle these problems. However, leaders gradually responded to rank-and-file demands and extended their inclusive leadership style to caucuses by supporting the institutionalization of caucuses and including caucus representatives in leadership legislative deliberations. This adaptation also enabled party leaders to use caucuses to meet leadership and institutional goals, even as it spurred caucus growth. As a result, a growing number of caucuses are active at points in the legislative process that bring them in contact with party leaders.

Caucuses are now accepted within Congress as policy actors. Their recognition as legitimate policy entities, and the development of organizational rules about caucuses and of regular ways of working with them, occurred gradually. Party leaders see the caucus system as a source of both problems and opportunities. Wary of caucuses, which they consider to be decentralizing and potentially divisive, leaders have nevertheless adapted to their existence. They often seek caucus assistance when it serves both their personal and institutional purposes. The sentiments of Speaker Thomas P. (Tip) O'Neill (D-Mass.) are typical, as is his ultimate adaptation to the new situation: "There were some terrific individuals in the class of 1974, but what really annoyed me about this group is that as late as 1979 they still had their own caucus. I could go along with the need for a freshman caucus, but I naturally assumed that after their first term was over, the new members would join the mainstream. But almost overnight, Congress was crowded with all kinds of caucuses: the freshman caucus, the sophomore caucus, the junior caucus, the black caucus, the Hispanic caucus, the steel caucus, the women's caucus—not to mention the various regional caucuses. As Speaker, I used to meet with them all" (O'Neill and Novak 1987, 285).

Caucuses proliferated in a period when party leaders were developing more inclusive leadership strategies. By including caucuses in party deliberations, leaders worked to keep "peace in the party" (Sinclair's term, in Sinclair 1983). By supporting, and later facilitating, the legitimacy and institutionalization of caucuses, leaders were able to bring caucuses under House regulations and gain some control over their operations.

An early action in caucus institutionalization was Congress's provision of office space to caucuses. Before 1976 only a few were given separate offices in the House office buildings. The Democratic Study Group occupied rooms in the Longworth Building, the Republican Study Committee was housed in the Cannon Building, and the Northeast-Midwest Congressional Coalition had offices in the House Annex. (Senate caucuses operate from senators' personal offices, although one Senate group, the Steering Committee, had separate offices for a few years in the 1980s.)

In 1976, further recognizing caucuses, the House established its Commission on Administrative Review (the Obey Commission) with the active support of the House leadership. Several commission recommendations were designed to stabilize and facilitate the operations of informal congressional caucuses, including certifying established caucuses as legislative service organizations, which could have caucus accounts but were required to submit financial reports and observe limits on the use of staff and office account funds (U.S. House of Representatives 1977, 73). The provisions were not adopted at the time, although most were subsequently implemented, but the effect of the recommendations was to legitimate an existing situation by recognizing the groups as separate entities and proposing procedures and disclosure regulations solely applicable to caucuses.

By 1979 additional recognition as legitimate entities was accorded caucuses by the House Administration Committee's action permitting House or bicameral caucuses to apply for designation as legislative service organizations (with caucus accounts and a required semiannual income and expenditure report to the clerk of the House). Two years later, following wide press coverage of an investigation of caucus funding by the Better Government Association, party leaders supported the establishment by the Committee on House Administration of an Ad Hoc Subcommittee on Legislative Service Organizations. After lengthy hearings and extensive consultation, further recognition was accorded caucuses by committee regulations, which required more detailed quarterly expenditure and income reports from legislative service organizations and prohibited caucuses that received any House monies (clerk hire, space, office expenses) from accepting outside funds.

Institutionalization increased gradually, primarily through further regulation of caucus operations, as leaders and some members continued to regard these congressional subunits with wariness. House Administration Committee task force reports in 1986, 1988, and 1990 recommended additional reporting and disclosure requirements, different space allotments, and curbs on the commingling of federal and private monies by caucuses associated with private institutes. Jim Bateman (D-Calif.), who served on two of the task forces, articulated a view held by some members that legislative service organizations were "out of control," that they were "another way of building staff, having chairmanships, contributing . . . money without any real limitations" (*Roll Call*, June 4, 1992, 14).

In June 1992, the House Administration Committee agreed to examine the operations of legislative service organizations after Republican members demanded increased supervision. An amendment to the FY1993 Legislative Branch Appropriations Bill, offered by Pat Roberts (R-Kans.) and included in the final bill, directed the General Accounting Office and the House Administration Committee to develop accounting standards and financial accounting guidelines for legislative service organizations. The Joint Committee on the Organization of Congress, established by H. Con. Res. 192 (102d Congress, 1992), considered the practices of legislative service organizations during its deliberations. In 1993, Charlie Rose (D-N.C.), chair of the House Committee on Administration (renamed House Oversight Committee in 1995), made caucus reform a priority, and Republican members of the committee, led by Pat Roberts (R-Kans.), asked the General Accounting Office to audit all of the legislative service organizations. Roberts announced that he would offer an amendment to the FY1994 Legislative Branch Appropriations Bill to abolish legislative service organizations (a similar amendment had failed in 1992; see *Roll Call*, March 15, 1993, 15, 28).

At the start of the 104th Congress in 1995, as part of the Republican changes in House rules, the legislative service organization designation for caucuses was abolished and caucuses were not permitted to have separate space in House buildings. Most of the twenty-eight legislative service organizations of the 103d Congress (eighteen of which had separate office space) continued operating out of members' offices as congressional member organizations—the term for caucuses that were not leg-

islative service organizations—with designated staff aides handling caucus work. Staff of a few former legislative service organizations continued
research and information gathering by establishing private sector research or publication groups. Republican Study Committee publications
were taken over by the House Republican Conference, and later, during
the 104th Congress, the Democratic leadership took over some of the information production and distribution previously handled by the Democratic Study Group.

Caucus representation on party committees has been institutionalized
by congressional leaders. Tip O'Neill used his at-large Steering and Policy Committee appointments to bring in representation from various caucuses, including the Congressional Black Caucus and the Hispanic Caucus, the Congressional Caucus on Women's Issues, and the Conservative
Democratic Forum (Boll Weevils). Appointments to the Democratic Caucus's Party Effectiveness Committee similarly ensured representation. Republican class clubs, too, elect representatives to their party committees
and whip organization. Since 1975, freshman class clubs have met with
party leaders and committee chairmen during the House organizational
meetings following biennial elections.

After the 1992 elections, the series of unprecedented meetings around
the country that House Democratic leaders held with newly elected members sought to socialize freshmen early to House, and leader, norms and
to encourage them to work within the party on reform and change—a
major theme for many during their election campaigns. Republican leaders also sought to include newly elected members early in party discussions and deliberations. At the start of the 104th Congress, several newly
elected freshmen Republicans managed sections of the resolution to
amend House Rules (part of the "Contract with America") during floor
debate. This was an extraordinary opportunity, and responsibility, for
first-term members.

Leaders have themselves joined caucuses when that served their goals.
In the Ninety-seventh Congress, Speaker O'Neill belonged to eleven caucuses, including two party (the Democratic Study Group, the United
Democrats of Congress), two regional (the New England Congressional
Caucus and the Northeast-Midwest Congressional Coalition), and two
industry groups. Minority leader Robert Michel (R-Ill.) belonged to four
caucuses—one party, one regional, and two industry groups. In the 104th
Congress, Newt Gingrich (R-Ga.), speaker of the House, belonged to
five caucuses, including the Grace [Commission] Caucus, the Law En-

forcement Caucus, and the Conservative Opportunity Society, which he helped establish. Richard Gephardt (D-Mo.), the Democratic leader, belonged to nine; he served on the executive board of the Congressional Arts Caucus.

Senate leaders, too, belong to and help lead caucuses. During the 103d Congress, majority leader George Mitchell (D-Maine) co-chaired the Senate Footwear Caucus and served on the Steering Committee of the Senate Textile Caucus. Republican leader Robert Dole (R-Kans.) co-chaired the Senate Rural Health Caucus. In the 104th Congress, majority leader Trent Lott (R-Miss.) belonged to eight caucuses, several of them industry oriented, others state/district and regional groups. Democratic leader Tom Daschle (D-S.D.) also belonged to eight caucuses and served as co-chair of the Alcohol Fuels Caucus, vice chair of the Populist Caucus, and Senate chair of the Vietnam Era Veterans in Congress Caucus. Both leaders were members of the Deficit Reduction and Economic Growth, Rural Health, and Travel and Tourism Caucuses, evidence of the bipartisanship of these three groups.

Analyses of leadership confirm that leaders seeking to maximize achievement of personal and institutional goals will shift their styles in response to contextual changes (see, e.g., Rohde and Shepsle 1987; Cooper and Brady 1981; Sinclair 1981, 1983, 1995). This also holds true for caucuses. Leaders' support has been an adaptive mechanism. The leadership has sought to constrain caucuses and, in 1995, supported the effort to abolish legislative service organization status, making it more difficult for some caucuses to operate. But leaders have also used caucuses to achieve access to groups of members important to coalition building or to keeping peace in the party. The new speaker of the 104th Congress met with various caucuses and frequently with the intraparty groups. By supporting regulation, and by working with caucuses and through caucus leaders, party leaders have legitimated caucus operations and even facilitated their establishment. They adapted to this new organizational phenomenon by defining the change in terms that permitted responsiveness to colleagues, by changing operating procedures, and by interacting with these new subunits to achieve personal and institutional goals.

CAUCUS LEADERSHIP ACTIVITIES

Providing information to their members is a major activity of most caucuses. Those in the House supplement the information available from the committee and leadership system, offering members alternative perspectives on pending issues and often distributing detailed factual information more widely. Some party caucuses carry out specific leadership information functions. For many years before 1995, the Democratic Study Group prepared briefing materials on the bills listed in the weekly whip notices, a function performed for the Republicans by the Republican Conference. Thirty-seven percent of House members, Democrats and Republicans, reported relying on Democratic Study Group material for information on floor legislation not handled by their committees (U.S. House of Representatives 1977).[1]

In the mid-1980s, Democratic leaders initiated discussions with the group about formally affiliating with the leadership. The group chose not to do so, believing it could be more effective outside the formal party structure. It was perhaps an inauspicious time for party leaders to propose formal ties with the Democratic Study Group, as its leaders were developing legislation to prohibit the reflagging of Kuwaiti tankers, an issue on which House Democrats disagreed. The group negotiated with members to develop language acceptable to a broad coalition and sought to put together a majority to support the bill on the floor. Such activity would have been severely constrained, and perhaps not even permitted, if the study group had become part of the leadership.

CAUCUSES AS A ROUTE TO LEADERSHIP

Caucuses offer junior members the opportunity to develop substantive expertise and leadership skills outside the committee system. Junior members disproportionately belong to caucuses (see table 5-1). Junior representatives, and most midlevel members, do not hold positions of institutional power and are unlikely to become important players in the subcommittee or committee policy process. Caucuses, operating outside the formal system but linked to it, provide an opportunity for representatives to start up the ladder to leadership in party, committee, or issue area. It is a well-established way for members to develop recognition that can be transferred to the formal system.

Caucuses offer junior members an opportunity to develop leadership skills and to supplement the formal structure in identifying, socializing, and training future leaders. Junior members often are active in establishing caucuses and are the most active group in many caucuses. During the Ninety-seventh Congress, fifty-nine junior members (holding office for one to three terms)—in contrast to thirty-eight midlevel members (four to seven terms) and thirty senior members (eight or more terms)—served in these positions. Thirty-one caucuses were chaired by junior members, twenty-six were chaired by representatives with midlevel seniority, and twenty-two were chaired by senior members. Interview data describe the leadership-socialization function of caucuses: "In many ways [the class club] was a proving ground, a place to practice becoming leaders . . . organizationally and also in parliamentary and legislative areas. [Members] were finding how to operate . . . the process of compromise and the way one functions in the United States House of Representatives. And they could then . . . take that learning to other activities in the House."

Caucus leaders guide caucus activity and serve as caucus spokespersons. If the caucus takes positions on legislative issues, caucus leaders work with committee and party leaders. In the 1980s, junior Republicans Newt Gingrich (Ga.), Vin Weber (Minn.), and Robert Walker (Pa.) led the Conservative Opportunity Society to major media attention, to an impact on the 1984 Republican platform, and to collaboration with the Republican leadership in the House. The COS tangled with Speaker O'Neill and supported Gingrich's ethics charges against Speaker Jim Wright. The group sought procedural and structural reform in the House more favorable to the minority party, such as a guarantee that one-third of committee staff aides would be appointed by Republicans. Their work with Republican leaders Michel and Lott, and their tactics in floor debate, enabled them to develop skills that brought recognition, responsibility, and election to formal positions of power. Weber won assignment to the Appropriations Committee in 1987 and was elected secretary of the Republican Conference in 1989. Walker became chief deputy whip in January 1989. And in March of that year, Gingrich was elected minority whip. In 1995, Gingrich became speaker of the House.

Both parties have seen junior members rise in the formal system through caucus work. Freshmen who have served as caucus chairs disproportionately go on to serve on major committees or in junior positions of party leadership. Buddy MacKay (D-Fla.), organizer of the Budget Study Group, and his caucus became major players on budget issues in his first term after he organized a group of members to vote against a continuing budget resolution as a protest about lack of attention to the deficit. At the start of the next Congress, he was appointed to the Budget Committee. Deborah Pryce (R-Ohio) and Eric Fingerhut (D-Ohio), 103d Congress freshmen, became identified as rising stars through serving as class club officers and taking a lead in congressional reform proposals. Serving as chair or as a party committee representative of the class club yields power-in-the-institution rewards and is highly prized. Gaining expertise and becoming an issue leader through caucus work offers similar rewards.

Because caucuses are diverse, a loose seniority system governs caucus leadership appointments. Junior members are most likely to serve as chairs of the smaller or more specialized caucuses, like the Budget Study Group and the Science and Technology Caucus. In the 100th Congress, 89 percent of junior members serving as caucus chairs or co-chairs were leading recently established caucuses. Apprenticeship on a caucus steering committee or an executive board also helps members with midlevel seniority establish eligibility to serve as chairs of the larger, longer-established caucuses. Of those serving as chairs or co-chairs of established caucuses during the 100th Congress, 11 percent were junior members, 37 percent had midlevel seniority, and 47 percent were senior members. Chairing a major caucus such as the Democratic Study Group, the Environmental and Energy Study Conference, or the Arms Control and Foreign Policy Caucus can give members with midlevel seniority further leadership training, recognition as issue leaders, and major contenders for formal positions of power. The alternate structure intersects the formal structure of the House, and caucus training has become a legitimate route to formal positions of power.

Party Leader and Caucus Interaction

House party leaders have adapted to caucuses by developing processes for within-party representation of caucus viewpoints and by including all caucus types in leadership policy and strategy deliberations. But party leaders' work varies with type of caucus, and their relationships with party and nonparty caucuses differ. Senate and House caucuses are dissimilar in their interactions with party leaders, reflecting the differences in the chambers' structures and rules (see table 7-1).[2] One-quarter of House caucuses report meeting with party leaders at their formal caucus meetings; no Senate caucuses do. Twenty-seven percent of the House caucuses, in comparison with 6 percent of the Senate caucuses, hold formal caucus meetings with committee leaders. A more highly organized House, with fewer committee assignments for each representative, makes negotiations over representation on various committees important to caucuses.

In the early 1980s, Charles Stenholm (D-Tex.) and the Boll Weevils,

Table 7-1.   Caucus and Party Leader Interaction, House and
Senate, 100th Congress (in percentages)

Interaction	House	Senate
Caucuses that meet with party leaders	25.0	0
Caucuses that talk with party leaders	40.6	72.2
Caucuses that work with party leaders	44.0	67.0
On committee assignments	12.5	5.6
On committee activities	26.6	16.7
On floor schedule	26.6	16.7
On floor issue content	26.6	33.3
On floor strategy	21.9	27.8
On whip counts for caucus use	21.9	11.1
On whip counts for leader use	12.5	0
Caucuses contacted by party leaders	29.7	0
For information	28.1	0
For strategy support	20.3	0
For votes	14.1	0
Occasionally	17.2	0
Frequently	9.4	0

who believed they were being penalized in committee assignments for deserting the party on some votes, argued with party leaders for more attractive assignments:

> The conservative voice in the Democratic Party basically believed that we were tolerated but had no input. We did a study on committees of the House. . . . [It] basically proved what we already knew was happening in the key committee assignments, that conservatives were not there. . . . It was not a shock, or should not have been a shock, to the speaker or the leadership. It means that when you bring a bill up, and the committee was already stacked, you would have divisions on the floor. Well, we actually heeded the advice of Speaker O'Neill. When we met with him he reminded us that the squeaky wheel gets the grease and that the liberals were squeaking louder. That wasn't his fault. But we ought to squeak louder. Therefore, we took his advice. And it worked.

Leaders agreed, and the Boll Weevils began working within the party, rather than opposing it, to achieve caucus goals.[3]

Other caucuses, the Black, Hispanic, and Women's Issues Caucuses, for example, achieved similar consideration. At the start of the 103d Congress, freshman Democrats and Republicans sought choice committee assignments. Party leaders in turn supported the appointment of freshmen to Appropriations, Ways and Means, Energy and Commerce, and Public Works. Freshmen of the 104th also received choice committee assignments: Republican freshmen were appointed to seven seats on Appropriations, three on Ways and Means, and one—a very unusual occurrence—on the Rules Committee.

In the egalitarian and less-structured Senate, caucuses are less likely to contact leaders about committee assignments for their members or about committee matters. Few Senate caucuses try to influence the floor schedule. But when legislation reaches the floor, a higher percentage (although a smaller number) of caucuses in the Senate than in the House report working with party leaders on the content of legislation and on floor strategy. Few Senate caucuses, though, join with party leaders on whip counts, and none reports doing whip counts that will be used by Senate leaders. (Although the proportion of House caucuses working with leaders is similar to or smaller than in the Senate, the actual number of House caucuses is higher, and often much higher, than in the Senate.)

House action in March 1993 on President Clinton's Budget Resolution and economic stimulus package illustrates both the opportunities and the problems of caucus activity. Charles Stenholm, leader of the Conservative Democratic Forum (the Boll Weevils), served on the Budget Committee in the 103d Congress. In committee, he was chief representative of the CDF and the chief negotiator in achieving a bill that had more spending cuts than the president's version. Having gained committee approval for the cuts, he held most of the CDF members together in support of the committee bill during floor votes, so that a unified Democratic Party supported the resolution and the new president. On the vote on the economic stimulus package, however, Stenholm and fifteen of his southern Democratic colleagues deserted the party and voted with most Republicans against the stimulus expenditures. A sixty-vote margin on the Budget Resolution was reduced to forty-five votes on the stimulus package.

PARTY CAUCUSES AND PARTY LEADERS

All party caucuses in the House work with their party leaders in some way (see table 7-2), participating, for example, in leadership meetings, whip counts, and similar actions.[4] As might be expected, party caucuses have the closest ties with leadership and cooperate with them to pursue common goals. And party caucuses are active at an earlier stage in the legislative process than other caucus types, seeking to influence party rules

Table 7-2.   House Caucuses and Party Leader Interaction, by
Caucus Type, 100th Congress (in percentages)

Caucus Type	Yes		No	
Party	100	(28)	0	
National constituency	75	(3)	25	(1)
Regional	21	(3)	79	(11)
State/district	14	(2)	86	(12)
Industry	29	(4)	71	(10)
Personal interest	16	(3)	84	(16)
Party	100	(28)	0	
Nonparty	23	(15)	77	(50)
Total no.	44		50	

Note: Based on semifocused caucus and leadership interviews; not all caucuses responded to this question. Party caucuses include class clubs. Number of
caucuses is given in parentheses.

and party agendas as well as the final legislative product. This is possible
because of their intraparty position. Even though nonparty caucuses work
with party leaders less frequently, such collaboration is usually spurred by
a common issue interest and a congruence of legislative goals.

Party caucuses seek to influence policy without fragmenting the party.
But party leaders view party caucuses as potentially fragmenting because,
if their views are not taken into account, they may upset fragile coalitions
or compromises on content. However, because all members share a common party label, caucuses offer potential assistance to party leaders for
coalition building and support in achieving collective party goals at an
early stage of the legislative process. Leadership respondents agreed that
party caucuses can play a prominent role in leadership's planning. A Republican, commenting on the Conservative Opportunity Society, said:
"They recognize the need for a party role. They want to be co-opted by
the leadership, not be a rump group of grenade throwers" (Center for
Congressional and Presidential Studies 1984, 87).

Leaders have adapted to party caucuses by accommodating diverse
views, thus enabling them to contain conflict and to face the opposition
party with a degree of unity. In the postreform era of independent candidates and fragmented congressional structure, the conditions for party
operation have changed, but parties appear to be adapting and reviving,
devising new integrative mechanisms. In this changed situation, congressional caucuses based on party have continued to be important actors.

Of the eleven party caucuses in the House during the 1980s that were not class clubs, seven worked on shaping party and leader agendas through long-range issue research and planning (for example, the Wednesday Group) or by placing issues on current agendas. Seven cooperated with committee leaders of their own party to shape legislation that takes account of a group position and is also acceptable to party members. Ten met regularly with party leaders to affect legislation scheduled for floor action. Five served an explicit leadership information-supplement role by distributing research reports or briefing information relevant to pending floor activity (e.g., the Democratic Study Group and the Democratic Research Organization).

Some party groups seek guarantees of representation and access from party leaders, as the Conservative Democratic Forum did. CDF links to the leadership include caucus members who also serve as party whips and on Democratic Caucus committees. At CDF meetings, held on Thursday mornings before Democratic whip meetings, members discuss legislation coming to the floor and whether the CDF wants to be involved. CDF members can then report caucus views at the whip meeting so as to factor them into party action. In 1994, CDF members urged in whip meetings that leaders do something about the discharge petition drive on budget reform, which was rapidly gaining signatures to bring a reform bill to the floor. The CDF was "part of the reason leaders decided to schedule votes on different reform bills—to draw the teeth of the discharge petition drive."

Both Democratic and Republican party caucuses influence long-range and pending congressional party agendas. In 1975, for example, proposals developed by the Republican Study Committee, including welfare and food stamp reform, were adopted by minority leader John Rhodes (R-Ariz.) for the Republican legislative agenda he had established (Feulner 1983). In 1985, the Conservative Opportunity Society was a major factor in the Republican response to the McIntyre election issue. It was also a chief sponsor of the 1986 Baltimore Conference III, working closely with the Wednesday Group and the Republican leadership to provide a "broad-based conference" to discuss "new ideas and the structure and procedures of Republicans in the House," according to participants. The '92 Group, established to seek a Republican House majority in 1992, "ginned up in eighty-five and presented an alternative budget." The caucus cooperated with Republican party leadership groups, although ironically "Budget Committee chairman William Gray leaned heavily on it . . . and it probably had more influence on the Democrats than the Republicans," according to one observer. Republican 104th Congress freshmen pushed

Speaker Gingrich to continue to schedule some of the more divisive "Contract with America" legislation for floor action.

Negative agenda setting by party caucuses also occurs. One such effort by the United Democrats of Congress, a moderate-to-conservative party caucus, was described by a participant:

> Let's say the leadership of the UDC . . . feels strongly about a piece of legislation. Very quietly they go to the speaker, or invite the speaker down for a very candid, off-the-record discussion of what membership is willing to do. The speaker [has] learned it is very important to pay very careful attention to UDC. . . . There are, you know, members who were tired of having to go on the line for certain issues that there was no chance in the world would ever be raised in the Senate. Why then should members of the House have to go on record? Why not have the speaker get some kind of a commitment from the Senate that they'll at least consider it before we go out on a limb on some controversial legislation that, to moderates and conservatives, would prove to be very, very harmful politically. . . . I think that perhaps the UDC is most influential in continuing to remind the leadership that there are Democrats who may not share their same views on all issues.

As partisan theories of congressional organization predict, party caucuses work through the formal party structures of the House and seek approval from the Republican Conference (of all Republican members) or the Democratic Caucus (of all Democrats). In the 1970s, the Democratic Study Group effected major reforms with passage of a Subcommittee Bill of Rights and changes in rules governing the election of committee chairs. The DSG and other informal groups have collaborated with the Democratic Caucus on budget resolutions; in the 1980s, for example, DSG meetings with Budget Committee members and with the speaker resulted in agreements on content and strategy—and party unification.

The revived Democratic Caucus served as a vehicle through which some informal groups could pursue their policy goals. The Party Effectiveness Committee, established in February 1981 by caucus chair Gillis Long (D-La.), sponsored strategy sessions, research, and long-range agenda and issues planning. The *Congressional Yellow Book 1982* and the "Blueprint for the Future" (released in January 1984 just before the Iowa presidential caucuses) laid out Democratic concerns and proposals. The changed operations and interests of the Democratic Caucus have allowed it to serve as an umbrella organization and a broker for interests represented by various congressional caucuses. Democratic Party leaders have sought to include all party viewpoints, as represented by party caucuses, and to represent concerns held by groups of Democrats in other caucuses, such as the Congressional Black Caucus and the Congressional Caucus on Women's Issues.

On occasion, however, party caucuses oppose party positions. In 1981, the Conservative Democratic Forum supported President Reagan and worked with Republicans to shape budget legislation. In that session, the strength of the Conservative Coalition increased by 20 percentage points, with CDF support a critical factor. It had a success rate of 92 percent on one roll call vote on a tax bill, with 64 percent of CDF members supporting the president's position (see *Congressional Quarterly Almanac 1981*, app. 35-C; also see Abramson, Aldrich, and Rohde 1986; Rohde 1989).

Caucus members are sensitive to the delicate position of party caucuses, particularly on issues that might bring the caucus into conflict with party leaders. The balance they must maintain—and the nature of the leader-caucus relationship—is demonstrated by freshman Democrats in the Ninety-eighth Congress. The '98 New Members Caucus (Democratic) united on the deficit issue. In 1983 the caucus began a Budget Study Group, which sponsored informational sessions and meetings with Budget Committee members and others. The following year, the group opposed the 1984 Democratic Budget Resolution. Democratic Party leadership sought to contain conflict by developing a compromise floor amendment and asked Buddy MacKay (Fla.), chair of the freshman group, to sponsor it. The MacKay Freeze Amendment, for an across-the-board spending freeze, failed in spite of strong freshman support, but the party leadership succeeded in avoiding a damaging party split at the height of Reagan's influence and success on Capitol Hill. In the Ninety-ninth Congress, the Budget Study Group became the Democratic Budget Group, whose meetings were regularly attended by leadership staff as well as more senior Democrats. Both consider it an informational, training, and occasional strategy group (interview data; but also see Calmes 1986).

By the 104th Congress, leaders of both parties worked with party caucuses. The Tuesday Lunch Bunch (moderate Republicans), in meetings with Speaker Gingrich, "forced concessions on the tax bill and got the limits on child care tax cuts lowered," according to a respondent not allied with the Lunch Bunch. Democratic leader Richard Gephardt met every other week with the Coalition (the Blue Dogs), which a senior observer describes as "very, very influential."

NONPARTY CAUCUSES AND PARTY LEADERS

In contrast to party caucuses, slightly less than one-quarter of the non-party caucuses work with party leaders on legislative matters (table 7-2). A number of factors determine whether leaders and nonparty caucuses work together (see figure 7-1). First, there must be agreement on an issue position; if caucuses and party leaders disagree, caucuses on occasion act against leaders. There must also be pending floor action, as nonparty caucuses collaborate with party leaders only on matters that are expected to come to the floor. In all instances, regularly scheduled agenda issues (e.g., authorizations and appropriations) or other mandated matters (e.g., extension of the ratification period for the Equal Rights Amendment) have been the vehicles for caucus-leader interaction. Bipartisan nonparty caucuses must also be able to adapt their organizations and procedures for meeting with party leaders on partisan issue positions. Some caucuses use task forces, with the understanding that not all caucus members are committed to the caucus or task force position. Members of some caucuses work under the general aegis of the caucus, but as individuals. Some caucuses focus on a general legislative approach and do not become involved in partisan conflict over scheduling or rules of debate.

If leaders and caucuses agree on an issue approaching floor consideration, leaders are more likely to bring the caucuses into the policy process. Established caucuses with a record of accurate information, expertise, and votes are most likely to be called on for assistance. Party leaders value reliable advice, information, whip counts, and work on legislative content and strategy. Access to caucus members or to constituent groups is also valuable. The multiple roles of caucus members also affect their work with leaders; for example, members who serve as party whips can raise caucus issues at whip meetings.

Many nonparty caucuses do not work with party leaders because their focus is elsewhere (see table 7-3). Nearly half of these caucuses are active only at early stages of the legislative process, that is, drafting legislation, or in committee hearings or at markup sessions. At these stages, nonparty caucuses generally seek policy goals only through committee work. Some nonparty caucuses, like the Environmental and Energy Study Conference, limit their activities to research and information. Others seek to affect agendas by keeping an issue salient but do not take positions that would require working closely with party leaders on specific policy issues. Some

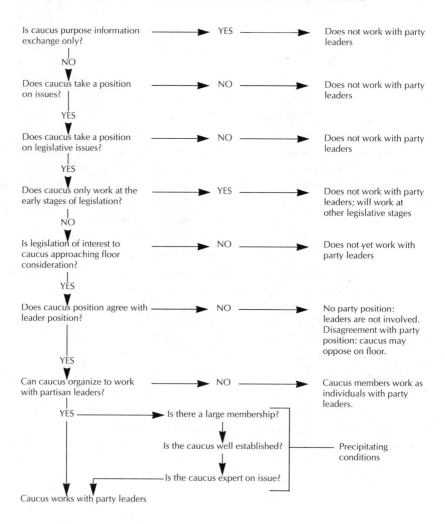

Figure 7-1. A Diagram of Factors Affecting Whether Nonparty Caucuses Work with Party Leaders

Notes: All the "events" (variables at the decision node) shown are conditional; that is, decision makers (leaders or caucus) know whether a variable is present. The last three (*x*, *y*, and *z*) may occur as individual events (e.g., the caucus is expert but not well established) or as joint events (e.g., the caucus is both expert and well established). (See Schlaifer 1969.) Any one (e.g., *x*), or any two (e.g., *x*, *y*), or all three (*x*, *y*, *z*) increase the likelihood of a caucus working with party leaders, and as the number present rises, the likelihood of working with party leaders increases. The decision tree depicting outcomes in the presence or absence of *x*, *y*, and *z* might be drawn in several different ways. The figure summarizes them as precipitating conditions, which can occur as a single event or in any combination.

Table 7-3. Reasons that Nonparty Caucuses Do Not Work with Party Leaders (in percentages)

Caucus Type	Information Only	Newly Established	Only Works Early in Legislative Process	Other
National constituency	0	0	100	0
			(1)	
Regional	9	9	72	9
	(1)	(1)	(8)	(1)
State/district	8	42	42	8
	(1)	(5)	(5)	(1)
Industry	10	20	60	10
	(1)	(2)	(6)	(1)[a]
Personal interest	38	6	24	31
	(6)	(1)	(4)	(5)
Total	18	18	48	16
	(9)	(9)	(24)	(8)

Note: Number of caucuses is given in parentheses.
[a]Cannot agree on legislation; does not work on legislation; or focuses on mobilizing the grass roots.

caucuses are too newly organized to be in touch with party leaders. Others do not become involved in legislation or oppose leaders' positions.

The purposes, policy role, and focus of activity of nonparty caucuses set the parameters of leader-caucus interaction. Issue agreement, the legislative schedule, and caucus procedures operate as further filters. When leaders cooperate with caucuses on legislative matters such as whip counts and floor amendments, they expand the group beyond the caucus to include their own advisers and close colleagues. The caucus may serve as a catalyst and may continue to form the core of the working group. In some instances, as compromises are hammered out, leaders may hold occasional meetings with a caucus to determine caucus views and perspectives. But the caucus does not control personnel, style, or strategy.

Two case studies illustrate nonparty caucus and party leadership cooperation. Both the Congressional Caucus on Women's Issues and the Arms Control and Foreign Policy Caucus have joined with leaders on strategy, scheduling, and whip counts for pending floor legislation. Both are bipartisan, but they handle the consequences of bipartisanship differently.

For the Congressional Caucus on Women's Issues, with its national constituency, the constraints of bipartisan membership affect its advocacy. The caucus decides agendas and issues by consensus, but members participate in drafting legislation or in deciding strategy as individuals. One respondent noted, "In developing legislation, it is often possible to work in a bipartisan fashion. But with scheduling, strategy, or rules, that often gets partisan. You must deal with majority and minority parties, so the caucus tends to stay out of those issues."

How does this work in practice? A cadre of Women's Caucus members helped draft the Civil Rights Act of 1984. Part of a broad-based working group, they participated because they were on the relevant committee or had been deeply involved in the issue. The caucus then circulated a "Dear Colleague" letter, with forty cosigners (including some leaders), asking representatives to support the legislation without substantive amendments. It was up to caucus members to testify and lobby individually. If members spoke for the caucus, they would support the content of the legislation without substantive amendments but would not take a position on the type of rule under which the legislation would be debated on the floor.

In the Ninety-eighth Congress, the caucus also worked with the Democratic leadership on extending the ratification period for the Equal Rights Amendment. The speaker tapped caucus expertise by seeking advice on floor strategy from Pat Schroeder (D-Colo.), caucus co-chair, and Don Edwards (D-Calif.). Caucus members and staff later did whip counts with the Democratic whip organization and the Leaders' Task Force on the ERA. The caucus took its own whip counts and also channeled the whip counts of citizen groups to the leadership.

The Arms Control and Foreign Policy Caucus sought to affect policy during the Ninety-eighth Congress on the MX missile program and on Central American issues, especially El Salvador and Nicaragua. On all three issues, the caucus cooperated with the Democratic leadership in the House, offering expertise, access to votes, and coalition-building assistance in exchange for leadership support of a caucus policy position. The caucus, based on members' personal interest, was bicameral and bipartisan. Advocacy was carried out through bipartisan task forces established to work on a specific issue. Agreement on a specific legislative position was reached within the task force, not by the entire caucus.

Long before caucus members sought out the House Democratic leadership, the caucus organized to work on Central American issues. George Miller (D-Calif.) was appointed head of a bipartisan Task Force on Central America by caucus chair James Leach (R-Iowa). The establishment of a task force offered its chair an institutional base, thus giving the effort legitimacy within the House and, eventually, extensive press coverage. The task force, with twenty members, reached consensus on one priority initiative, which became the Foley Amendment to the FY1985 Department of Defense Authorization Bill.

The caucus initiated the amendment, which prohibited the sending of U.S. combat troops to Central America, and asked majority whip Foley (D-Wash.) to sponsor it. After Foley agreed, the caucus task force began to build support, and Democrats on the task force and caucus staff attended leadership strategy sessions, working closely with the speaker's office and the Democratic whip organization. The caucus, and especially the task force, was in contact with constituent groups active on U.S. policy in Central America and became a "kind of conduit" between these groups and the congressional leadership. It also drew on citizen groups' whip counts (considered extremely accurate), to supplement the counts of the Democratic whip organization. The amendment passed with a five-to-one margin. One observer believed that a major factor in that margin was the caucus strategy of developing the amendment and having it sponsored by a member of the leadership and supported by well-organized caucus activity.

CAUCUSES, LEADERS, AND LEGISLATION

Caucus influence depends on accuracy of information, especially whip counts. Their influence also is affected by their commitment to the issue; committed caucus members will attend meeting after meeting and will contact members one-on-one to get an accurate whip count or to line up support. Some participants believe this to be a major factor in whip count accuracy and in caucus achievement. Leaders also look at previous caucus successes. For example, the success of the Arms Control and Foreign Policy Caucus in the MX debate helped it in subsequent work with the leadership. And leaders know that caucuses can serve an early-warning function analogous to the Rules Committee's field commander role (Oppenheimer 1977), because they work in a different time frame and can be alert to the potential advantages and problems of various long-range strategies.

SUMMARY

Caucuses developed in part as a reaction to the failure of party leadership to handle the demands of a changed congressional environment. Subsequently, leaders adapted to the emerging caucus system and supported caucuses as legitimate congressional subunits of the policy process. Caucuses now supplement House leadership work by identifying and training future leaders and through various informational and legislative activities.

Leader-caucus work is an exchange relationship. Caucuses want leaders to respond to their concerns and to support their policy positions, while leaders need caucus help. Caucuses are an efficient mechanism to give leaders access to blocs of members with expertise and votes and can help leaders' centralization efforts. Leaders can bestow benefits on caucus members and give visibility and support to caucus positions.

The adaptive response of party leaders to party caucuses has been to try to keep differences within their party. Party caucuses work with party leaders in Congress at all stages of the legislative process. These caucuses have been granted representation within party councils and have opportunities to influence party agendas, the content of bills, and legislative strategy. They can persuade leaders to keep items off a legislative agenda or to modify the substance of legislation to include a broader coalition of party members, because party leaders want to build broad-based coalitions within the party.

The relationship between nonparty caucuses and party leaders is different. Cooperation requires agreement on an issue position, and floor action must be pending. Caucus maturity, expertise, voting strength, and previous success are additional factors that determine whether or not nonparty caucuses work with party leaders.

Variation among caucus types working with party leaders (significant at the .001 level, Pearson chi-square) is affected by the groups' constituency base and by the issues they focus on. Few personal-interest caucuses interact with party leaders, because many of these groups are not active in legislation or because they emphasize agenda setting. The proportion of constituency-based caucuses that report activity with party leaders decreases as the constituency becomes more localized and the issues of interest more narrow. Subsystem politics and the handling of issues by the executive seem to be the primary explanation.

The relationship between the caucus system and the formal party system is sometimes conflictual, but it can also be mutually beneficial. Not all caucuses work with party leaders. But those caucuses that do work with the leadership are increasingly important actors in the legislative system.

8/ Working with the Executive Branch

Although caucuses work primarily within Congress, they also seek to affect executive branch policy decisions. Caucuses are most likely to work with the executive branch if the issues with which they are concerned depend on executive branch decision making. Caucuses that focus only on providing information seek information from the executive but do not try to influence decisions. The issue stage is also important. For example, the White House may contact caucuses, which represent votes, if a bill is scheduled for floor debate. Party control of the White House also affects caucus action, because the White House is more accessible to caucuses of the president's party. There are also Senate-House differences.

Every type of caucus, and senators and representatives as well as caucus staff, work with the executive branch (see table 8-1). Caucuses vary in the locus of their efforts, interacting with agencies or the White House, with staff or political appointees, or with the president. They seek information and pursue policy goals, which may be a change in regulations, the development of bills and amendments, administration support for caucus positions, or assistance in strategy and coalition building. Executive agencies seek similar assistance from caucuses, such as help on developing legislation, advice on strategy, or voting support.

About one-third of party, personal-interest, state/district, and industry caucuses host executive branch officials as speakers or meet with them for discussion at regularly scheduled caucus meetings. Higher proportions of the national constituency and regional caucuses report such meetings. A substantial group of caucuses hold meetings with White House officials. The party caucuses have the most such meetings, reflecting access to high-level executive branch policy makers enjoyed by same-party caucuses. Party caucuses regard party affinity with the president as an opportunity to achieve their policy goals. The administration may use caucuses in a search for votes or in developing legislation acceptable to Congress.

Party caucuses, and to a lesser extent national constituency caucuses,

Table 8-1. Meetings and Activities between Caucuses and the Executive Branch, 100th Congress (in percentages)

			Caucus Type			
Variable	Party[a]	Personal Interest	National Constituency	Regional	State/ District	Industry
Formal, scheduled meetings						
With White House	50	17	20	25	0	6
officials	(5)	(4)	(1)	(3)	(0)	(1)
With other executive	50	33	60	42	30	33
officials	(5)	(8)	(3)	(5)	(3)	(6)
Informal meetings						
With cabinet official	60	38	20	58	30	39
	(6)	(9)	(1)	(7)	(3)	(7)
With subcabinet official	60	42	40	42	0	50
	(6)	(10)	(2)	(5)	(0)	(9)
With White House	60	38	20	17	10	39
official	(6)	(9)	(1)	(2)	(1)	(7)
With president	40	8	40	25	0	17
	(4)	(2)	(2)	(3)	(0)	(3)
With bureaucrat	30	29	0	42	20	39
	(3)	(7)	(0)	(5)	(2)	(7)
Letters to administration	60	54	60	75	60	44
officials	(6)	(13)	(3)	(9)	(6)	(8)
Phone conversations with	40	38	60	17	10	28
administration officials	(4)	(9)	(3)	(2)	(1)	(5)
Working with executive	50	71	60	75	60	67
branch	(5)	(7)	(3)	(9)	(6)	(12)
Purpose						
Policy	30	50	60	42	50	44
	(3)	(12)	(3)	(5)	(5)	(8)
Representation	20	8	0	33	10	17
	(2)	(2)	(0)	(4)	(1)	(3)
Oversight	0	4	0	0	0	6
	(0)	(1)	(0)	(0)	(0)	(1)
Congressional structure	0	8	0	0	0	6
	(0)	(2)	(0)	(0)	(0)	(1)
Election	10	4	0	0	0	0
	(1)	(1)	(0)	(0)	(0)	(0)

(Continued)

have frequent contact with the president, White House staff, and high-level administration appointees. Personal-interest caucuses also actively meet with high-level officials. Regional and industry caucuses seek policy goals primarily through executive agencies, on occasion contacting high-level officials within these agencies. Regional groups are particularly active in meeting with cabinet officials, while industry groups contact sub-cabinet appointees. State/district caucuses are the least active, reporting working frequently with executive branch agencies but infrequently with

Table 8-1. *(Continued)*

Variable	Party[a]	Personal Interest	National Constituency	Regional	State/ District	Industry
			Caucus Type			
Executive made contact						
For information	30	33	20	50	40	22
	(3)	(8)	(1)	(6)	(4)	(4)
For strategy support	20	21	20	42	20	17
	(2)	(5)	(1)	(5)	(2)	(3)
For votes	20	17	20	42	0	11
	(2)	(4)	(1)	(5)	(0)	(2)
White House made contact						
For information	30	21	40	17	0	11
	(3)	(5)	(2)	(2)	(0)	(2)
For strategy support	30	17	20	8	0	6
	(3)	(4)	(1)	(1)	(0)	(1)
For votes	30	12	20	8	0	6
	(3)	(3)	(1)	(1)	(0)	(1)

Note: Number of caucuses is given in parentheses.
[a]Excluding class clubs.

officials and even staff. Caucuses are also contacted by the executive branch for information, strategy assistance, and votes. The White House contacts caucuses less frequently; party, national constituency, and personal-interest caucuses are the most likely to be contacted.

These patterns reflect shared party or issue interests as well as public-agenda-setting and support-seeking strategies. Party caucuses work within the party. They have easy access to political officials in the executive branch, including the president, when their party controls the White House. The distributive issues with which regional, state/district, and industry caucuses are often concerned are handled at the agency subsystem level. The low activity of state/district caucuses perhaps reflects the issues with which these caucuses deal: they are diffuse and crosscutting, with executive responsibility shared among several agencies, and it may be too difficult for a caucus to work with all the relevant agencies. Alternatively, many state/district caucuses report that a major focus is coordination of the various parts of a diverse issue area. This takes time and organization and may result in a focus on information or on coordinating congressional activity rather than on work with executive agencies. Many personal interest caucuses are organized to serve the information-gathering and analysis needs of members and explicitly eschew policy advocacy. Meetings with cabinet and White House officials largely reflect the information sweep of these caucuses and the issues of interest to them and the executive. For national constituency caucuses, meetings with high-level political officials increase the visibility of their concerns, and work with agency personnel moves forward their policy goals.

PARTY CAUCUSES

Many party caucuses regularly seek information from the executive branch on legislative and other policy issues and often are in regular and continuing contact with agency personnel. Their work with the executive branch often goes well beyond information gathering, as the following examples make clear. They influence agendas, propose alternative policies, develop legislation, and negotiate specific legislative language to effect policy changes.

The House Northeast-Midwest Republicans (Gypsy Moths), a moderate Republican group, worked closely with the White House, and particularly with David Stockman, director of the Office of Management and Budget, as President Reagan's FY1982 budget was developed. The Gypsy Moths sought changes in the budget reconciliation measure, consisting of a smaller increase in the defense budget and a smaller decrease in domestic programs than the administration sought. The administration needed Gypsy Moth votes, so negotiations began, with Stockman meeting several times with the group on budget and (later) tax issues. The situation was fluid, and an initial caucus list of proposed cuts, mostly from Defense Department spending, was continually revised as the provisions of the budget bill changed. The caucus also met with Treasury Department officials on tax issues in the budget bill, conveying information and concerns about the impact of the tax proposals on their states. Subsequently, Treasury Department officials contacted the group and held meetings with them and Office of Management and Budget officials, including Stockman. A participant described these: "At the most recent meeting—you name the issue and it was brought up. They went around the whole Gypsy Moth group. There were twenty-something people there, and everybody brought up something different." The caucus staff director remained in close touch with the White House congressional liaison for the House. The caucus never met as a group with President Reagan, but members met individually with him on a number of occasions. The picture is one of serious negotiation, including proposals and counterproposals (although no specific deals were made). Contact established during the initial negotiations continued as the caucus and high-level administration officials subsequently discussed other issues, policy positions, and concerns.

Gathering research information is the major reason for contact between the Wednesday Group (moderate and liberal Republicans) and executive agencies. On occasion, however, members of the group move beyond research and seek agency assistance in developing legislation. During the Carter presidency, the Wednesday Group worked closely with the Justice Department on the caucus's civil rights project. Caucus staff and leaders received feedback from the department, including an unofficial evaluation of their draft legislation. The caucus then worked with the department to refine the bill.

Caucus relations with the executive branch can be ongoing and routine even without specific immediate concerns. During the Carter presidency, the United Democrats of Congress, active through the mid-1980s, held a monthly breakfast meeting with members of the president's cabinet or senior White House staff such as Hamilton Jordan, the president's chief of staff, and Zbigniew Brzezinski, national security adviser. The group of 125 Democratic members used these meetings as opportunities to touch base with administration officials:

> The president had UDC down to the White House twice. . . . The president is not against our using him as a sounding board. We got many of the cabinet secretaries calling and asking if they could come to the [monthly caucus] meetings. They thought they were very worthwhile because they were off the record, closed, and members-only (with the exception of the executive committee staff), and they could come and say about anything they wanted to say. But more importantly, they could hear [a congressional view]. It was one thing to listen to the leadership; it was quite another to go to this cross section where you've got very senior members, very junior members, chairmen. It really covers a cross section of the nation, and even politically [within the party].

The executive committee of the caucus "guarded the confidentiality of the meetings . . . to encourage exchange" and discouraged comments to the press following a meeting.

The Conservative Democratic Forum (CDF) has met regularly with executive branch officials to discuss pending issues and legislation. The CDF is a bloc of swing votes, and both Democratic and Republican presidents have sought their support on critical roll calls. Groups of members met, particularly on budget and tax issues, with President Reagan and with Treasury Secretary Donald Regan. Other meetings and telephone calls—often from White House staff, congressional liaison staff, Office of Management and Budget, and Treasury Department officials—also occurred. In 1995, in an effort to keep them from voting for Republican "Contract with America" initiatives, President Clinton met with the (newly formed) Coalition (the Blue Dogs), a spin-off from the Conservative Democratic Forum (the Boll Weevils).

The Midwest Conference of Democratic Senators was established to develop alternative policies, particularly on agriculture and rural development matters, to those proposed by Presidents Nixon and Ford. At times they worked with executive agencies, but their purpose was to formulate alternative proposals, to have the data to back up those ideas, and to be a focus for alternate policy making—a kind of shadow government. After President Carter was elected, the group's purpose shifted, and more coordination and cooperation with executive agencies ensued. The caucus worked with the Farmers Home Administration on rural development issues and, "very occasionally," with Office of Management and Budget personnel and White House staff. The group met with officials of the Agriculture Department on a number of occasions. It would voice objections to administration policy, but with a change in control of the White House to their party, they worked within the system rather than seeking press coverage and congressional support for alternative policies.

The Senate Steering Committee (conservative Republicans) reports a similar experience. They enjoyed frequent meetings and close contact with high-level officials on a wide range of issues during Republican administrations and contacts with Democratic administrations that were constructive but more constrained. A former staff director characterized the differing relationships with the executive:

> During the Carter administration, quite clearly, you had a totally adversary situation. During the Republican administrations, we worked with the executive branch when people were inclined to do so. There were times when the [Republican] executive branch took positions which were not pleasing to the majority of senators on the Steering Committee—at which point the Steering Committee members would take action—they had better contacts and more response than with the Democrats. What was principally done was that the administration would be requested to make officials available for a Steering Committee meeting. I don't imagine that person probably welcomed that, but nevertheless they would come, and matters could be discussed at very close range.

On issues on which the Steering Committee and a Republican White House agreed, there could be close coordination between the two, and on occasion Steering Committee staff operated as a congressional staff arm of the White House. Their work on an amendment to the funding measure for the Legal Services Corporation during the Reagan administration exemplifies this. The Steering Committee's general counsel worked on two amendments to the measure, drafting amendments, gathering information and data, helping prepare material for speeches, and handling floor support for the senators. Steering Committee staff and members were in constant contact with the White House by telephone or in person. When, infrequently, the caucus and the White House disagreed, the caucus made its concerns known to the White House or even organized and led Senate opposition to the White House.

Party groups thus work quite frequently with the executive branch, usually through meetings, often with high-level officials and on occasion with the president. These serve as early-warning or sounding board sessions for the administration. Full and frank exchange or working together to develop legislation generally requires a shared party affiliation. Vote negotiating sessions may occur with caucuses of either party, but for these meetings the determining factor is that caucus members represent swing votes—votes a president may seek to keep in his party or to peel off from the other party.

PERSONAL-INTEREST CAUCUSES

Many personal-interest caucuses see their role as coordinating and disseminating information and do not take caucus positions on issues. Typically, they are in contact with executive branch agencies primarily for information. They seek information, for example, on the status of pending decisions, on agency activity and views on legislation, and on implementation criteria and activity. These caucuses work, as a senior aide noted, "to maintain open channels . . . hoping to piece together the picture on an issue." If the executive branch has "policies or issues they are lobbying for, we are certainly in touch with them." When administrations, and top administration officials, change there is often a period of confusion and uncertainty while new channels of information are established.

These caucuses seek information on the whole range of their concerns. For the Environmental and Energy Study Conference, for example, issues "run across the board and across the executive branch." The caucus is in touch with, among others, the Office of Management and Budget, the White House, the Environmental Protection Agency, and the Energy Department. The Senate Caucus on the Family also has concerns that cut across executive agencies; it works with Health and Human Services, the Commerce Department (including the Census Bureau), the Justice Department, and the White House. The Human Rights Caucus, with a more specific interest, works with offices in the White House and in the State Department—the Immigration and Naturalization Service, the Human Rights and Humanitarian Affairs Bureau, and the Refugee Programs Bureau. The Military Reform Caucus reported extensive contact with the Defense Department, including occasional meetings with the secretary and officials on specific caucus stands. A senior staffer said, "There are a number of people [in the Defense Department] who are aware of the caucus and realize it can be a formidable and influential group. The caucus is now known at the Pentagon, and there are those that fear it."

A caucus may work through Executive Office of the President agencies, White House offices, administrative departments, or independent agencies that handle its issues. Meetings between the Arts Caucus and the special assistant for the arts in the White House and the Presidential Task Force on the Arts and Humanities were primarily informational, but they led to closer collaboration. As a senior caucus staffer said: "There is no formal set of meetings, but we send them all of our material, and they, in turn, keep us informed of theirs. . . . Each time the task force met, both the White House and the task force called us, and we sent a representative. The task force chair came up to the Hill and had lunch with our executive board, and there was an exchange of information on what the task force might well look into and what specific issues the task force and the executive board of the caucus might combine forces on."

The concerns of the Clearinghouse on the Future dictate a different approach. Contacts within agencies are broad but personal. There is no formal contact on any particular issue of agency jurisdiction, as a caucus respondent noted: "We have contact with people within agencies that are interested in futures. We haven't done it in any strategic fashion. . . . It's people who hear of our efforts through the World Future Society, or something. . . . [They] call us, and we'll have contact that way." But in the mid-1980s, the caucus considered a change, and a more systematic approach: "It's been debated often, within [caucus] staff, what should be the relationship between the clearinghouse and executive agencies. In the past, the clearinghouse primarily served the legislative organization" and kept itself "from involvement with the executive branch. We're becoming less inclined to do that, because involvement of some of the people in the executive branch, at least some of the dialogues that we have, may prove beneficial to everybody concerned."

Three factors affect the work of personal-interest caucuses with the executive: whether the caucus and the executive agree on an issue, the timing of executive branch decision making, and whether legislation of interest to the executive branch is being considered on Capitol Hill. During the Reagan administration the Pro-Life Caucus worked with Health and Human Services, the Office of Personnel Management, and the White House on abortion issues; the administration shared the caucus's views and supported its efforts on the floor. When caucus chair Christopher Smith (R-N.J.) drafted an amendment to an appropriations bill deleting federal funds for abortions for federal employees, the Office of Personnel Management supported the caucus's efforts on the House floor. Agency staff gave the caucus information, and agency head Donald Devine sent the caucus a letter, used in floor debate, "explaining point after point after point why Smith's amendment falls directly in line with the administration's position and current law." The caucus worked with White House staff and with staff at Health and Human Services on other aspects of the abortion debate. For international issues regarding abortion, it worked with the director of the Agency for International Development and his staff.

Just as presidents' issues influence caucus efforts, caucuses sometimes influence the White House. In these efforts, timing can offer the caucus its opportunity. The National Security Caucus (formerly the Peace through Strength Caucus) sought to influence the internal decision process in the White House on various issues: "When the president was deciding on the defense strategic mix, we had a letter on the B-1 bomber signed by seven of our eight caucus co-chairmen. We had that letter delivered to the president by [Senator] Paul Laxalt at a meeting of the Republican leadership that we knew was called to discuss the B-1 bomber, because the B-1 decision would pretty much be made at that meeting. . . . The real impact was a letter at an appropriate time and in an appropriate place to try and influence the decision-making process." When the caucus held a conference on defense issues, it "communicated with the White House prior to the conference, trying to give signals on holding the line as far as defense cuts are concerned." The caucus also worked with the Office of Management and Budget, the Defense Department, and the State Department on defense-related issues. It works on both substance and strategy ("political operations," according to one staff aide).

Many personal-interest caucuses also meet regularly with high-level agency officials. The Environmental and Energy Study Conference, for example, arranged meetings with the secretary of the Interior Department, the director of the Environmental Protection Agency, and other high-level appointees. The Military Reform Caucus held sessions with the secretary of the Defense Department. Caucuses seek to establish a format for an exchange of views between members and departmental officials; and agency officials have likewise found that meetings can develop channels for meaningful communication. The Space Caucus, for example, at first had a problem meeting with NASA officials, whose attitude seemed to be, "We understand the process as it works on the Hill. . . . We know the players. We are not interested in dealing with a new body. We are not interested in having to track the activities of a space caucus." Later, however, when the caucus numbered sixty to seventy members, "NASA began to think that maybe this is something they had better look at with a little more seriousness, because it doesn't look like it's going to fizzle out and go away. And then, we started having a series of very rigorous briefings on issues." NASA began to understand that the caucus "would not interfere with NASA, it would not hurt NASA, and if NASA were intelligent it would use it to create a higher-level profile for space." After caucus statements in the *Congressional Record* supporting NASA, telephone conversations with NASA staff, and favorable comments about the caucus from "people in the business, scientists with companies involved in a particular program," it became clear that the caucus could be useful to the agency, and the relationship with NASA became cordial.

Executive branch contacts by personal-interest caucuses depend on issue interest and whether the caucus serves an information-exchange function only or whether it takes a position on issues—and whether it agrees with the administration.

NATIONAL CONSTITUENCY CAUCUSES

National constituency caucuses, like other caucus types, need information from executive agencies, but their primary concern is in influencing executive decisions and actions. These caucuses are interested in a broad range of issues, many of which cut across agency jurisdictions, so they interact with a range of agencies. The Congressional Caucus on Women's

Issues reports contacts with Health and Human Services (and with several agencies within this department), the Defense Department, the Labor Department, the White House, and the Office of Management and Budget. The Hispanic Caucus, about one-fourth of whose activity is with the executive branch, worked with the Justice Department, the Commerce Department, Health and Human Services and its subcabinet agencies, the Office of Management and Budget, and the White House. The Vietnam Era Veterans in Congress Caucus, with the narrowest issue parameters of the national constituency caucuses, is primarily oriented toward the Veterans Affairs Department but has also worked with the Defense Department, Health and Human Services, the Department of Education, and the White House. The caucus regularly attended meetings of two executive branch groups: the President's Task Force on Agent Orange and the Veterans Affairs Advisory Committee. Caucus members or staff are in touch with executive officials at all levels. Contacts range from the president (with whom the Congressional Black Caucus and the Hispanic Caucus meet) and the president's and vice president's wives (with whom the Women's Caucus usually meets) to agency political appointees, commissioners, and staff.

Both the Congressional Black Caucus and the Caucus on Women's Issues report contacts with the Office of Management and Budget on budget issues. The Women's Caucus interacted with the Defense Department on women in the military and military spouse issues. The Hispanic Caucus was in contact with the Justice Department regarding immigration issues, and because the caucus "focuses on allocation of funds for programs [that impact] Hispanic constituencies," it also worked with Health and Human Services, the Department of Education, and the Labor Department. The Vietnam Veterans Caucus worked with the Veterans Administration on implementation of a law passed in the previous Congress affecting Vietnam veterans' health care. The caucus considered the Veterans Administration preliminary draft of the guidelines for its hospitals "extremely good," but it had "also received a document that they've been sending out to their regional hospitals and offices which was very, we thought, one-sided on the issue of Agent Orange. . . . It's prejudiced and not very factual. . . . They were encouraging their representatives in the field to use this when they talked to the media. We [looked at] that and really went to town on them."

National constituency caucuses on occasion take on federal projects. For the Congressional Black Caucus, an issue involved them with the Department of Housing and Urban Development, "a problem down in Miami, Dade County, where there were 8(a) contractors, minority contractors in the area, who were approved by the Carter administration to get funding to help build a senior citizens home and hospital in the same complex.[1] [When] the Reagan administration came in, they wanted to award the 8(a) contract to another group. The group [originally awarded the contract] asked that we intervene on their behalf, since this was a case that had to deal with a federal law that caucus members [had] helped to implement." The caucus contacted the secretary of Housing and Urban Development, and the chair of the relevant caucus task force eventually worked with department officials on the problem.

National constituency caucuses also monitor agency actions and proposals. When the members of the Women's Caucus "found out that the new head of the National Cancer Institute [under Reagan] was considering abolishing a central task force on breast cancer, we wrote a letter saying that he ought not to do that, and he backed off his position." The letter "apparently sensitized him to the fact that there is a constituency out there and he just can't make an offhand remark in a New England medical journal and not expect to have to live with it." The caucus continually monitors National Institutes of Health activities and has successfully pushed the institutes to include women in clinical trials and women's health issues in programs and research. The meeting between the Hispanic Caucus and the secretary of education is another example: "He said that because of its regionality bilingual education would not be put into the block grant program—which was a major victory we thought. He said that we would be consulted on [the director of a major program]. . . . He went down through a laundry list of things. . . . We didn't even have to bring out our agenda. And that was a pretty significant victory."

As representatives of national constituencies, national caucuses gain access to all levels of the executive, from presidents to lower-level agency staff. They sometimes seek access through members of their own national constituencies who hold high-level positions. During the Bush administration, for example, the Hispanic Caucus gained entree to the administration through Manuel Lujan, secretary of the Interior Department and a former member of the caucus. Or the vehicle for access may be formal caucus meetings, issue seminars, or even caucus events featuring speakers from the executive branch. For the Vietnam Era Veterans in Congress, the overlap of members and staff with the Veterans' Affairs Committee of the House has given the caucus ongoing executive agency access.

National constituency caucuses also seek to influence executive branch nominations and appointments. A Hispanic Caucus staff aide described the beginning of the Reagan administration:

We had meetings with Hispanic staffers who worked for powerful Senate Republicans and who represented strong constituencies, Hispanic constituencies, in their states. And we really worked with Republicans in general, to try and see if we couldn't get [appointments] regardless of party. . . . We worked with everyone: the White House, the campaign, the transition office, Senate staff, House staff, national organizations, everyone. . . . You're talking about thirty people, maybe, that are working together to pull in all of these resumes and make sure they get on somebody's desk, and . . . people rounding up support for people, and the caucus writing letters when they would support somebody. . . . How much of an impact were we able to make? Probably every Hispanic that was appointed within the administration, we probably had some contact with—either wrote a letter, made some phone calls, or did something.

Perhaps because they deal with issues that cut across department and agency jurisdictions, national constituency caucuses sometimes serve as catalysts for executive branch coordination. A Vietnam Era Veterans in Congress aide describes how caucus information sharing prompted coordination:

In 1980, Max Cleland [administrator of the Veterans Administration] came to the Veterans Committee and pooh-poohed Agent Orange [a defoliant widely used by U.S. Armed Forces in Vietnam], said there was no evidence that even suggests any health problems [for U.S. service people exposed to Agent Orange]. . . . We shortly thereafter got hold of five European epidemiology studies, which EPA had from the previous year. . . . We brought these to [Cleland's] attention in a rather abrupt fashion. We had a press conference one day. . . . From then on, the VA always at least mentioned these studies and said, well, there is a suggestive link here, but it's not definitive. I think we really made them much more careful and also forced them to coordinate more with the other agencies here in town, especially EPA, which had a big case against Dow Chemical to ban 2,4,5-T [the suspect ingredient in Agent Orange]. The VA hadn't even talked to them over there. They didn't know what the hell they had. So we had to tell them what EPA had, and from then on I think they've been much more conscientious in talking to these other agencies and finding out what information they've got, what they don't have.

This effort also illustrates a typical national constituency caucus strategy, that is, the use of highly visible events, reported to the public, to affect executive action and policy making. Black Caucus and Hispanic Caucus meetings with the president, the Black Caucus Weekend each autumn (which often includes a presidential speech), the meetings of the women members of the Congressional Caucus on Women's Issues with the wives of presidents and vice presidents, these are all are high-visibility events designed to make caucus issues more salient and to activate caucus constituencies to work for executive support of caucus positions.

National constituency caucuses are also likely to meet with top decision makers from other countries. The Hispanic Caucus met with King Juan Carlos of Spain. The Vietnam Era Veterans in Congress wrote to the Australian minister of veterans affairs about Agent Orange and Vietnam veterans' issues after the minister had returned to Australia from a trip to Washington and, according to a caucus aide, "seemed to be misreading the actual views of people over here who really are concerned about these issues." The minister responded, "Please, we do want to hear your views since we are making policy over here on these issues." The caucus has stayed in touch.

REGIONAL CAUCUSES

Regional caucuses work at all levels of the executive and are often in touch with high-level executive officials, including department secretaries, agency heads, and presidential assistants for domestic affairs or national economic policy. These caucuses need information about regional demographics, industry, and other subjects as well as information on administration positions and decisions. They often represent a large geographic area (Northeast, Midwest, West, New England) and are bipartisan, both of which appear to encourage information flow. According to one respondent, his caucus had "no complaints whatsoever." The caucus received the information it needed, regardless of the party in power. The Office of Management and Budget, even though it was sometimes in an adversarial role with the caucus, had been "very forthcoming. We were on their mailing list; and as soon as things came up to the Hill, they had their person stop here. They had their documents on time, complete." Information flow differs from one president to another, but the difference is apparently due to differences in efficiency and organization, not to party affiliation.

Regional caucuses are typically in contact with a range of agencies. The Northeast-Midwest Congressional Coalition, for example, works with the White House, the Office of Management and Budget, the Defense Department, the Treasury Department, the Department of Housing and Urban Development, and the Economic Development Administration. During the Carter presidency, the New England Caucus met with the president and interacted with the Interstate Commerce Commission, the Civil Aeronautics Board, the State Department, and the Department of Energy. The Great Lakes Caucus, a group of members from states around the lakes, reports contacts with the Maritime Administration, the State Department, the Department of Transportation, the Office of Management and Budget, and the White House.

Senate caucuses, particularly, work with officials at the highest levels. Senate rules and multiple and overlapping committee memberships are important factors in the interaction. As a Western Coalition staffer pointed out: "The two branches have to work together pretty closely. . . . The managers in the executive branch really have to be concerned, because many of the caucus members are in positions to offer legislation and appropriations. A senator who is on the Appropriations Committee, a natural resources subcommittee, and other committees that deal with natural resources and western issues can offer funding in areas that we think are important or can cut money in areas that we think aren't important." Both Senate and House caucuses report ready access when caucus and committee membership overlap. Many of these caucuses are also consulted by the executive.

Information flow and issue discussion are often based on high-level personal relationships. When asked how his relationship with the executive branch worked, a senior staffer of the Northeast-Midwest Congressional Coalition answered, "largely on interpersonal relations. We enjoy very good relations with the executive branch. In the White House, we tend to work very closely with the head of the domestic policy staff and, increasingly, with the senior officials of OMB."

At the department and agency level, caucuses work primarily with staff and officials who are responsible for certain issues, rather than with congressional liaison staff. One aide remarked: "I think the more involved you get with an issue the more apt you are to be dealing with the more senior people, especially if you're speaking for more than just one member. . . . We do work with the congressional liaison people, and I guess our interns get information from them, but often we work at a more senior staff level." A Senate Western Coalition aide remarked that most of their communications were at the cabinet level. "That's the beauty of this—a cabinet member will come over and talk to a number of senators. Often, they're very wary of what the purpose is and if they're going to walk into a shooting gallery or what have you, so usually it's somewhat negotiated at the staff level as to whether press is going to be there, whether it's off the record, on the record, or what."

Because regional caucuses rely on government data for many of their analyses, they are interested in executive branch information gathering. During the early 1980s, the Northeast-Midwest caucus fought to maintain the Energy Information Agency: "We were up front in [the] fight. . . . That agency is just absolutely vital. [It is important] that information on supply, consumption, and price be provided by the government and not be turned over to the industry, as the American Petroleum Institute would prefer. OMB had almost signed off on [elimination of the agency] before we came in and at least put somewhat of a hold on it . . . by unloading a frenzy of letters, phone calls, etc. from our members." The caucus was also part of the effort to press every federal department and agency for district-specific information.

The New England Caucus sought the establishment of a regional petroleum reserve as part of the U.S. strategic petroleum reserve: "After pushing for many, many years on this thing, we finally got it in the president's budget, and it looks like we're finally getting a regional petroleum reserve. . . . We use letters to the president, lobbying by outside groups, a lot of meetings. . . . In most cases, I know the executive branch people very well, and they call up, we work together. It's incredible, on [mid-level] issues like this, you can win if you really persist and just keep at it. On the big-level issues you don't necessarily win."[2]

Regional caucuses also work with executive branch agencies in developing legislation. Here, the relationship is often mutually beneficial, and caucuses are consulted by executive agencies. As a caucus respondent said, "We're considered an interest group [by the agency]. . . . Interest groups tend to have more impact than members of Congress, so we have the best of both worlds. We consult with them as members and as an interest group. . . . They have clearly figured out [that internal groups can be useful]. They sound us out on proposals—the White House more than the agencies, especially as power centers become more centralized."

These consultations are sometimes formalized and ongoing. The Border Caucus, for example, worked with a White House interagency task force established by the president to examine problems along the Mexican border. An aide recalls: "The White House contacted us [before meetings in border cities]. . . . We provided them with background information . . . and what we saw as some problems they might look into." The New England Caucus reported an arrangement that, while not as formal, promotes the same kind of long-term cooperation: "We're working with the administration on a bunch of things in which they come and ask our views [about] how legislation might be improved. It's clear that they're trying to use us to a large extent, and they want to push legislation that we might not normally want—although if they know we're going to oppose it, obviously they don't bother, because they know that just gives us an opportunity to mobilize. . . . But . . . they will very often come over and say, 'Can we deal on this?'" The Northeast-Midwest Coalition had a somewhat different ongoing relationship with the Carter White House on developing the president's urban policy. They worked with the two top domestic policy officials: "His staff came to us, and we essentially wrote the procurement aspect of that policy." Later, the caucus badgered the White House because "they hadn't done anything about it."

These caucuses also work to influence administration positions on pending legislation before it is considered by congressional committees. If unsuccessful with the administration, caucuses seek to influence subcommittee, committee, and if necessary, floor action, but influencing the executive is often the first goal. The Northeast-Midwest Coalition's activity regarding the funding of a block grant program is a good example of how a caucus, when enough is at stake, may follow an initiative from its earliest stages in the executive branch through committee review and, if necessary, floor consideration. A senior staffer reflected on caucus efforts:

> The issue is very simple. There were enormous amounts of funds to be distributed for very broad purposes. The question was, how was it going to be divided up? Who was going to get how much? Our contention was that those cities that are growing of their own accord . . . don't have as great a need for federal assistance in development as the cities that aren't growing. In other words, the Phoenixes of the world shouldn't be getting the same amount of money as the Clevelands, even if they have the same population and the same amount of poverty. Certainly size, in and of itself, wasn't the most important factor.
>
> We came up with some thoughts. The administration was basically going in the same direction and felt that we had to focus on older, decaying cities.

The method that we agreed to employ was the use of aging housing stock, which turned out to be a good statistical proxy for distress and need. It didn't degrade things for Phoenix, you see, but it wasn't primarily the new money in the bill which would be focused in that fashion. In fact, it was a dual formula arrangement: [a city] could choose whichever [formula] provided them with the most funds. We were successful through our task force, made up of members on the committee, to advocate a strategy and a position. By and large, the administration was supportive of it.

Although the caucus achieved a major success through working directly with the executive, that success was incomplete, and the caucus later shifted its activity to the committee and opposed the administration on some issues.

Regional caucuses generally work in a bipartisan fashion with executive branch agencies. However, when caucuses work with the White House or Executive Office of the President agencies, they organize differently. Democratic White Houses are especially accessible to Democrats; Republican ones, to Republicans. Bipartisan caucuses, therefore, often organize a Republican or Democratic group from the caucus to work with presidential agencies and White House staff and officials.

The Western caucus illustrates caucus strategy, access to high-level officials, and the effect of representing a geographic region.[3] When a Department of Natural Resources was proposed, Western Coalition senators went to the White House to meet with the vice president, the secretary of the interior, and presidential aides. They made clear that the proposal would not have their support because of "the way it was organized. There were too many weak spots. They didn't see any real reason for it, so why do it? And nobody could give us a good answer. And I think that's pretty much where it died." Caucus members also met with the secretary of the interior on funding for water projects: "The government was putting out money for a lot of projects; we asked them to come over. . . . The secretary came over, we talked with him, and compromises were struck. . . . We tried to attract attention [to the fact] that there are states and people out there that should . . . be recognized."

Two factors may be particularly important in regional caucus interaction with the executive branch. First, these caucuses represent geographic regions and, hence, blocs of states and constituents; and second, members of these caucuses often sit on committees that oversee or fund an issue of interest to the caucus. It is likely, therefore, that the incentives for executive officials and staff to be responsive are particularly compelling. The pattern of interaction is not that of a completely closed subsystem but, rather, of contact with a broad range of agencies, departments, and quite frequently, the White House. When caucus members are involved, Senate caucuses, particularly, appear to gain high-level access. But other meetings and contacts also take place with high-level officials, including political appointees, when specific issues are discussed or negotiated.

STATE/DISTRICT CAUCUSES

These caucuses seek information from the executive branch and work with departments and agencies to develop legislation, to seek changes in appropriations or formulas for program authorizations, and particularly to affect the implementation of regulations. Their interests often cut across department jurisdictions. Success varies, in some instances because caucus issues are peripheral to agency concerns or necessitate cross-agency coordination. More than other caucus types, state/district caucuses work with cabinet departments and independent agencies and with lower-level officials and staff.

When close working relationships are established, information often travels in both directions. But a senior staffer of a caucus, who works closely with a number of agencies, reported that he often "had to go after the agencies . . . [because] they don't tell you a damn thing they don't want to. . . . We've never had any big problem once we've asked for information, but I don't think they are going to provide weekly input . . . unless we ask for it and stay on them." This experience contrasts strongly with that of regional caucuses, perhaps because state/district caucus issues are more diffuse and have less clearly defined or interested constituency groups.

Some Senate state/district caucuses report more interaction with high-level officials than do the parallel House caucuses. Shortly after the establishment of the Senate Family Farm Task Force, the caucus and the secretary of agriculture held a successful press conference on the decline of family farms. The secretary spoke, the task force members presented their views, and a roundtable discussion ensued. The Senate Export Caucus has met with the secretary of commerce and the U.S. trade representative to talk about various trade and export matters. In contrast, the House Export Caucus meets primarily with agency and office heads within the Commerce Department. Senate meetings appear to be wide-ranging, while House meetings are more focused on specific legislation, which may explain the difference.

The concerns of these caucuses bring them in contact with a number of agencies. Because numerous agencies deal with small cities and rural development, the Rural Caucus works with the Department of Housing and Urban Development, the Department of Agriculture, the Economic Development Administration, the Environmental Protection Agency, the Small Business Administration, and others. The Export Caucuses have worked with the Departments of Commerce, State, and Agriculture, and the U.S. trade representative. Caucuses report success in putting their concerns on executive agendas, working with agencies to craft legislative language, and producing occasional change through oversight.

For some of these caucuses, incentives for agency response flow from overlap between caucus and committee leadership or membership. In the mid-1980s, for example, the chair of the House Export Caucus was Don Bonker (D-Wash.), who also chaired the Foreign Affairs Committee's Subcommittee on International Economic Policy and Trade. William Roth (R-Del.) chaired the Senate Export Caucus and the Governmental Affairs Committee and was ranking majority member on the Finance Committee's Subcommittee on International Trade.

A respondent from the Rural Caucus described its range of activities: "We were involved in the Rural Development Policy Act. We've had an active dialogue with the Labor Department over job training programs and activities. . . . We have dialogues with HUD on matters related to small cities and rural areas." The caucus also advised the Community Services Administration (and successor agencies) on low-income issues. It worked on sewage treatment programs with the Environmental Protection Agency, on farm, community, business, and housing programs with the Farmers Home Administration in the Department of Agriculture, and on rural health issues with Health and Human Services.

Caucus respondents describe some success: "A while back, the Rural Caucus and its advisory team were responsible for keeping the Economic Development Administration; otherwise, the administration would have chopped it." The caucus later "helped write the budget recommendations [on program authorization levels] for the Farmer's Home Administration"; these recommendations were submitted to the House Agriculture Committee. The caucus sued the Office of Management and Budget over the Nixon administration's impoundments: "We went to federal court and sued them for 4.5 billion bucks. . . . We were going to sue them for impounding another $9 billion in EPA sewage treatment monies, but we backed off because Nixon got into trouble, and we notified the White House that when Mr. Ford took over as president we wanted to stay off his back, so we withdrew the suit." Ford subsequently released a lot of the funds.

The Senate Family Farm Task Force's concerns helped push the Department of Agriculture into a study of the structure of U.S. agriculture. Caucus establishment and the start of the study occurred at about the same time. A senior aide said:

> The fact that there were people making noise up here convinced the department that the issue, the structure of agriculture, wasn't going to go away, and they had to make some sort of response to it. For those who were defenders of traditional agriculture, increasing productivity and more and greater use of technology on the farm was a good thing, because we were producing more. And therefore the people who were talking about the fact that mechanical agriculture was having a deleterious effect on one sector of the farming community, namely the small farmers, were kind of debunked as the lunatic fringe and radical. But I believe that the caucus definitely had an effect on the department's beginning to take a look at it.

A Senate Export Caucus experience illustrates an occasional focus on unlikely departments and a flexibility in strategy and approach. Early in the Reagan administration, forty-six members of the caucus sent a letter to the president asking that ambassadors be instructed to place a high priority on promoting trade and that they be evaluated on this basis. The president agreed, and the State Department then sent a cable instructing ambassadors that this was to be a high priority. Later, an amendment by Senator William Roth (R-Del.), which was attached to the State Department authorization bill, confirmed this as a priority.

INDUSTRY CAUCUSES

More than any other group, industry caucuses engage in subsystem politics, working outside the limelight with executive agencies and private sector interests. These caucuses work with the executive branch because that is where their interests—trade, tax, regulation, and implementation—are handled. Many issues are complicated and highly technical, and the general media usually do not report this caucus work, although the specialized media sometimes follow it carefully. For many of these caucuses, a major part of their work is bringing private sector adversaries (e.g., business and labor, consumers and producers), caucus members, and administration personnel together to exchange information or to engage in policy negotiation.

A higher proportion of these caucuses than others work primarily on administrative agendas (see table 6-1), meet with agency staff (see table 8-1), and view the primary purpose of contact with the executive branch as representation, all of which would be expected of subsystem actors. Also, these caucuses, more than others, tend to be headed by senior members of Congress, and caucus-committee overlap is therefore a significant factor in administrative response to caucus concerns. A number of the caucuses in this category are Senate caucuses, a fact that enhances the committee-caucus overlap for the groups.

Because each of these caucuses focuses on the relatively narrow issue of one particular industry, contact with the executive branch is usually with a single department. The Travel and Tourism Caucus, for example, works mostly with the Commerce Department. When industry caucuses expand their administrative contacts, they move up to the Office of Management and Budget and the White House rather than laterally to other departments. However, some caucuses are in contact with several agencies because each works on a different aspect of a subject of caucus concern. The House and Senate Coal Caucuses, for example, work with the Interior Department, the Labor Department, and the Environmental Protection Agency. The Jewelry Manufacturing Coalition interacts on trade, tax and industry assistance issues with the U.S. trade representative, the Treasury Department, the Commerce Department, the Small Business Administration, the Economic Development Administration, and the White House.

Information exchange for industry caucuses follows the pattern of all caucuses in that they need information from executive agencies, and the agencies sometimes want information from them. At times there is trust; at other times, caution. Typically, caucuses meet with administration officials for information and exchange of views; Senate industry caucuses are more likely than House caucuses to meet with high-level political officials. On occasion, a caucus uses a high-profile meeting to gain its ends. The Senate Steel Caucus has held caucus hearings to publicize an issue, the administration's position, and caucus concern. If the issue is hot, television, the general press, and the trade press may cover the hearing.

What strategies do these caucuses use? How effective have they been? The Travel and Tourism Caucus approached the executive to appoint an undersecretary of commerce, to create an independent agency to deal with industry issues, and to develop a coordinated national government approach to these issues. The caucus eventually prevailed—but not in the executive: legislation establishing a Commerce Department undersecretary for travel and tourism and a U.S. Travel and Tourism Administration within the Department of Commerce was passed by Congress and signed by the president after long negotiation with the administration to develop the legislation.

The Jewelry Manufacturing Coalition achieved partial success on a trade issue. The coalition "couldn't get a presidential decision [on imports] reversed," after meetings with the U.S. trade representative, the Commerce Department, the Economic Development Administration, and White House staff, but "did get the International Trade Commission to study the issue." The caucus also supported an application by the jewelry industry for a federal grant to study industry problems and propose solutions. The effort was successful, "in part because of the coalition making it clear . . . that this was something that was important and helping to spell out the problems the industry was facing." A senior caucus aide concluded that the "caucus was a catalyst for creating a new sensitivity on the part of administration officials and agencies as to this industry. . . . Decisions in the past . . . were made without any thought given to the jewelry industry, because it was so small and it had no voice. Now it's realized that it has to be considered before the president, or the trade representative, or the Department of Commerce makes a decision."

The Senate Steel Caucus has regular contact with agency bureaucracy and high-level officials. The tripartite process (industry, labor, and government) to develop legislation affecting the steel industry was generated in part by caucus pressure. There has been caucus-committee overlap since the caucus's founding. To make access smoother, caucus chairs match the party controlling the White House, switching parties when the presidency changes party. Other caucuses seek access with co-chairs, one from each party. Although industry caucuses do not automatically support and argue for every industry position, they generally seek consideration of industry issues in executive decision making. A few industry caucuses follow a different model. The Senate Rail Caucus, for example, operates as a broker among interested parties rather than as an advocate of a specific position.

Summary

All caucus types work with the executive branch. All are strategically flexible, moving easily between levels of the executive or shifting the locus of activity to Congress when executive remedies fail. Caucuses exchange views with executive officials and seek to influence policy. There is cooperation, but there is also negotiation and hard bargaining. Caucuses are often at least partially successful in achieving their policy goals.

In contacts with the executive branch, congressional caucuses represent concerns important to their constituencies and serve as oversight watchdogs. In their focus on an issue, they deal with a number of agencies and may coordinate agency actions. Committee membership affects the relationship of a caucus to the executive. The role of Congress in establishing executive programs and overseeing executive actions is not forgotten: executive agencies may be more responsive if a senator or representative who is a caucus leader is also a member of a relevant subcommittee. If members do not achieve policy goals through the executive, they may seek that goal through legislation. This is particularly true in the Senate, in which caucus and committee memberships often overlap.

Variation among caucus types is also evident. Party caucuses disproportionately work with presidential agencies or White House staff. Party and national constituency caucuses more than others meet with presidents. The contacts of industry caucuses with the executive branch are more narrowly focused (as to both issues and agencies); they work less with high-level officials, following a typical subsystem politics model. They eschew the public arena and focus specifically on representation of constituency interests, which are often quite narrow. Party caucus contacts with the executive branch are affected by control of the White House. Meetings are frequent if the caucus's party controls the presidency; less so if the opposition party controls. Bipartisan caucuses, if structured to work with the party in power, are not generally affected. This is particularly true for distributive caucuses (regional, state/district, and industry). Their contacts with the bureaucracy are stable.

Contacts with the executive may be directed at specific decisions, such as increasing program authorization or appropriations, changing grant formulas, or achieving a decision on imports. But much caucus work with the executive is dialogue, directed at influencing attitudes, sensitizing agencies to a constituency or a problem, putting an issue on the executive agenda, bringing in new thinking or program formulas, or giving impetus to a study. These are important factors in the Washington policy equation. Whether representing industry interests or a more general national interest, caucuses function as crucial information brokers in the federal policy-making process.

9/ WORKING WITH CONGRESSIONAL COMMITTEES

Congressional caucuses of every kind work in some way with committees, but not every caucus is active in this arena. Caucus relationships with committees range from collaborative to cool and are affected by the caucus's primary mission, issue focus, and membership overlap with committees. Caucuses established to deal with subjects that are being neglected by committees are often viewed as challenging committee leadership, even though caucus leaders may serve on the committee.

FOUR MODELS OF CAUCUS-COMMITTEE RELATIONS

The Senate Family Farm Task Force, for example, faced a hostile committee. The caucus was founded in the late 1970s by Donald Stewart (D-Ala.) to focus attention on the plight of the family farm and to develop and coordinate legislative action. Although Stewart served on the Senate Agriculture Committee, the committee chair, Herman Talmadge (D-Ga.) and staff distrusted the caucus and feared it would impinge on committee turf. Few committee members joined the caucus. It became inactive and, finally, disbanded after Stewart's electoral defeat.

For other caucuses, an initially chilly climate gradually changed. When the House Space Caucus was established, the House Science and Technology Committee was also concerned about its territory. One observer noted that, "historically, space, and especially colonizing space and having manned missions to Mars, have been left largely to space enthusiasts. There has been a problem . . . with long-term projects being perceived as flaky. . . . So committee members weren't sure that this wouldn't turn out to be a very peculiar, sort of spacey, flaky, nonserious caucus." When it became clear that serious members had established and joined the caucus and the caucus began to work on increasing the understanding of— and support for—space programs, the committee's view changed, and caucus assistance was welcomed. One of the founders and first co-chairs of the caucus was Newt Gingrich (R-Ga.), a space buff who was worried that without investment in space research and development the country's future ability to develop technology would be significantly curtailed.

The Arms Control and Foreign Policy Caucus exemplifies another model. There has been considerable membership overlap between it and the House Foreign Affairs Committee (renamed the International Relations Committee in the 104th Congress) and some overlap between the caucus and the Armed Services Committee (renamed the National Security Committee), but many caucus members do not serve on these committees. One participant noted that, other than caucus membership, they "don't have any foreign affairs or military affairs outlet. . . . People who are on Rules, for instance, really want to belong, really come to our meetings" and participate. Nevertheless, relationships with the committees, and particularly with Foreign Affairs, were close, even though committee chairs did not belong to the caucus. A staff aide observed, "I think the Foreign Affairs [Committee] people regard us more as sort of an extension and an opportunity to be bipartisan, when their committee is often more partisan." The caucus also cooperated with the Armed Services Committee's staff on some issues, with smooth, even friendly, relationships.

A fourth model, which is rare, consists of total cooperation, with committee chairs also serving as caucus chairs and committee aides staffing the caucus. In the 1980s, the chairs of the Port Caucus also chaired the Public Works Committee and the Merchant Marine and Fisheries Committee, and committee staff served as caucus staff. The larger and more diversified membership of the caucus expanded the information exchange system and provided links to additional outside groups. Caucus members and staff emphasize that caucuses are formed to work within the system. As one caucus staff director emphasized: "We have . . . kept the committee very informed of what we are doing because we are not trying to pull support away from the chairman. . . . We see the caucus as being able to pull in support from other members for the chairman, rather than vice versa. We don't want to parallel the activities of the committee in any way."

CAUCUS GOALS, COMMITTEE NEEDS

A caucus that focuses solely on education and information or that can be useful to a committee will have cordial relations with that committee.

A caucus that also seeks specific policy outcomes may not. A former staff director of the Senate Rail Caucus observed that, if the caucus took "mandatory positions on some of the issues before this subcommittee and [tried] to galvanize people on them, we'd have a different relationship than we do." As it is, the caucus focus is "to get everybody educated, because the committee doesn't have time, with its broad jurisdiction, to focus in detail on this issue, and we do, and so it's an advantage to them, too." This caucus stays out of legislative specifics and holds meetings and briefings on issues, not on bills. It seems to work. When long-time caucus chair David Durenberger (R-Minn.) achieved passage of major rail legislation, he did so in a way typical of Senate caucuses, acting as an individual, distinct from the caucus but informed by its work.

The timing and the issue are also important. A caucus staff director noted that "there are certain occasions where committees are interested in educating and other times when they are not. There are certain occasions when they want to float trial balloons and tip their hand, and there are other occasions when they do not. The degree to which they cooperate with us depends on their motives. . . . They generally see us—minority, majority, or whatever—as an aid in their work [because] a lot of their work is education . . . and we can help them do that. We save them time and phone calls." The chairs of the House Human Rights Caucus, too, gained recognition as helpful participants in the policy process. They "established themselves as forces in the area of human rights and are frequently asked by other members to cosponsor things. The subcommittee [on Human Rights] recognizes that and, on certain issues, will work with us." The caucus was founded in 1985; in 1993–94, caucus co-chair, Tom Lantos (D-Calif.), also chaired the Human Rights Subcommittee.

CAUCUS-COMMITTEE OVERLAP

Caucuses offer an opportunity for noncommittee members to work on committee-related issues. Caucus members who are also members of a relevant committee can focus on issues that are overlooked by the committee or gain support for questions that are before the committee. Junior members disproportionately belong to caucuses, but senior members also join and participate in caucus work and can be significant in achieving caucus legislative goals. For senior members who chair a caucus and serve on a relevant subcommittee, caucus and committee activity often mesh to achieve a desired policy goal.

Several party and national constituency caucuses seek to place members on committees that handle issues of caucus concern or to bring that caucus's perspective to committee deliberations. A former senior staffer described Congressional Black Caucus efforts:

> We'll look at the committees where we don't have any caucus members sitting, and we'll look at the issues that we were confronted with last year. Say, for instance, that we have no members sitting on Agriculture, but that committee handles food stamp legislation. OK, do we need somebody strategically there? Also, Agriculture may deal with black land grant colleges and with the small southern cooperative farming groups that have started in the South (some of which are black) and the loss of land in the South by black farmers—so we need someone on Agriculture. So then if another caucus member from the South comes in, then the caucus will talk to him about sitting on the Agriculture Committee to deal with the large constituency out there that has those particular concerns and interests.

Larger caucuses and those with a wide issue focus—like the Democratic Study Group, the Environmental and Energy Study Conference, and the Northeast-Midwest Congressional Coalition—generally have members on most, if not all, House committees (see table 9-1). Caucuses with an explicit information exchange function, such as the Wednesday Group, and small caucuses with a specific interest in a range of committee memberships for their caucus members, such as the Boll Weevils, also have members on virtually all House committees. Most caucuses with a specific issue focus have members who serve on the relevant committee or committees. Industry and state/district caucuses, in particular, are helped by senior members who are also in committee leadership positions.

As caucus members gain seniority, they also gain leadership clout. In the Ninety-seventh Congress, members of the Congressional Black Caucus served on a wide range of committees, and two of them chaired committees (District of Columbia and House Administration). By the 103d Congress, twelve subcommittees and three major committees were chaired by CBC members. The major committees were Armed Services (Ron Dellums, D-Calif.), Government Operations (John Conyers, D-Mich.), and Post Office and Civil Service (William Clay, D-Mo.).[1] In the intervening Congresses, Bill Gray (D-Pa.) chaired the Budget Committee and later served as Democratic whip; other caucus members had gained leadership positions in the formal congressional system.

Table 9-1. Caucus/Committee Membership Overlap, House of Representatives, Ninety-seventh Congress (percentage of committee seats occupied by caucus members)

Caucus	Agriculture (43)	Appropriations (55)	Armed Services (45)	Banking (45)	Budget (30)	District of Columbia (12)
Democratic Study Group	51	55	37	47	53	50
Republican Study Committee	28	25	31	24	37	25
Conservative Democratic Forum (Boll Weevils)	19	11	22	7	10	0
Wednesday Group	2	7	2	4	7	0
Congressional Black Caucus	0	6	2	2	0	33
Congressional Caucus on Women's Issues	0	4	7	4	7	8
Hispanic Caucus	2	2	0	4	0	0
Vietnam Era Veterans	7	2	4	7	13	8
Northeast-Midwest	26	47	38	60	43	33
Sunbelt	5	9	16	4	0	8
Export	23	20	13	33	30	17
Family Farm	30	6	7	4	7	0
Federal Government Service	2	9	7	9	0	42
Rural	79	31	40	24	27	0
Automotive	7	11	18	11	7	8
Coal	16	18	16	4	10	8
Mushroom	21	31	27	29	23	50
Steel	9	29	20	13	23	0
Textile	7	6	9	0	3	0
Arms Control	14	29	11	29	27	50
Baltic	0	20	24	24	20	25
Military Reform	14	9	29	9	13	8
Environment and Energy	54	58	40	51	50	75
Pro-Life	2	0	4	0	3	8

Table 9-1. *(Continued)*

	Education and Labor (34)	Energy and Commerce (42)	Foreign Affairs (37)	Government Operations (41)	House Administration (19)	Interior (43)	Judiciary (28)	Merchant Marine (36)
Democratic Study Group	44	57	51	51	47	44	39	39
Republican Study Committee	26	43	30	27	32	33	21	28
Conservative Democratic Forum (Boll Weevils)	3	12	11	10	10	7	7	17
Wednesday Group	9	2	11	10	5	5	11	6
Congressional Black Caucus	8	5	5	7	5	0	11	0
Congressional Caucus on Women's Issues	3	5	3	5	5	2	4	6
Hispanic	0	0	0	0	0	2	0	0
Vietnam Era Veterans	3	14	5	5	0	16	0	8
Northeast-Midwest	59	52	68	59	47	28	54	53
Sunbelt	0	7	3	12	5	5	11	11
Export	21	17	41	17	21	28	25	19
Family Farm	15	5	8	5	0	7	14	3
Federal Government Service	3	7	11	7	0	5	7	8
Rural	35	29	22	24	21	44	25	39
Automotive	6	7	11	20	0	12	11	11
Coal	18	21	5	10	16	30	17	6
Mushroom	29	31	38	29	42	28	32	33
Steel	32	29	24	32	21	23	17	11
Textile	3	10	14	5	0	7	4	6
Arms Control	21	19	35	27	21	19	29	22
Baltic	18	33	35	20	21	7	25	33
Military Reform	12	5	5	12	10	12	4	14
Environment and Energy	65	74	60	61	21	65	69	69
Pro-Life	6	7	5	0	0	2	14	8

(Continued)

Table 9-1. *(Continued)*

	Post Office and Civil Service (27)	Public Works (48)	Rules (16)	Science and Technology (40)	Small Business (40)	Veterans' Affairs (34)	Ways and Means (35)
Democratic Study Group	44	50	56	48	50	32	60
Republican Study Committee	26	35	6	28	25	38	31
Conservative Democratic Forum (Boll Weevils)	0	8	0	13	13	21	11
Wednesday Group	0	2	0	3	3	3	6
Congressional Black Caucus	15	2	6	2	5	0	6
Congressional Caucus on Women's Issues	11	4	6	2	2	3	0
Hispanic	4	0	0	2	2	0	0
Vietnam Era Veterans	4	4	12	8	5	9	6
Northeast-Midwest	52	46	37	55	63	41	46
Sunbelt	0	10	12	5	0	15	6
Export	0	6	19	25	28	9	29
Family Farm	4	4	0	10	10	9	0
Federal Government Service	22	8	0	2	0	0	9
Rural	18	35	31	35	30	35	17
Automotive	4	15	12	15	12	15	14
Coal	11	21	6	18	18	26	6
Mushroom	33	27	25	28	25	35	29
Steel	30	31	19	22	32	29	23
Textile	7	10	19	15	2	12	14
Arms Control	26	8	25	25	18	6	14
Baltic	26	17	25	32	25	18	20
Military Reform	7	6	6	5	5	9	3
Environment and Energy	52	56	62	82	52	35	57
Pro-Life	4	4	0	5	12	3	0

Note: At the start of the 104th Congress (1995) three committees were abolished: District of Columbia, Merchant Marine and Fisheries, and Post Office and Civil Service; nine committees were renamed: Armed Services became National Security, Education and Labor became Economic and Educational Opportunities, Energy and Commerce became Commerce, Foreign Affairs became International Relations, Government Operations became Government Reform and Oversight, House Administration became House Oversight, Interior (later Natural Resources) became Resources, Science and Technology became Science, and Public Works became Transportation and Infrastructure.

[a] The number of members of each standing committee is given in parentheses in each column head.

House Caucuses

Party caucuses, operating as factional groupings within a party, generally hold a wide range of committee memberships and have significant caucus-committee overlap. Members are well positioned to share information about committee activity, to place issues on a committee agenda, or to seek specific legislative goals. Democratic Study Group members in the Ninety-seventh Congress, for example, served on every standing committee except one. On ten of the standing committees, half or more of the committee members belonged to the caucus. The Republican Study Committee was similarly well represented: members served on every committee and were a majority of minority party members on most of them.

The committee membership of the smaller Boll Weevil Caucus (the Conservative Democratic Forum) in the Ninety-seventh Congress reflects its successful push to gain assignments on major committees and in party positions. Caucus members served on all but three of the standing committees, with a major presence on committees that particularly interested the caucus, such as Agriculture, Armed Services, Merchant Marine and Fisheries (with jurisdiction over ports), Public Works, and Veterans' Affairs. The caucus also had members on two of the major (exclusive) committees (Appropriations and Ways and Means) and on Budget. The (Republican) Wednesday Group also achieved wide representation. One of its main purposes is to serve as an information-exchange group and early-warning system on committee action. To achieve this, the caucus must have members on a wide range of committees. Although the Wednesday Group had only twenty-two members in the Ninety-seventh Congress, they were on all but three standing committees, including all of the most important policy committees except Rules.

National constituency caucus members do not serve on all standing committees, but they are well represented on committees of particular interest to the caucus. Membership overlap between the CBC and committees reflects the concerns of the representatives' constituencies as well as the priorities of the caucus. Although the caucus had only seventeen members during the Ninety-seventh Congress, caucus members served on most of the standing committees, including all of the exclusive committees (Appropriations, Rules, and Ways and Means).

Some small national constituency caucuses can have trouble achieving the committee representation they want. The Congressional Caucus on

Women's Issues, however, overcame its size limitations with multiple assignments; the seventeen members of the caucus served on most standing committees. In contrast, the small Hispanic Caucus was able to place its six members on only seven committees, including Agriculture (caucus member Kika de la Garza, D-Tex., was committee chair), Appropriations, Interior, and Banking. The caucus had to rely on honorary members to expand committee representation. Members of the Vietnam Era Veterans in Congress Caucus found that, despite their small number, they could gain representation on all committees of interest to them: Appropriations, Armed Services, Government Operations, Veterans' Affairs.

Size and concerns govern the caucus-committee overlap of regional caucuses. On some committees, a caucus's members occupy a majority of the seats (see table 9-1). The large Northeast-Midwest Congressional Coalition (211 members) had no difficulty finding members who served on committees with jurisdiction over the issues of particular importance to the caucus: Agriculture (11), Banking, Finance, and Urban Affairs (27), Education and Labor (20), Energy and Commerce (23), Public Works (23), Small Business (25), Appropriations (25), Rules (6), Ways and Means (16), Budget (13). This is one of the best-represented caucuses, and the opportunities for sharing information on committee activities and influencing committee work are many. State/district caucuses target specific issues, and most have members on relevant committees. Members of industry caucuses may serve on divers committees, but they also have members on committees particularly important to the caucus, and often those members are committee leaders. Five members of the Automotive Caucus, for example, served on Ways and Means, four of them as subcommittee leaders; three were on Energy and Commerce, all in positions of leadership (the committee chair was a caucus member); six members served on Appropriations, with three in leadership positions. The pattern for personal-interest caucuses is similar to that of state/district caucuses, with caucus members serving on committees that have jurisdiction over issues of interest to the caucus. Members of the 249-member Environmental and Energy Study Conference, for example, served on all standing committees, with a major presence on committees of particular relevance to the caucus.

The Pro-Life Caucus presents a somewhat different picture. Typically, the caucus has proposed abortion-banning amendments to appropriations bills and to Defense Department and District of Columbia authorization bills. During the Ninety-seventh Congress, one or two caucus members served on the Armed Services Committee and the District of Columbia

Committee, but there was no caucus member on the Appropriations Committee. This may have pushed the caucus to propose floor amendments, because it was largely unable to affect legislation at the Appropriations Committee stage.

Senate Caucuses

In the Senate, caucus-committee overlap is considerable. In conjunction with Senate rules, which permit senators to participate to some degree in the work of any committee, and the increase in individualism, activism, and amending activity, caucuses typically seek policy results at the committee level. The Senate Export Caucus is typical. Most members from exporting states belonged to it, and caucus members served on all the committees concerned with trade. Because any senator can introduce legislation and see it through committee, the interests of the caucus are covered at all the formal legislative points.

CAUCUSES AS SOURCES OF COMMITTEE INFORMATION

Caucuses are important parts of the congressional information and early-warning system. Written material from the Democratic Study Group, the Republican Study Committee, the Environmental and Energy Study Conference, the Arms Control and Foreign Policy Caucus, and others has been widely distributed and used. Publications offer information on committee agenda items and actions and on legislation scheduled for floor action. Twenty-two percent of House members used materials from the Democratic Study Group for information for committee work (U.S. House of Representatives 1977). Many members also reported using Republican Study Committee publications. Other caucuses rely primarily on caucus meetings for information exchange. The House Wednesday Group, which explicitly seeks members with a range of committee assignments, meets each week to discuss committee activities and pending floor action. Other caucuses find face-to-face discussions are important for sharing information on both committee and floor activity: "There is such a barrage of legislation and it is so complicated that, if you're not a specialist on the particular committee in which that legislation originated, you may not understand that much about what you're actually voting on. And that's one of the things this particular group has accomplished—there is a pretty widespread cross section of committees represented and people with varying degrees of expertise in their various areas. And since they share a political and fiscal philosophy, they can exchange information on various bills." Another respondent emphasized a caucus's early-warning role: "The members are really the types that are good legislators. . . . They're genuinely interested in finding out about an issue before it happens, and getting as much information as they can."

Caucuses with the primary purpose of information exchange seek to highlight the importance of issues and the factors to be considered in addressing problems, but they do not take a position on issues and so do not work with committees. Caucuses that do take issue positions, however, generally stay away from omnibus bills. The Rural Caucus could not "take on a farm bill," one respondent noted, "because it's so damn diversified."

Most caucuses are bipartisan, and although members may agree that an issue is important, there may not be unanimity on legislative policy or on how to achieve a desired outcome. To take a position on an issue, a caucus must first decide how that will be done. A few caucuses, like the Congressional Caucus on Women's Issues, require unanimous agreement to take a position. For many years, until the 103d Congress, this policy kept abortion off the caucus agenda. Most caucuses, however, give the authority to take a caucus position to a group within the caucus—caucus leaders, executive or steering committees, or a task force—or caucus members as individuals take the lead in seeking a caucus coalition to support a position. Both ways seem to work. Alternatively, members speak as individuals but identify themselves as members of the caucus, and the caucus does not, technically, take a position on the issue. Variation in the House does not occur systematically by caucus type. However, all Senate caucuses follow the individual model.

For example, the Arms Control and Foreign Policy Caucus used bipartisan task forces, which studied an issue and developed legislative proposals. Democrats and Republicans on the task force worked with their party colleagues on committees and in the leadership to achieve passage of task force proposals. The Democratic Study Group's legislative proposals are approved by the caucus's Executive Committee, which has wide representation of caucus members. In one of the smaller caucuses, the leaders speak not for the caucus but for themselves. The Northeast-Midwest Congressional Coalition uses ad hoc task forces.

A task force can be set up very simply by a member who serves on a relevant committee, being concerned about a particular piece of legislation. [The member] sends out a "Dear Colleague" letter, which says, "I'm concerned about this legislation. We should set up a task force to analyze it and have a united front when we deal with it in the subcommittee. If you're interested in joining, come to a meeting in this room on this date and at this time." And then the members meet, try to decide what's in the best interest of the region, try to present a united front during subcommittee hearings and markup and so on—and push our legislation through. Positions are taken on behalf of the coalition task force—not on behalf of the coalition, and not on behalf of anyone whose name is not signed at the bottom of that letter. But it does not have to be approved by the executive or steering committees.

The purpose of a task force is to educate, to work on legislative strategy, and to put together a voting bloc.

Republicans and Democrats in the Northeast-Midwest Congressional Coalition also use task forces to work separately with their party leaders. One respondent recalled the coalition's work in the review of appropriations legislation, during the Reagan administration, for the Economic Development Administration and for urban development action grants (appropriations to cities or towns, which then lend to local businesses at a favorable rate): "It was with a sense of frustration that our members on the Republican side began trying to consider how they could best influence the process. . . . They had two choices: through the coalition or as Republicans, working with their party's leadership and [the] president. . . . They rightly chose the latter. . . . They found their niche in the policy-making process and worked it quite well. . . . It's not a threat to the coalition at all."

Ad hoc caucus groups, led by individual members, are the most typical way of organizing to work on a specific policy issue. Two or three Wednesday Group members link up on each research issue. Individual members of the Ad Hoc Monitoring Group on Southern Africa signed statements distributed on caucus letterhead. The (conservative Republican) Senate Steering Committee is one of the most individualistic caucus operations; it does not take specific stands on issues, and members do not need to agree on a matter before working on an issue as individuals. The caucus serves as a means for like-minded senators to share resources and to coordinate policy activity. Caucus staff, especially during the 1980s when the caucus employed a separate staff, helps individual senators pursue legislation at both the committee and floor stages.

CAUCUS-COMMITTEE INTERACTION

National constituency and regional caucuses are the most active in working with committees, closely followed by party caucuses, and then by personal-interest caucuses (see table 9-2). Industry caucuses are less active, as would be expected for a group whose principal focus is on executive action. State/district caucuses are the least active, reflecting lower activity in general.

More than half the national constituency and regional caucuses hold formal meetings with committee leaders, testify at committee hearings, and hold caucus hearings. If class clubs are excluded, this pattern also describes party caucuses. Industry and personal-interest caucuses testify less frequently at hearings and only infrequently meet with committee leaders. Using the Pearson chi-square, the differences among the types of caucuses on committee meetings are significant at the .006 level; on testifying, they are nearly significant (.10 level).

When class clubs are excluded, party caucuses are the most involved in all aspects of committee work: 40–50 percent of these caucuses draft bills and amendments and work with committee and subcommittee leaders and committee staff (see table 9-2). The activity pattern of national constituency caucuses and regional caucuses is more varied, but in many areas it is also high. Both caucus types work with committee staff, the nationals more at the full committee level, the regionals at the subcommittee level.

About one-third of the personal-interest and state/district caucuses draft bills for committee consideration; fewer draft amendments. State/district caucuses work more at the subcommittee than at the full committee level and work with committee leaders rather than staff. Few industry caucuses work on legislation at the committee level, because many of the issues with which these groups are concerned are handled by executive agencies.

The issues that caucuses worked on in 1987 reflect important agenda matters in the 100th Congress; the focus of the various caucus types indicates their concerns.[2] Industry caucuses are primarily concerned with business, labor, the economy, and trade. State/district and regional caucuses also focused on these topics, although unlike industry caucuses, they were also concerned with the functioning of government and social benefits. National constituency caucuses focused on economic and social

Table 9-2. Caucuses and Congressional Committee Activities, by Caucus Type, 100th Congress (in percentages)

Activity	Party		Party without Class Clubs		Personal Interest		National Constituency		Regional		State/District		Industry	
Hearings and formal meetings														
Meeting with committee leaders	31	(4)	40	(4)	8	(2)	40	(2)	50	(6)	10	(1)	17	(3)
Holding hearings	8	(1)	8	(1)	17	(4)	40	(2)	42	(5)	0		6	(1)
Holding hearings with other caucuses	0		0		4	(1)	0		8	(1)	0		0	
Holding solo hearings	8	(1)	8	(1)	12	(3)	40	(2)	42	(5)	0		11	(2)
Testifying at hearings	38	(5)	50	(5)	17	(4)	60	(3)	50	(6)	0		33	(6)
Testifying at House hearings	31	(4)	40	(4)	8	(2)	60	(3)	50	(6)	10	(1)	22	(4)
Testifying at Senate hearings	8	(1)	10	(1)	4	(1)	40	(2)	25	(3)	10	(1)	28	(5)
Legislative and committee work														
Drafting bills for committee consideration	38	(5)	50	(5)	33	(8)	40	(2)	42	(5)	30	(3)	17	(3)
Drafting amendments	31	(4)	40	(4)	21	(5)	20	(1)	25	(3)	10	(1)	6	(1)
Working with subcommittees	38	(5)	50	(5)	17	(4)	40	(2)	42	(5)	20	(2)	11	(2)
Working with subcommittee chair	31	(4)	40	(4)	17	(4)	20	(1)	33	(4)	20	(2)	11	(2)
Working with subcommittee ranking minority member	31	(4)	40	(4)	21	(5)	0		25	(3)	0		6	(1)
Working with subcommittee staff	38	(5)	50	(5)	17	(4)	20	(1)	33	(4)	0		6	(1)
Working with full committee	31	(4)	40	(4)	17	(4)	60	(3)	33	(4)	10	(1)	11	(2)
Working with committee chair	23	(3)	30	(3)	17	(4)	40	(2)	17	(2)	10	(1)	11	(2)
Working with committee ranking minority member	31	(4)	40	(4)	17	(4)	0		17	(2)	0		6	(1)
Working with committee staff	38	(5)	50	(5)	12	(3)	40	(2)	17	(2)	0		6	(1)
Working solo to draft legislation	16	(2)	20	(2)	8	(2)	0		8	(1)	10	(1)	6	(1)
Opposing chair or ranking minority member to draft legislation	15	(2)	20	(2)	8	(2)	0		0		0		0	
Caucus contacted by committee leader														
For information	15	(2)	20	(2)	17	(4)	60	(3)	50	(6)	30	(3)	11	(2)
For strategy support	23	(3)	30	(3)	17	(4)	40	(2)	42	(7)	10	(1)	6	(1)
For votes	15	(2)	20	(2)	12	(3)	20	(1)	33	(4)	0		6	(1)

Note: Number of caucuses is given in parentheses.

benefits; party caucuses on appropriations, budget, foreign policy, and military matters. Personal-interest caucuses worked on a wide variety of issues.

Nearly 90 percent of the sixty-eight caucuses listing a major concern sought to influence congressional policies. Two-thirds worked at the committee level (all of the party caucuses, four-fifths of the regional caucuses, two-thirds of the industry caucuses, three-fifths of the national constituency caucuses, three-fifths of the personal-interest caucuses, and slightly less than half of the state/district caucuses). The picture is one of a major effort by caucuses to affect committee decisions.

Hearings and Legislation

One-third of the caucuses testify at hearings: some work with subcommittees to set up hearings, and a few have held caucus or joint caucus-subcommittee hearings. Typically, chairs of national constituency and industry caucuses testify as representatives of the caucus. For other caucus types, representatives and senators often identify themselves as caucus members but testify as individuals, rather than as caucus members.

Caucuses place issues on committee agendas by holding caucus hearings or by persuading committees to do so.[3] Work with committees to set up hearings, choose topics, and develop witness lists can affect the parameters of later debate. Testifying at hearings is likewise an effort to affect policy outcomes. The Hispanic Caucus, for example, testifies at hearings and also works with subcommittees to set up hearings—for example, on immigration issues with the Judiciary Committee and on census and population issues with the Post Office and Civil Service Committee (a subcommittee of the Government Reform and Oversight Committee since 1995).

An informal hearing that the Vietnam Era Veterans in Congress Caucus called for veterans groups was eventually held under the auspices of the Veterans' Affairs Committee, when that committee established an Ad Hoc Select Subcommittee-for-a-day. It was chaired by Tom Daschle (D-S.D.), a committee member and officer of the caucus. Caucus and committee members and other interested representatives were invited to attend and participate or to sit on the subcommittee. Veterans had demanded a hearing as a condition of ending a hunger strike protesting the lack of official attention to concerns about Agent Orange. The caucus, perceived as sympathetic, had been in continuing contact with the veterans. The committee saw the hearing as a way to handle a difficult situation. A close observer said: "It was just kind of the circumstances at the time. . . . I don't think the committee felt comfortable with taking this on; everybody wanted to end this thing, and an ad hoc hearing organized by the caucus but under the auspices of the committee could help."

Subcommittee chairs who are also caucus members may use their committee leadership positions to hold hearings on topics of interest to the caucus and the committee. When Al Gore (D-Tenn.) was chair of the Congressional Clearinghouse on the Future and also of the Subcommittee on Investigations and Oversight of the Committee on Science and Technology, he held subcommittee hearings on the greenhouse effect and on genetic screening in the workplace. Both issues were on the agenda of the caucus.

One-third of caucuses draft legislation or amendments to be offered at the committee stage of the legislative process. Proposals by party caucuses include rules changes, party issues, and concerns that split members along party lines. Negotiations between party factions occur initially among the party members on the committee but may spill across party lines if party groups need support from opposition party members. If the issue splits members along party lines, simultaneous sessions on both substance and strategy may be held with both committee and party leaders, as occurred on the tanker-reflagging legislation. Members of bipartisan caucuses work separately with members of their own party on a committee, or they may seek a coalition of committee members from both parties in support of a bill or an amendment.

Issues and Approaches

Caucuses also play a role in integrating issues at the committee stage by, for example, proposing amendments on issues overlooked by the committee or, on occasion, developing bills that cover diverse aspects of a subject. In the early years of the Reagan administration, the Senate Export Caucus developed and introduced the National Export Policy Act, an omnibus bill (a compendium of legislation) that took into account a number of export issues, including "legislation, programs, and matters which were already either on a congressional agenda or which people were thinking about." The bill was cosponsored initially by sixteen caucus members and, eventually, by thirty. The caucus sought to pull the various issues together and to use the bill as a tool for promoting trade in a comprehensive and rational way.

The bill brought together programs of the Export-Import Bank, the Commerce, Agriculture, and State Departments as well as policies viewed as disincentives to trade, including the Corrupt Practices Act that addresses bribery of officials overseas, taxation of U.S. nationals abroad, and some antitrust laws. The bill was referred to the Senate Banking Committee, where it languished. However, some pieces of the omnibus bill, which were introduced as separate bills, were referred to various committees and were approved. The omnibus bill, according to a senior staff aide, was "really partly used as a tool to bring attention to the issues and the need for an overall perspective, rather than with the thought that it would be passed."

The Congressional Caucus on Women's Issues uses a similar approach. In April 1996 the group introduced the Women's Equity Health Bill, a package of thirty-six bills addressing various aspects of women's health. In June 1996 the caucus introduced the Economic Equity Act, a group of five bills. Such omnibus measures draw attention to an umbrella issue. Caucus members then took the lead within committee on the separate bills. The caucus achieved passage of portions of these packages.

A Republican member of several caucuses described caucus membership as an information source and a supplement to committees. The Arms Control and Foreign Policy Caucus "was a forum for members to feel their way along on issues that weren't being talked about in the Foreign Affairs or Armed Services Committees. You can't learn much if you have only your own subcommittee of Public Works." It was also useful for building bipartisan understanding and, at times, cooperation; it reveals how bipartisan caucuses can develop issue positions that have bipartisan support. As a Republican representative noted, "I did some work with [a very liberal Democrat]. . . . There turned out to be a lot of things we agreed on, and he was pretty practical."

Caucuses try to affect committee work in various ways. They may present caucus concerns to the committee through members, or work with committee staff, or offer research or analytical information. Caucus concerns dominate here, rather than committee needs. A regional caucus "analyzes what we think is coming out of the committees and tries to put some policy consideration into the process before it reaches the floor. . . . We work through [our members on a committee] to use some of the caucus material, or at least consider it when drafting the final proposal. . . .

We don't sit over staff and make sure they are using all our material in drafting this legislation . . . but we do work with staff and put forth our ideas and suggestions." The Rural Caucus, concerned about reduced rail service to small cities and rural areas, "took on the Interstate Commerce Commission on the Rail Act—behind the scenes" when they were alerted by constituent groups. The caucus mobilized, met with committee staff, and worked with members and outside groups. A respondent recalls: "They came up with some changes, and the changes were eventually included in the act as it came out. And we did it within the system."

On occasion, caucus staff functions as an extension of committee staff, on both substantive and procedural matters. A senior caucus staffer noted that "sometimes [the committee] asks for our help, sometimes we offer help, sometimes we will work with them on [matters before] another committee. . . . It will be very much a joint effort. We'll do our things, and we'll basically be another constituency for the . . . committee, so they don't look like they're out for their own jurisdiction or saving their own skin. We'll also ask them for advice." This particular caucus had been very involved in an amendment (offered by one of its members) that linked arms control and weapons procurement by holding back release of funds for weapons systems until progress had been made on arms control negotiations. The staffer continued, "I found myself spending hours there [with the committee] . . . trying to figure out a way around a parliamentary situation that was going to come up, redrafting our amendment, and being sure they had all the background on a point of order that was going to be made [on the floor]." The amendment was ruled out of order, and the "practical effect was that you can't offer an arms control amendment to an arms bill. . . . [But] if we had [had] another couple of hours we would have worked out a solution. As it was, we didn't."

While caucuses prefer the committee arena to the larger, less predictable, floor, they are also strategically flexible and can shift their point of activity. For instance, the Rural Caucus has worked with the Agriculture Committee to write authorization levels for the Farmers Home Administration. Although it might have acted at the Office of Management and Budget stage, the caucus believed it would have far more effect at the committee stage. Subsequently, the caucus followed the issue through Budget and Appropriations Committee considerations. The Northeast-Midwest Congressional Coalition, after working with the executive branch to develop a method to target distressed cities for assistance, opposed the administration in committee on the range of discretionary responsibility given to the secretary of housing and urban development. A caucus participant described it: "We started in subcommittee and fought them there. We didn't want to go to the floor. . . . We wanted the whole thing to be taken care of and not be an issue [on the floor], but it didn't turn out that way. We won in the subcommittee, we won in the full committee, and then it went to the floor. . . . The southerners were a bit put out, and it was a very, very heated floor battle—which we lost."

Even when caucuses oppose committee leaders, the overlap of caucus and committee membership serves caucuses well. In 1985, Ed Jenkins (D-Ga.), chair of the Textile Caucus and member of the Ways and Means Committee's Subcommittee on Trade, introduced a textile trade bill in response to industry concerns about increased textile imports. Frustration with the administration's trade policy was one reason Jenkins shifted his focus from the executive branch to Congress. The move also gained support for the bill from colleagues who were not caucus members. Jenkins, an influential issue and regional leader, was opposed by the committee but supported by party leaders. He used his positions in the formal and informal systems of Congress to build a winning coalition, coordinating other industry caucuses (the Competitiveness Caucus, the Export Caucus, and the Steel Caucus) in support of the legislation. The bill went to the floor and was passed. (The president, however, vetoed it, and a veto override effort failed.)

Caucus strategic flexibility can mean losing at the committee level and moving the fight to the floor. As a result, some caucuses appear before the Rules Committee, as the Pro-Life Caucus did after losing a vote on an antiabortion amendment in the Appropriations Committee. Not wanting to have a proposed floor amendment struck down on a point of order, the caucus co-chair successfully went before the Rules Committee for a rule permitting his amendment to be offered without later being amended.

Although most caucus-committee collaboration is initiated by caucuses, committee leaders also seek the assistance of caucuses. Caucus information and coordination of adversarial groups and interested colleagues can be useful. And caucuses can serve as access points to groups of members and interested outside groups, and can mobilize blocs of votes. One-third of all caucuses are contacted by committee leaders: 25 percent for information, 20 percent for strategy assistance and support, and 13 percent for votes. More national constituency, regional, and state/district caucuses are contacted than other caucus types.

Caucuses, the Senate, and the House

Senate caucuses are less active than House caucuses at the committee level (see table 9-3). A lower proportion of Senate than of House (including bicameral) caucuses meet with committee leaders, hold hearings, draft legislation, and work with committees or subcommittees. Committee leaders contact House and bicameral caucuses more than Senate caucuses. There are few differences in the issues on which Senate and House caucuses worked.

Senate caucus efforts are more individualistic than House activities. A senior aide of a loosely organized Senate caucus described the process as a focus on "instantaneous things—floor strategy, emergency work. . . . The caucus has weekly meetings. . . . There are few rules, but one was that senators could never be replaced by staff. . . . The senators never voted, but they had a caucus position insofar as committing staff effort to something. . . . One senator on one issue disagreed with all the rest of them" but was "perfectly happy to have the staff work on it."

In the Senate, particularly, the overlap of committee and caucus leadership positions is helpful in achieving caucus goals. Jennings Randolph (D-W.Va.) chaired the Senate Steel Caucus and also the Committee on Environment and Public Works. He introduced an amendment to the Clean Air Act extending the compliance deadline for air pollution standards for steel plants. The bill was "written by committee, EPA, and steelworkers," a tripartite process generated by caucus pressure. The bill was referred to Randolph's committee. The bill's progress through the Senate illustrates caucus bipartisanship and the integration of Senate caucus and committee operations.

Randolph held a hearing on the proposal, but neither house completed action before Congress adjourned. The bill was introduced again in the next Congress, and hearings were held by the now Republican-controlled committee. A Republican had also become chair of the caucus, a pragmatic response of a bipartisan caucus to the shift in party control. The new caucus chair, John Heinz (R-Pa.), testified for the caucus, and shortly thereafter Randolph and three caucus colleagues (Heinz, John Glenn, D-Ohio, and Richard Lugar, R-Ind.), all cosponsors of the bill, sent a "Dear Colleague" letter to senators on the importance of the bill, putting it into the perspective of the Steel Caucus. Both Randolph and Heinz appeared for the caucus and in support of the bill at committee hearings. Subsequently,

Table 9-3. Senate and House Caucuses, Committee Activities, 100th Congress (in percentages)

Caucus activity	House (N = 64)	Senate (N = 18)
Holds hearings	17	11
	(11)	(2)
Holds hearings with other caucuses[a]	3	0
	(2)	
Holds solo hearings[a]	11	11
	(7)	(2)
Testifies at hearings	31	17
	(20)	(3)
Drafts legislation	27	6
	(17)	(1)
Drafts bills	36	17
	(23)	(3)
Drafts amendments	19	17
	(12)	(3)
Works with subcommittees	28	11
	(18)	(2)
Works with subcommittee chair	23	11
	(15)	(2)
Works with subcommittee ranking minority member	16	17
	(10)	(3)
Works with staff	20	11
	(13)	(2)
Works with full committee	25	11
	(16)	(2)
Works with committee chair	19	11
	(12)	(2)
Works with committee ranking minority member	12	17
	(8)	(3)
Works with committee staff	17	11
	(11)	(2)
Works alone to draft legislation	6	17
	(4)	(3)
Contacted by committee leaders	36	6
	(23)	(1)

Note: Bicameral caucuses are included in the House column because much of the work of bicameral caucuses occurs on the House side. Number of caucuses is given in parentheses.

[a]104th Congress regulations of the House Oversight Committee prohibited House caucuses from holding hearings.

Randolph shepherded the bill through committee and worked to coordinate with the House. The bill was passed by both chambers and signed by the president. Although managed by Randolph, a Democrat, the process and outcome were basically bipartisan. Party mattered only to the degree that the majority party actors changed (because party control shifted).

SUMMARY

Caucuses work with committees in many different ways, in response to the needs of both. Some caucuses do not work on legislation. Others do, but not at the committee level. Or they put issues on a committee agenda but do not pursue support and passage during committee deliberations. Some caucuses do work at the committee level, monitoring committee activity, giving early warning of committee issues and strategy, and providing information for members and, on occasion, for interested outside groups. They develop and introduce bills and amendments and build committee coalitions in support of caucus positions. Some caucuses coordinate diverse issues, colleagues, and outside groups. Caucuses also serve as an access point to groups of members for committee leaders in search of information, assistance, or votes. In committee work, as elsewhere, caucuses decentralize an institution because they offer independent sources of information and sometimes oppose committee or party leaders. But the integrative effect is more prominent.

Variation among caucus types is evident. As with agenda setting, the representational or interest base of the caucus (constituency, party, or information) determines differences among caucus groups in committee work and affects the issues they work on and the activities they emphasize. National constituency caucuses and regional caucuses are the most active on all measures, including hearings that raise the visibility of issues. Party caucuses (except for class clubs) are also very active but do not hold hearings. State/district and industry caucuses are the least active, and personal-interest caucuses present a mixed picture.

On legislative drafting and other work with committees, the party, national constituency, and regional caucuses also rank high, followed by personal-interest, state/district, and industry caucuses. The three types of distributive caucus—regional, state/district, and industry—are primarily concerned with economic, trade, energy, and environmental issues. Party, personal-interest, and national constituency caucuses work more on other issues. Committees initiate contact most frequently with national constituency and regional caucuses, least frequently with industry caucuses.

The distinction between caucus and committee prerogatives is a sometimes touchy question. What seems clear is that caucuses are adjuncts to the committee system and perform tasks traditionally reserved for committees. Committees have adapted to the system, although their relationship with caucuses is not without tensions.

10/ CAUCUSES AND CONGRESSIONAL FLOOR ACTION

Caucuses are likely to be active during floor deliberations. And because caucus information and activity can increase members' understanding of issues and, thus, of the effects of proposed legislation, caucuses are also likely to affect the votes of their members on issues of caucus concern. Two variations in floor activity stand out: Senate and House caucuses differ, and party groups are more active on the floor than other caucus types. The analysis reveals that most caucuses are more unified than the rest of the House on votes of particular interest to them. And for more than half the caucuses, membership in a caucus is a significant factor in how representatives vote.

Most congressional caucuses are, at least tangentially, involved in congressional floor action through informational activities, such as discussing pending floor legislation in meetings or circulating issue briefs and materials about legislation scheduled for floor action. Nearly one-third establish a floor strategy, and two-fifths offer floor amendments (see table 10-1). Caucuses are unlikely to participate in floor action if they emphasize information exchange over legislative battles, if issues of interest are handled in the executive branch, or if their issues were defeated at the committee level.

All caucus types, especially party, personal-interest, national constituency, and regional, offer information on legislation scheduled for the floor. "Many observers have seen members scanning DSG reports on bills as they go to the floor" (Maisel 1981, 261). "I rely heavily on information from the DSG. If you can just digest all of that—which isn't easy—you are on your way to real understanding," said one respondent.

Party and national constituency caucuses are most likely to hold meetings to discuss and develop caucus floor strategy, followed by regional, personal-interest, and industry caucuses. Twenty percent of all caucuses offered floor amendments during the first session of the 100th Congress (1987). Party caucuses are the most active in offering floor amendments,

Table 10-1. Caucus Floor Activity, by Caucus Type, 100th Congress (in percentages)

Floor Activity	Party	Personal Interest	National Constituency	Regional	State/ District	Industry
			Caucus Type			
Meetings to set caucus	54	17	60	50	0	11
floor strategy[a]	(7)	(4)	(3)	(6)		(2)
Information on pending	70	67	80	58	40	39
floor legislation (oral)	(9)	(16)	(4)	(7)	(4)	(7)
Written	46	50	60	50	30	39
information	(6)	(12)	(3)	(6)	(3)	(7)
Offering floor amendments	31	17	20	25	0	22
(1987)	(4)	(4)	(1)	(3)		(4)
Working with other caucuses	15	0	20	0	0	6
on amendments	(2)		(1)			(1)
Working with Democratic leaders	0	4	20	8	0	0
re caucus amendments		(1)	(1)	(1)		
Coordinating strategy with						
Democrats re caucus	8	4	20	8	0	0
amendments	(1)	(1)	(1)	(1)		
Coordinating strategy with						
Republicans re caucus	0	12	0	8	0	0
amendments		(3)		(1)		
Working with outside groups	31	38	60	25	20	39
re pending floor legislation	(4)	(9)	(3)	(3)	(2)	(7)

Note: Columns do not add to 100% because of multiple responses. Number of caucuses is given in parentheses.

[a]Differences among caucus types are significant at the .002 level (Pearson chi-square).

followed by regional, industry, and national constituency caucuses. One-third of the caucuses work with groups outside Congress on pending floor legislation to develop floor strategy, to take whip counts, and sometimes to generate citizen action.[1]

Senate caucuses are less active on the floor than House caucuses, except in working with other caucuses on a floor amendment (see table 10-2). Fewer develop caucus floor strategy, provide information on pending legislation, offer floor amendments, or work with party leaders. In the more egalitarian and individualistic Senate, caucuses are more loosely organized and rely more on individual members than on group initiative.

Providing Information on Bills

The packaging and distribution of caucus information on pending floor action range from ad hoc sharing of caucus materials to full-blown

Table 10-2. Caucus Floor Activity, Senate and House, 100th
Congress (in percentages)

Activity	House	Senate
Set caucus floor strategy	30	17
	(19)	(3)
Information on pending floor legislation (oral)	61	44
	(39)	(8)
Information on floor legislation (written)	50	28
	(32)	(5)
Offer floor amendment (1987)	22	11
	(14)	(2)
Work with Republican leaders		
First-priority issue	11	11
	(7)	(2)
Second-priority issue	5	0
	(3)	
Work with other caucuses on floor amendment	3	6
	(2)	(1)
Work with Democratic leaders		
First-priority issue	19	6
	(6)	(1)
Second-priority issue	5	0
	(5)	

Note: House caucuses include bicameral caucuses. Number of caucuses is given in parentheses.

efforts to organize voting on the floor. Caucus information on pending floor issues is important to members and is often distributed widely. Dick Conlon, long-time staff director of the Democratic Study Group, described how party leaders controlled this information before caucuses took on these tasks:

In the 1960s, the party leadership put out a one-page whip list every week of matters which were coming to the floor. [Speaker] Rayburn felt, if you're on the committee [of jurisdiction] you should know about the issue. If you're not on that committee, you ought to find a member you trust who knows about the issue and ask how to vote. The information [on bills] was closely held by the committee and, especially, the committee chair. A vote against a committee bill, by a committee member, was unheard of. So all the cues went together to support committee chairs, and, ultimately, to support, of course, the party leadership. Members . . . who had voted against the committee would hear about it later. So the whole thing was very closely held, and staying in line was very important.

Caucuses, as alternative information sources, were important in changing this system and now are significant sources of information for members.

In sharing information, caucuses can perform both the informational and coordinating functions once reserved for the party system. Members of the House Wednesday Group meet weekly to discuss committee action and legislation scheduled for the floor. The group has provided research studies on issues not yet on the congressional agenda and backgrounders on other issues. These are used by individual members in newsletters, press releases, briefing reports, and speeches, and members may provide them to constituents. They are typically released to focus attention on an issue and to sketch out policy possibilities and are not designed as reports on pending committee or floor legislation. Occasionally, however, release of a research report coincides with a scheduled floor vote. A staffer described what happened when the caucus released a report on U.S.-China trade: "I had to carry copies to the floor because one of our senior [caucus] members was distributing them to every member on the floor for the vote. Every member was grabbing them. . . . The member read the report two days before [the vote], and he told other members . . . on both sides of the aisle, and we got calls and requests. . . . But that's very atypical, because our reports for the most part are not legislative reports [on pending committee or floor issues], they're issue reports. . . . On that one, the vote happened to come up at the same time."

The Arts Caucus, in identifying for its members the arts issues in pending legislation, provides a service once left to chance and has raised the visibility of arts issues on the Hill. Before the Arts Caucus was established, many members did not know where to find provisions in pending legislation that affected the arts. A senior staffer explained that funding "historic preservation [is] not a line item. It's locked in with land and water conservation. . . . Even the National Endowment for the Arts is under [the] postsecondary education subcommittee." The caucus serves as a coordinating group for members on diverse and apparently unrelated arts issues. The Northeast-Midwest Coalition provides continuing information on pending bills and amendments: a background paper, legislative alerts, and "finally a piece of paper distributed to members on the floor outlining the specifics of the bill and how it will be of concern to their area, their state, and their district." The Environmental and Energy Study Conference fine-tuned its legislative information and developed materials with different levels of detail. The purpose is to make the information readily accessible in whatever format a caucus member finds most useful.

Caucuses and party leaders sometimes share informational and organizational tasks. A respondent from an industry caucus with members in leadership and senior committee positions described working with party leaders on floor scheduling: "We [need] advance notice sometimes, and sometimes they'll say, 'Hey, don't tell anybody, but we are going to do this bill next week.' That gives us a head start. . . . We help them, too. . . . They have to get some sense of what's coming—how long is this bill going to take, are we going to have problems, who are we going to have problems with? . . . We can give [leaders and our] members a pretty good fix on what controversies are likely to come up on the floor, and who's going to be involved, and where the committee is coming from." The party leadership was the caucus's eyes and ears, and the caucus could use advance notice to develop strategy.

BUILDING SUPPORT FOR LEGISLATION

Before floor consideration, caucuses seek to shape legislation as part of developing floor strategy. Caucuses share information, participate in discussions and negotiations as the legislation is being drafted, and begin to build supporting coalitions for their viewpoint. The negotiations on the first Reagan budget that the Gypsy Moths (moderate House Republicans) held with David Stockman, head of the Office of Management and Budget, are described by both Stockman (1986) and by interview respondents (see chap. 8). The caucus was partially successful in shaping the bill debated on the floor. Members of the National Security Caucus worked on the same legislation with Phil Gramm (R-Tex.) and Delbert Latta (R-Ohio) on "what their figures were and what the impact would be, what the arguing points were for floor debate, and how other aspects could be handled."

Caucuses use various strategies to organize floor action. The Populist Caucus, a bicameral caucus of Democrats that focuses on agriculture, tax, and energy issues, drafted two amendments to an Agriculture Committee bill, which were rejected during committee markup.[2] The caucus then offered the amendments during floor debate. A staffer's account of the caucus's efforts reveals considerable strategic flexibility. The caucus organized the floor battle:

We had the right issue, on which there was a convergence of small farmer and urban concerns. We circulated six "Dear Colleagues," focusing on particular issues. Each [caucus member's] office did their own. We worked with the member who had introduced the amendments in committee—where they failed by a considerable margin. And then we basically called around to get sufficient numbers of Republicans in support, raised the issue as a nonpartisan one, and then wrote up floor statements for the members who were going to speak on it. . . . It was caucus-organized, and populist in approach, but we didn't say "as the Populist Caucus, we did this." It didn't make political sense to do that.

Both amendments won on the floor.

National constituency caucuses often seek to activate grassroots groups when an important issue is pending on the floor. A Congressional Black Caucus senior staffer described a successful effort to mobilize caucus constituents: "We had told people that they had to call or send their telegrams, or whatever they were going to do, before noon on Monday. . . . I'd say 65 percent of the people that we called, called back to say that they had sent telegrams, that they had called, that they had talked to their member, that they had gotten hold of them in the district that weekend to let them know how they felt they should vote on the Voting Rights Act."

These groups sometimes undertake longer-term efforts to activate the support of their constituents in the policy-making process. The Hispanic Caucus educated grassroots organizations on voting rights legislation in anticipation of floor debate: "The caucus got together two years ago, saying, 'This is going to come up, and its important, [we should] let local community groups know what [a provision] means and the problems with it.' . . . Bilingual ballots are in serious jeopardy. . . . So, starting two years ago, people were talking, it was in newsletters. They take stuff from our newsletter and reprint it in their local newsletter. . . . So you start building a coalition of black and Hispanic groups, insert things in the *Congressional Record*."

Information sharing in Congress was an important adjunct to the caucus's outreach program. It involved "members talking to members, making sure all the members know about it. Because, let's face it, if you're the chairman of the Agriculture Committee, voting rights legislation isn't going to be on the agenda until it's up that week. . . . You've got a lot of things to think about, like getting a farm bill out. So [we are] just making sure that they all know what's happening. . . . And that's [how we built a coalition] for passage in the House." With a coordinated and sustained effort, the Hispanic Caucus and its constituents and the Populist Caucus and its supporters achieved the kind of legislative result once controlled by the congressional leadership and a relatively small group of power brokers. Thus, caucuses are part of the shift to wider participation and a more inclusive leadership style, hallmarks of contemporary congressional operations.

Caucuses also coordinate groups within the House, drawing together those from the formal and informal systems. The Ad Hoc Monitoring Group on Southern Africa, active until 1991, coordinated several groups within Congress, including a subcommittee of the formal system, on floor strategy and debate on concerns of the caucus: The caucus

> is the nucleus, and carries out behind-the-scenes strategy sessions with other interested groups. . . . [We] meet together and talk about what we should do, split the workload of contacting other members, divide it up state by state. The groups that usually work together on this kind of an issue are the Ad Hoc Monitoring Group, the Congressional Black Caucus, the Arms Control and Foreign Policy Caucus . . . and the African subcommittee [of the International Affairs Committee]. In the last few Congresses [the subcommittee] has seen the issue in the same way we did, so we get together with them, as well, and pretty much decide what line of argument to take: a moralistic argument on the floor or facts of American interest.

The caucus's highly organized floor strategy also includes an awareness of the importance of a good presentation: "Everybody is using the same line of argument—but through different speakers, who speak from our side but [who] present it in different ways or emphasize different things. . . . We try to mobilize a few good speakers and make sure they're not all saying the same thing."

Some caucuses count votes. In the 103d Congress, the Space Caucus worked with NASA on a close vote on the space station. The Congressional Caucus on Women's Issues has worked with party leaders on both vote counts and floor strategy. On the Equal Rights Amendment in the 1980s, as well as on other votes, the caucus relied on outside groups for accurate counts, coordinated them, and worked with the leadership on final whip counts. The influence of the whip system of the Democratic Study Group has been documented (Stevens, Miller, and Mann 1974). A few other caucuses also use a whip system, wherein the executive committee or a group of caucus members alert members to a pending roll call vote to seek support for the caucus position.

Caucuses claim success in keeping some issues from coming to the floor. One party caucus described meeting with the speaker to argue that, if an issue was not going to come up in the Senate, there was no point in having it come to the House floor, where members would have to go on record about it. The same caucus also approached colleagues who were not caucus members for support. A senior participant reported successes with this kind of caucus organizing. Another caucus respondent reported success in keeping certain provisions out of bills at the committee markup stage: "We were involved in getting a [proposed floor] amendment to the Older Americans Act withdrawn." The amendment did not take account of population shifts, so the money for a useful program did not correctly follow the target population. "We checked with the leadership, got clearance to proceed, and did normal whip work on it. This office called 119 congressional offices. And the net result was that enough of them zeroed in on the sponsors of the amendment . . . [that it was] not offered."

The caucus system intersects the formal party system at the floor stage. All caucus types report working with party leaders at the floor stage, and more than half the caucuses in four categories report such work (see table 10-3). Caucuses support and work with party leaders on scheduling legislation for floor consideration, on the content of the legislation, and on floor strategy and whip counts. All caucus types also report being contacted by party leaders for information, with all but the state/district caucuses also contacted for assistance on floor strategy and for votes.

SUCCEEDING ON THE FLOOR

Caucuses succeed because they build successful coalitions, sometimes over a long period, or go to floor votes with committees behind them. Other times, caucuses fail at the committee level and then bring the issue to the floor and succeed; other times, they anticipate failure in committee and make their first effort on the floor.

The Northeast-Midwest Congressional Coalition culminated a four-year coalition-building effort in September 1980, when the House voted 220–179 to repeal the Maybank Amendment. A large membership, caucus cohesion, and well-positioned caucus leadership resulted in success, although repealing the amendment was widely perceived as a threat to the economies of areas of the country such as the Sunbelt, which had less

Table 10-3. Caucuses and Party Leaders, Floor Activities, by Caucus Type, 100th Congress (in percentages)

Activity	Party	Personal Interest	National Constituency	Regional	State/ District	Industry
			Caucus Type			
Caucus contacted	54	12	40	33	20	6
by party leaders	(7)	(3)	(2)	(4)	(2)	(1)
For information	46	12	40	33	20	6
	(6)	(3)	(2)	(4)	(2)	(1)
For strategy	38	8	40	25	0	6
	(5)	(2)	(2)	(3)		(1)
For votes	15	4	40	25	0	6
	(2)	(1)	(2)	(3)		(1)
Caucus works with	62	54	20	58	10	56
party leaders	(8)	(13)	(1)	(7)	(1)	(10)
Floor schedule[a]	38	21	40	25	0	28
	(5)	(5)	(2)	(3)		(5)
Issue content[a]	46	21	40	17	0	44
	(6)	(5)	(2)	(2)		(8)
Strategy[a]	31	25	40	8	0	33
	(4)	(6)	(2)	(1)		(6)
Whip counts	38	17	20	25	0	17
(caucus use)[a]	(5)	(4)	(1)	(3)		(3)
Whip counts	31	12	20	0	0	0
(leader use)	(4)	(3)	(1)			

Note: Number of caucuses is given in parentheses.
[a]Significant at the 0.01 level (Pearson chi-square).

unemployment than the Northeast and the Midwest. The effort, led by Defense Appropriations Subcommittee chair Joseph Addabbo (D-N.Y.), had lost at the committee level. Northeast-Midwest leaders then decided to muster their strength on the floor, shifting the conflict to more favorable territory. Nearly 90 percent of the 213 coalition members voted for repeal, thus allowing states with high unemployment to have a competitive edge in bidding on certain nonstrategic defense items.

Another floor effort built on caucus planning but required quick action. In one day, the House Export Caucus turned around a vote that had cut funds for the Export-Import Bank. David Obey's (D-Wis.) legislation to increase funds for the International Development Association to make soft loans to poor countries failed on the floor. Obey was so angry that he introduced a floor amendment, which was approved, to reduce funds for the Export-Import Bank (which lends money to businesses in developed countries). The Export Caucus subsequently changed the outcome by working with subcommittee and personal staff and by mounting a major effort to contact representatives who had voted to cut the Export-Import Bank's funds and to explain the effect of the vote. They persuaded most members who had voted that way to reverse their positions on a subsequent vote and to support full funding for the bank.

A central focus of the Vietnam Era Veterans in Congress Caucus has been to obtain medical and educational benefits for Vietnam veterans. Initially at odds with leaders and many members of the Veterans Committee, who were mostly of an earlier generation, caucus efforts led during the 1980s to committee support and floor success. The chair of the caucus introduced two bills (supporting Agent Orange victims' health care and vocational training benefits for Vietnam veterans), which were incorporated into an omnibus veterans bill at the committee level. On the floor, the provisions were passed overwhelmingly.

Long-range strategies and quick tactical thinking by both caucuses and their adversaries can combine for surprising last-minute floor efforts. Members of the Pro-Life Caucus have typically offered—and until the 103d Congress (1993–94) had been successful in obtaining passage of—floor amendments prohibiting federal funds for abortions.[3] One year, the caucus (after losing an Appropriations Committee vote to include their amendment) succeeded in getting a floor amendment offered without being subject to a point of order. There was a close vote on adopting the rule, but the House approved it.

Favorable circumstances sometimes also help caucus success. During the Reagan and Bush presidencies, the Travel and Tourism Caucus was remarkably successful in achieving structural and procedural changes designed to promote travel and tourism, including an undersecretary of commerce for travel and tourism, a bill facilitating visa waivers, and tax breaks for conventions. A large caucus, wide geographic distribution of membership, strategic flexibility, and appeal to American small business values all helped caucus success. The Rural Caucus's floor victories are in part attributed to its success in committee, which led to committee support on the floor. Committee-caucus membership overlap and strong bipartisan support of caucus positions by caucus members on the committee and in leadership positions have all been part of this caucus's successful strategy.

Occasionally, caucuses are adversaries in floor fights. Two caucuses opposed each other in seeking floor support in 1985–86 for their positions on aid to the Nicaraguan contras, who opposed the Nicaraguan government.

The Central America Task Force of the bipartisan Arms Control and Foreign Policy Caucus, chaired by George Miller (D-Calif.), produced reports, drafted amendments, and worked with Democratic leadership
groups to achieve passage of amendments that limited U.S. intervention
in Nicaragua. One caucus study "became the basis for critics' charges
that the contra military leadership was largely made up of former Somoza
National Guard officers" (Brenner and LeoGrande 1991, 235). On the
other side, the Republican Study Committee assisted the administration
with a whip system in support of President Reagan's policy (ibid.).

The fight over the Balanced Budget Amendment in the 104th Congress
is a classic example of how a smaller caucus can leverage its influence. The
Republican "Contract with America" included bringing to a vote on the
floor of the House a constitutional amendment requiring a balanced federal budget. Nearly all Republicans and some Democrats strongly supported such an amendment. But after the 104th Congress convened in January 1995, Republican unity began to erode. A House group of moderate
Republicans and many Democrats, as well as several senators, announced
that they did not support the contract's incorporation in the amendment
of a requirement for an "extraordinary majority"—three-fifths of the
House—to increase taxes. Charles Stenholm (D-Tex.), leader of the Boll
Weevils (the Conservative Democratic Forum), and cosponsor Dan
Schaefer (R-Colo.) introduced a version of the amendment that did not
include this provision. This alternative measure had wider support—
reportedly the 290 votes necessary for passage. The Republicans scram-
bled to arrange a rule that, if necessary, would use a Stenholm version as
a fallback but that would not have Stenholm's name attached. Stenholm
and the Boll Weevils had led the drive for a balanced budget amendment
for years, and he was able to use that experience and expertise to continue
his leadership on the issue in the 104th Congress after the majority party
changed hands, much to the chagrin of the newly dominant Republicans.
The Stenholm version of the amendment was passed by the House in January 1995; Republican efforts were partially successful, as many news accounts credited the Republican cosponsor, Schaefer, as the author.

As Republicans took control of the House at the start of the 104th
Congress and began their drive to enact the measures in the "Contract
with America," some Republicans' misgivings prompted longer-range
efforts. An incipient caucus of twenty to thirty party moderates, the Republican Discussion Group, first met on January 3, 1995, to discuss ways
to dilute the contract. Specific topics included the proposed extraordi-

nary majority requirement for tax increases and their own organization, including regular meetings, a possible whip system, and working with the speaker (Novak 1995). Because the measures in the "Contract with America" were scheduled for early and fast consideration by committees and the House, the group successfully focused on floor action. The new group demonstrated both the strengths and weaknesses of the caucus system. Establishment is easy, strategic flexibility facilitates success, and access to a group of swing votes is efficient for leaders and can magnify caucus influence. But the price of caucus activity is some party fragmentation and sometimes a more difficult negotiating job for party leaders.

The difference between Senate and House caucuses is particularly evident at the floor stage. House caucuses often have regularized structures and procedures in place to decide a group position, develop legislation, and work with party leaders. Senate caucuses rely on the work of individual members, which is not always explicitly caucus supported, and Senate caucuses rarely work with party leaders.

The Senate Steering Committee is typical. According to a respondent, it "will often give a lot of staff support to a senator who will never mention the Steering Committee . . . and, furthermore, would not want the Steering Committee affiliation mentioned at all. There is no requirement that the members agree on specific items . . . [and] no formal position-taking by the caucus." The Steering Committee helps senators act independently, even as it supports their actions. There is apparently no effort to touch base with other members when a senator undertakes either committee or floor action. Steering Committee aides work mostly with personal staff and less frequently with committee staff, because "the Steering Committee is working on developing amendments with a senator as an individual rather than as a member of a Senate committee."

By the early 1980s, the Steering Committee's "agenda had been a success and senators had gone to the floor with coordinated strategies, had defeated legislation that was odious to them, and had passed a number of amendments by virtue of their cooperation with each other—which otherwise weren't going to be passed." The caucus was so successful that it was able to exercise one of the most powerful tools in politics: "At one point it got to be strong enough . . . that the threat of conservative action became almost as good as the action."

An action by the Senate Western caucus illustrates how Senate rules are used by senators to achieve caucus goals and individual preferences. A caucus respondent recalled that at one point the National Park Service "was at odds with a lot of western senators on the management plan for the Grand Canyon National Park [regarding] motors on the river. So a couple of [caucus] senators simply came to the floor and offered an amendment to a bill which legislated what they wanted to accomplish." Senate rules, which allow amendments to be offered at any time, gave caucus members this chance, almost literally at the last minute. It also illustrates that executive branch managers have incentives to respond to Senate caucuses before floor action can occur.

Caucuses do not talk about, or even remember, their failures, as one caucus respondent pointed out. The fast-paced world of Capitol Hill requires a focus on the present—today's vote, the issue before the committee tomorrow, or planning for arguments before the Rules Committee on a proposed rule. Caucuses do, of course, fail—both at the committee level and on the floor. Recall the efforts of the Arms Control Caucus on an arms control amendment, which was ruled nongermane during floor debate (chap. 9).

Miscalculation, inadequate effort, or simply not having enough supporting votes can doom caucus initiatives. Like many participants in federal Washington, caucuses rely heavily on others' perceptions and try to avoid being seen as ineffectual. Timely and reliable information, well-placed members and allies, and careful preparation can do more than make an impression. They can deliver votes. With these tools, caucuses can leverage their influence and affect policy outcomes. The more interesting story may be how caucuses achieve success.

AN ANALYSIS OF CAUCUS FLOOR ACTION

Caucuses can create blocs of swing floor votes on issues by delivering their own votes and organizing or threatening to organize those of other members. One caucus member said of caucuses: "Basically, if you're going to have any effect, whatsoever, you've got to have the votes." He recalled how a major political change gave his group the appearance of having established positions and strategy and of operating as a cohesive voting bloc: "It wasn't until Reagan was elected—and all of a sudden we became a large enough group to affect the outcome of a vote—that things began to happen. From that point forward, we were seen to be something that we weren't." The White House and party leaders negotiated with the caucus on the provisions of legislation, and the caucus was courted by both Republicans and Democrats in search of votes. The respondent explained: "There were forty-seven members of our group in 19——, but we seldom all went one direction. We usually split twenty-four to twenty-three." In fact, the caucus never voted unanimously: "It was just phenomenal, the divisions. . . . We're not a group that marches in lockstep. We've got our different districts; we've got our different philosophies." When asked whether the group nevertheless counted votes, he said, "Oh, absolutely! Wherever the votes are! We usually begin on whether you're for it or against it. We're trying to win."

Caucus information and positions on legislation can influence caucus members, and formal caucus action on positions is widespread. For example, 35 percent of all caucuses (47% of House caucuses) hold meetings to establish a caucus position; 80 percent of national constituency, 67 percent of regional, 50 percent of party groups (class clubs excluded), and nearly 40 percent of industry caucuses hold such meetings; few personal-interest or state/district caucuses do. (These differences are significant at the .05 level, using the Pearson chi-square.) The pattern is similar for meetings to develop overall caucus strategy on an issue: 80 percent of national constituency, 75 percent of regional, 70 percent of party groups (class clubs excluded), and 21 percent of personal-interest caucuses. Caucuses also work with party leaders on floor whip counts and procedure; they debate, serve as coordinators, and offer channels of access to outside groups. But does caucus concern and support translate into bloc voting on the floor? And does caucus membership significantly affect the individual member's voting decisions? The data indicate that many caucuses are cohesive on votes that matter to the caucus and that caucus membership is a significant variable in the members' voting decisions.

Two types of analysis are reported here. First, using a difference-of-proportions test, caucus unity is compared to the unity of other House members on floor votes on issues of concern to a caucus. Then the effect of caucus membership on representatives' votes, on votes of interest to the caucus, is assessed, using regression, or logit, analysis.

The floor votes of a subset of seventeen caucuses, a representative group of typical caucuses, are analyzed, some from each caucus type. The caucuses profiled include three party caucuses: the Conservative Democratic Forum (CDF, or Boll Weevils), the Democratic Study Group, and the Republican Study Committee, which vary by party, size, and ideology. The other caucuses analyzed are bipartisan and are diverse in size, date of establishment, range of issue focus, and issues of interest. Five caucuses are based on members' personal interests: Arms Control and Foreign Policy, Balanced Budget, Environmental and Energy Study Conference, Pro-Life, and Science and Technology. The three national constituency caucuses analyzed, the Congressional Black Caucus, the Hispanic Caucus, and the Congressional Caucus on Women's Issues, focus on a broad range of issues and vary in size. They are bipartisan, although until the 103d Congress there were no Republican members of the Congressional Black Caucus. Two regional caucuses profiled here, the New England Caucus and the Northeast-Midwest Congressional Coalition, also differ in size and they focus on a number of issues, many of which are economic. The Northeast-Midwest Coalition is one of the largest caucuses in Congress.

The two state/district caucuses, the Federal Government Service Task Force and the Rural Caucus, focus on quite different issues and also vary in the number of committees that have jurisdiction over their issues. The Federal Government Service Task Force, which is concerned only with the federal civil service, deals primarily with one committee. Before 1995, this was the Post Office and Civil Service Committee; since the start of the 104th Congress it works with a subcommittee of the Government Reform and Oversight Committee. The interests of the Rural Caucus are spread among several authorizing committees—Agriculture, Banking, Commerce, Economic and Educational Opportunities, Transportation, and Ways and Means. The two industry caucuses analyzed—Coal, Travel and Tourism—also differ. Coal is smaller and has a narrower issue focus; Travel and Tourism is large, with interests in virtually every congressional district and before several committees.[4]

The votes of interest to each caucus that were selected for the analysis were chosen from Ninety-seventh Congress roll call votes, based on interview and caucus survey data supplemented by media reports. The votes cover such issues as budget, foreign policy, civil rights, trade, education, and labor. Votes on which there was a split of 90 percent to 10 percent (or smaller) were excluded from the analysis. Routine procedural votes (election of the speaker, dispensing with the reading of the *Journal*) were also excluded. All other procedural votes, such as adoption of the rule governing debate, were included because these votes, particularly if they are conflictual, often mask substantive disagreement.

Caucus Unity

Caucuses are more likely to have an effect on floor voting if their members vote as a group. Caucus activity and the information learned from being a member should solidify members' support of the issues and the positions of the caucus. And caucus members should be more united than the rest of their House colleagues on votes of concern to their group.

For each caucus, the cohesion of the caucus was compared with the rest of the House on caucus votes—that is, on votes of concern to the caucus and on all other votes during that Congress (excluding those votes described above), giving caucus member and nonmember unity scores on both sets of votes (see table 10-4).[5] The analysis does not indicate or assume causality; the interest is in examining whether or not caucuses are more unified than the rest of the House on caucus votes. If so, the finding offers support for the argument that caucuses as blocs of votes are attractive to coalition builders, including party and committee leaders, and offers some explanation for caucus success in achieving modification of bills coming to the floor and during floor debate.

For each caucus, table 10-4 reports the percentage of the caucus members voting in the same direction on all caucus roll call votes and on the noncaucus votes. It also reports the same figures for noncaucus members.

Thirteen of the seventeen caucuses analyzed display significantly greater unity on the caucus roll call votes than did the rest of the House: two of the three party caucuses, four of the five personal-interest groups, two of three national constituency caucuses, all the regional and state/district caucuses, and one of two industry caucuses. The unity of an additional caucus, the Congressional Caucus for Women's Issues (a national constituency caucus) is nearly significant (.10 level), and if included, brings the total to fourteen of the seventeen.

To determine whether caucus unity on caucus votes was unique or whether the caucus was unified on all House votes, caucus unity on noncaucus votes was also examined (either way, coalition builders could be interested in working with a caucus). Some caucuses do display significantly greater unity than noncaucus members on noncaucus votes as well as on caucus votes. However, for five of the seven caucuses, the magnitude of the difference between caucus and noncaucus members was less than on caucus votes. The Democratic Study Group differed; its members were significantly more unified than noncaucus members on noncaucus, but not on caucus, votes, which may reflect the liberal ideology of these caucus members on all votes, whether or not they were caucus votes. Most caucuses, however, were more unified than the rest of the House on votes of interest to a caucus. This finding offers justification for considering caucuses as blocs of votes in floor voting and is a partial explanation

Table 10-4.   Unity of Caucus Members and Noncaucus Members on Caucus and Noncaucus Votes, Ninety-seventh Congress

Caucus	Number	Caucus Members Voting Unity (z)	Noncaucus Members Voting Unity (z)
PARTY			
Conservative Democratic Forum			
Members	47	47.8	57.5
		(4.21)***	(3.25)***
Nonmembers	387	20.3	33.4
Democratic Study Group			
Members	210	44.9	57.5
		(0.08)	(5.04)***
Nonmembers	224	44.5	33.4
Republican Study Committee			
Members	139	68.1	54.4
		(8.69)***	(1.65)*
Nonmembers	295	24.6	45.9
PERSONAL INTEREST			
Arms Control and Foreign Policy Caucus			
Members	87	51.1	64.4
		(2.71)**	(4.73)***
Nonmembers	347	35.3	36.4
Balanced Budget Caucus			
Members	43	33.6	43.6
		(1.24)	(1.29)
Nonmembers	391	24.9	33.7
Environmental and Energy Study Conference			
Members	249	50.8	37.2
		(6.12)***	(–0.21)
Nonmembers	185	21.9	38.2
Pro-Life Caucus			
Members	16	93.3	35.7
		(9.38)***	(0.16)
Nonmembers	418	10.8	33.8
Science and Technology Caucus			
Members	7	67.6	50.8
		(2.6)**	(0.94)
Nonmembers	427	23.9	33.9
NATIONAL CONSTITUENCY			
Congressional Black Caucus			
Members	17	80.6	84.4
		(4.92)***	(4.26)***
Nonmembers	417	25.9	33.9

(Continued)

Table 10-4.   *(Continued)*

Caucus	Number	Caucus Members Voting Unity (z)	Noncaucus Members Voting Unity (z)
Hispanic Caucus			
Members	5	70.0	52.5
		(2.22)*	(0.89)
Nonmembers	429	25.9	33.5
Congressional Caucus on			
Women's Issues			
Members	17	40.8	41.3
		(1.50)ᵃ	(0.68)
Nonmembers	417	24.7	33.4
REGIONAL			
New England Congressional Caucus			
Members	24	78.4	57.9
		(3.97)***	(2.43)**
Nonmembers	410	37.6	33.6
Northeast-Midwest Congressional			
Coalition			
Members	211	46.0	37.8
		(3.46)***	(0.02)
Nonmembers	223	29.9	37.7
STATE/DISTRICT			
Federal Government Service Caucus			
Members	29	40.2	49.4
		(4.11)***	(1.72)*
Nonmembers	405	12.5	33.7
Rural Caucus			
Members	142	54.2	39.0
		(1.88)*	(1.42)
Nonmembers	292	44.6	32.1
INDUSTRY			
Coal Caucus			
Members	66	27.2	40.6
		(0.05)	(1.2)
Nonmembers	368	26.9	33.0
Travel and Tourism Caucus			
Members	198	78.9	37.7
		(12.25)***	(1.53)ᵃ
Nonmembers	236	20.0	30.7

Note: Roll call votes number 524 (routine procedural votes and those with a 90–100% split or less are not included; see appendix). Caucus votes vary from 2 (coal caucus) to 47 (Congressional Black Caucus). Noncaucus votes are roll call votes minus caucus votes. The z-test is between caucus and noncaucus members; z-score is given in parentheses.

ᵃSignificant at .1 level.
* $p < .05$, one-tailed test
** $p < .01$, one-tailed test
*** $p < .001$, one-tailed test

for caucus success in modifying pending legislation to accommodate caucus views and in building voting coalitions.

Caucus Membership and Votes

Various factors such as constituency, members' party, ideology, seniority, and electoral security can affect members' floor voting.[6] The regression model draws on this literature and adds caucuses. Caucus membership should have an independent statistical effect on a caucus member's voting on caucus votes, after controlling for party, ideology, position within the House, and constituency characteristics. The model includes members' party, ideology, leadership position in the House, membership on prestige committees, electoral security (measured by percentage win in the election), seniority, and caucus membership. Constituency characteristics include economic data on employment, manufacturing, agriculture, and mining; the percentage of urban constituents; ethnic data (the percentage of black, Hispanic, and foreign constituents); other committee assignments; other constituency characteristics relevant to a particular caucus; and caucus membership. (Regression analyses are reported in table 10-5.)[7]

For each caucus, the regression equation is:

$$y = a + bX_1 + bX_2 \ldots bX_n + e,$$

where y = support of caucus votes, X_1 = membership in a caucus; X_2 = party (Democratic or Republican); X_3 = ideology (conservative coalition score recomputed to eliminate absences); X_4 = seniority, measured by number of terms in the House; X_5 = leadership positions in the House; X_6 = percentage of vote received in the last election (to capture any marginality influence); X_7 = membership on prestige committees (Appropriations, Rules, Ways and Means); $X_8 \ldots X_n$ = variables relevant to the caucus. These variables might be the percentage of urban, black, or Spanish heritage constituents; the percentage of constituents employed in manufacturing or agriculture; the percentage of constituents employed in coal mining and related industries; and membership on committees relevant to the caucus.

Disentangling the effects of caucus membership and relevant constituency characteristics is difficult. Even a survey of constituency preferences on caucus issues might be an imperfect measure, because it would

Table 10-5. Representatives' Voting, by Caucus, on Caucus Votes, Ninety-seventh Congress: Composite Table of Regression Results (coefficients and t-ratios)

Variable	Party Caucuses				Personal-Interest Caucuses			
	Conservative Democratic Forum (Boll Weevils)	Democratic Study Group	Republican Study Committee	Arms Control and Foreign Policy	Balanced Budget	Environmental and Energy Study Conference	Pro-Life	Science and Technology
Caucus membership	0.270 (6.267)***	•	•	•	0.065 (1.806)*	0.085 (2.583)**	3.776 (10.971)***	•
Party	−0.777 (−23.717)***	1.036 (22.854)***	−0.644 (−19.665)***	•	−0.534 (−18.297)***	0.702 (17.121)***	−0.605 (3.27)a	0.744 (11.668)***
Conservatism	0.007 (12.447)***	−0.008 (−12.070)***	0.009 (16.983)***	−0.011 (−11.161)***	0.006 (11.015)***	−0.008 (−9.976)***	0.056 (39.001)***	−0.013 (−12.188)***
Vote margin	•	−0.002 (−2.274)*	−0.010 (−3.390)***	0.004 (3.262)***	•	•	0.007 (0.391)***	•
Seniority (no. of terms)	−0.005 (−2.000)*	0.011 (3.243)***	•	•	−0.006 (−2.247)*	0.008 (1.903)*	−0.082 (3.481)a	•
Leader	•	•	•	−0.112 (−2.522)**	•	•	•	•
Prestige committee		•	−0.057 (−2.337)*	•	•	•	•	0.117 (2.053)*
Employed (civilian)		−1.394E-06 (−1.723)a	1.322E-06 (1.914)*	2.044E-06 (2.027)*	•	•	•	•
Manufacturing employment	−1.346E-06 (−1.889)a	•	•	−2.425E-06 (−2.068)*	•	•	•	•
Percentage black		•	•	—	•	—	−3.339 (5.513)**	•
Percentage Hispanic	0.258 (2.025)*	•	•	—	—	—	—	•
Mining employment	•	•	•	—	—	•	—	•

	(1)	(2)	(3)	(4)	(5)	(6)	(7)
Coal employment	—	—	—	—	—	—	—
Percentage foreign	—	-0.330 (-2.908)***	•	•	-0.456 (-2.522)**	0.267 (1.698)[a]	2.932 (2.593)[a]
Percentage urban	•	•	-0.159 (-1.653)[a]	•	•	-0.421 (-3.854)***	•
Percentage rural	—	•	•	—	—	•	—
Agriculture employment	—	—	—	•	6.618E-06 (1.943)*	—	-6.1E-05 (4.572)*
Federal workers	—	—	—	—	—	•	—
Agriculture Committee	—	—	0.125 (2.506)**	—	—	—	—
Armed Services Committee	—	—	—	—	•	—	—
Banking Committee	•	—	—	—	—	—	—
Budget Committee	•	•	•	•	—	—	—
Education and Labor Committee	•	—	—	—	—	—	•
Energy and Commerce Committee	—	—	-0.103 (-2.399)*	—	—	-0.106 (-2.025)*	—

(Continued)

Table 10-5. (Continued)

	Party Caucuses			Personal-Interest Caucuses				
Variable	Conservative Democratic Forum (Boll Weevils)	Democratic Study Group	Republican Study Committee	Arms Control and Foreign Policy	Balanced Budget	Environmental and Energy Study Conference	Pro-Life	Science and Technology
Foreign Affairs Committee	—	—	—	•	—	—	—	—
Interior (Resources) Committee	—	•	—	—	—	-0.118 (-2.221)*	—	—
Judiciary Committee	—	—	—	—	—	—	—	—
Post Office and Civil Service Committee	—	—	—	—	—	—	—	—
Public Works and Transportation Committee	—	—	—	—	—	—	—	—
Science and Technology Committee	—	—	—	—	—	—	—	0.284 (3.542)***
Small Business Committee	—	—	—	—	—	—	—	—
Constant	-0.417 (-3.222)***	0.390 (1.876)[a]	-0.210 (-1.432)	0.036 (0.151)	-0.189 (-1.386)	.535 (2.154)*	-6.026 (6.521)**	0.466 (1.138)

Note: Except for the caucus membership variable (which uses a one-tailed test), all reported significance levels are for two-tailed tests. For the Pro-Life caucus, coefficients and significance (Wald) are reported from a logistic regression model because only one vote was analyzed. A dash indicates that a variable was not included in the regression; t-ratios are reported in parentheses.

[a] $p < .1$
* $p < .05$
** $p < .01$
*** $p < .005$
• Insignificant coefficient.

(Continued)

Table 10-5. *(Continued)*

	National Constituency Caucuses			Regional Caucuses		State/District Caucuses		Industry Caucuses	
	Black	Hispanic	Women's Issues	Northeast-Midwest	New England	Federal Government Service	Rural	Coal	Travel and Tourism
Caucus membership	•	0.776 (2.756)***	0.180 (1.827)*	0.154 (4.017)***	•	•	0.078 (1.346)[a]	0.095 (2.594)***	0.557 (8.074)***
Party	0.457 (10.181)***	0.438 (8.184)***	0.628 (12.170)***	0.692 (18.023)***	0.674 (14.647)***	-0.150 (-4.540)***	0.378 (6.209)***	0.341 (10.822)***	0.215 (2.383)*
Conservatism	-0.012 (-13.761)***	-0.010 (-9.437)***	-0.011 (-12.484)***	-0.009 (-11.818)***	-0.010 (-11.226)***	•	-0.008 (-7.533)***	-0.001 (-2.409)*	-0.007 (-4.477)***
Vote margin	•	-0.003 (-1.699)[a]	•	•	•	•	•	•	•
Seniority (no. of terms)	0.009 (2.156)*	0.010 (1.798)[a]	•	0.010 (2.736)**	•	•	•	•	•
Leader	•	•	•	•	•	•	•	•	•
Prestige committee	•	•	•	•	•	-0.078 (-2.716)**	•	0.074 (2.680)**	•
Employed (civilian)	•	•	•	•	•	•	•	•	-4.691E-06 (-2.600)**
Manfacturing employment	•	•	•	•	•	•	•	•	—
Percentage black	•	-0.334 (-1.956)*	•	•	•	0.219 (2.022)*	•	0.172[a] (1.835)	—
Percentage Hispanic	•	-1.244 (-3.968)***	•	-0.320 (-1.674)[a]	•	—	—	•	—
Mining employment	—	—	—	—	—	—	—	•	—

(Continued)

Table 10-5. (Continued)

	National Constituency Caucuses			Regional Caucuses		State/District Caucuses		Industry Caucuses	
	Black	Hispanic	Women's Issues	Northeast-Midwest	New England	Federal Government Service	Rural	Coal	Travel and Tourism
Coal employment	—	—	—	—	—	—	—	•	—
Percentage foreign	•	0.471 (1.973)*	—	•	0.477 (2.298)*	0.472 (3.258)***	•	0.237 (1.914)[a]	—
Percentage urban	•	•	•	-0.310 (-2.917)***	-0.477 (-3.710)***	-0.213 (-2.280)*	—	—	•
Percentage rural	—	—	—	—	—	—	0.664 (3.904)***	—	—
Agriculture employment	—	•	•	-9.203E-06 (-2.840)***	•	-9.353E-06 (-3.577)***	•	—	—
Federal workers	—	—	—	—	—	5.734E-06 (2.244)*	—	—	—
Agriculture Committee	•	•	•	0.127 (2.274)*	0.113 (1.618)[a]	—	•	—	—
Armed Services Committee	—	—	—	—	—	—	—	—	—
Banking Committee	•	•	•	•	•	—	—	—	—
Budget Committee	•	•	•	•	•	—	•	—	—
Education and Labor Committee	•	•	•	•	•	—	—	—	—
Energy and Commerce Committee	—	•	—	•	•	—	—	•	•

Foreign Affairs Committee	—	—	—	—	—	—	—	—	—
Interior (Resources) Committee	—	—	—	—	—	—	—	—	—
Judiciary Committee	•	•	—	—	—	—	—	—	—
Post Office and Civil Service Committee	—	—	—	—	—	•	—	—	—
Public Works and Transportation Committee	•	—	—	—	—	—	—	—	—
Science and Technology Committee	—	—	—	—	—	—	—	—	—
Small Business Committee	•	•	•	•	•	—	—	—	•
Constant	0.798 (2.639)**	0.080 (0.176)	1.038 (3.080)**	0.620 (2.626)**	0.621 (2.132)*	0.422 (2.426)*	0.358 (1.061)	1.482 (9.354)***	0.698 (1.504)

Note: Except for the caucus membership variable (which uses a one-tailed test), all reported significance levels are for two-tailed tests. For the Pro-Life caucus, coefficients and significance (Wald) are reported from a logistic regression model because only one vote was analyzed. A dash indicates that a variable was not included in the regression; *t*-ratios are reported in parentheses.

[a] $p < .1$

* $p < .05$

** $p < .01$

*** $p < .005$

• Insignificant coefficient.

be drawn from the geographic constituency and so might target the wrong constituency for that issue. In an effort to capture constituency effects, constituency variables relevant to a particular caucus were used: the percentage of federal employees in a district for the Federal Government Service Task Force analysis; the percentage of constituents employed in coal mining and related industries for the Coal Caucus; the percentage of rural constituents for the Rural Caucus equation.[8]

The dependent variable, the caucus support score, is the sum of all votes for or against a caucus position divided by the total number of caucus votes on which the representative voted.[9] A vote for the caucus was coded one, a vote against the caucus was coded negative one, and no vote was coded zero. If a member voted on fewer than half the selected caucus votes, the member was considered missing for this caucus score. The result is a support measure ranging from minus one to one; the higher the score, the higher the caucus support. For nine of the caucuses, caucus membership was a statistically significant variable (.05 or more significance level) in members' votes on caucus issues.[10] If the Rural Caucus (at the .10 significance level) is included, caucus membership was significant for ten of the seventeen caucuses. Two other independent variables, party and ideology, were statistically significant for most caucuses, ideology for all but the Federal Government Service Task Force, and party for all except the Pro-Life Caucus and the Arms Control Caucus.

Caucus membership was significant on votes of interest to the caucus for only one of the party caucuses, the Conservative Democratic Forum. Caucus membership was not significant for the Democratic Study Group or the Republican Study Committee; there are several possible explanations, the most likely being the large membership of these caucuses. More than half of all Republicans and Democrats belonged to these caucuses, many for the caucuses' information and publications rather than to support caucus positions. Caucus membership is diverse, and on specific issues members may not agree. Members may not have supported a caucus position (recall that few caucuses require unanimity on an issue before taking a position and that many delegate position setting to a group within the caucus). When positions are taken, caucuses may not whip members on a vote. Or it may be that, for these caucuses, the selected caucus votes are not accurate indicators of caucus activity and position on issues. Members' seniority was also a significant variable for these party caucuses, although its direction differs.

Caucus membership was a significant influence on caucus votes for three of the five personal-interest caucuses analyzed: Balanced Budget, Environment and Energy, and Pro-Life. Variables other than caucus membership were significant in determining the votes of Arms Control and Foreign Policy and Science and Technology Caucus members. For two of these caucuses, membership on committees relevant to caucus interests appears as a significant variable. Science and Technology Committee members are more likely to support Science and Technology Caucus votes, which perhaps reflects the fact that committee members view the caucus as supportive of the committee because it emphasizes science and technology training and research. Energy and Commerce Committee members were less likely—but Interior (now Resources) members were more likely—to support Environmental and Energy Study Conference votes.

Caucus membership was significant for two of the three national constituency caucuses analyzed. Party and ideology were significant for all of the caucuses. Committee membership was not significant. The percentage of black constituents in a district was not significant for Congressional Black Caucus members; the percentage of Hispanic constituents was significant for members of the Hispanic Caucus, but in a direction contrary to expectation.

Caucus membership was statistically significant for the Northeast-Midwest Congressional Coalition but not for the New England Caucus. Membership on the Agriculture Committee was significant for Northeast-Midwest members and nearly significant for New England caucus members, although membership on other committees was not. For both caucuses, the level of urbanization in the district was significant: the higher the percentage of urban constituents, the less support representatives gave to caucus votes. The Northeast-Midwest Coalition chose its issues carefully, had overlap (even at senior levels) with relevant committees, presented the results of major research studies to members, and distributed extensive informational materials, which included the Northeast and Midwest perspectives and the expected impact of proposed legislation on these regions and their congressional districts. A result was a high level of cohesion and caucus membership as a significant variable on caucus votes.

Caucus membership was not a significant variable for either of the state/district caucuses (although it was nearly significant—at the .10 level—for the Rural Caucus).[11] The percentage of rural constituents was also significant for Rural Caucus members. For Federal Government Service Task Force votes, the size of the federal government workforce in a district, prestige committee membership (less likely to support caucus positions), and the percentage of urban constituents were significant variables. For both of the state/district caucuses analyzed, caucus membership likely has a direct influence on agendas and on identifying votes that affect caucus members' districts but only an indirect influence on support for caucus votes.

For industry caucuses, caucus membership, party, and ideology were significant. A constituency variable, the number employed in mining and mining-related services (a measure of the importance of the coal industry in a member's district) was not significant for Coal Caucus members. It may have an indirect effect through the caucus.

These committee-caucus patterns reflect caucus membership characteristics identified earlier. Junior representatives who do not serve on committees relevant to caucus concerns disproportionately join caucuses, and senior committee members may be wary of a caucus working in a similar area. Junior members are more likely to support caucus positions than are senior members. And in some instances, members of prestige committees, often the more senior representatives, are less likely to support caucus positions.

Caucus Types

A majority of the seventeen caucuses display unity and membership effect on caucus votes at a statistically significant level. Party caucuses differ considerably from the other types: only one of the three party caucuses analyzed displays a significant effect of caucus membership. Party caucuses work first with party leaders and seek success on issues within their parties. To the extent that they are successful at that stage (and interview data indicate that they often are), the caucus position at the floor stage may not vary as much from noncaucus members as is likely with other caucus types. The measures used in this analysis may not capture a difference because concerns are resolved earlier and a majority (or minority) coalition is in place.

Personal-interest caucuses display a somewhat varied pattern. For three of them, both unity and caucus membership are significant. However, for the other three, the pattern is mixed. These caucuses may be the purest test of caucus impact, because members join for interest in policy not filtered through party or constituency. Even when caucuses empha-

size information and do not take an advocacy position, caucus membership matters (at a significant level). As with other caucuses, when there is
no statistical significance, the caucuses are still often effective in setting
agendas and the parameters of debate or in ensuring committee or floor
consideration.

For five of the nine constituency caucuses, caucus membership affects
caucus floor votes.[12] If the Women's Caucus (significant at the .10 level)
is included, 89 percent (all but the Coal Caucus) display significant unity
on these votes. These caucuses enable members to coordinate strategy,
understand an issue and the legislation's potential impact, and serve as a
force to coordinate constituency interests. They are effective.

Floor Votes

Caucus membership does affect members' voting. It has an independent effect at a statistically significant level on voting support for caucus
positions for a majority of caucuses. Membership on committees relevant
to caucus interest is not significant for national constituency, state/dis-
trict, or industry caucuses, but it is for some caucuses of each of the other
types. Committee membership, however, may either increase or decrease
support for caucus votes.

Constituency variables that are significant generally reflect characteristics relevant to the caucus. Marginality in the most recent election was
significant only for the Democratic Study Group, a rather surprising
finding since members of most constituency caucuses who come from
marginal districts might be expected to cast votes for caucus positions in
order to claim credit and to gain constituent support for re-election. Seniority is a significant variable for nearly half of the caucuses analyzed. It
was significant for the three party caucuses, two of the three personal-
interest groups, and for one of the national constituency and regional
caucuses. Holding a leadership position is significant for only one caucus,
the Arms Control and Foreign Policy Caucus (leaders support caucus positions less). The size of the caucus does not seem to be important. Membership is significant for some large and small caucuses and not significant for others. For more than half the caucuses, membership matters in
votes on caucus issues. Although other variables also are significant, caucus membership has an independent effect on the floor vote even when the
primary purpose of the caucus is information rather than advocacy (recall the Environmental and Energy Study Conference).

SUMMARY

The focus on policy, which caucuses report as a primary emphasis, is confirmed by these data on floor activity and votes. Caucuses bring issues to the floor or keep them off the floor; share information on the content of legislation and the strategies of floor debate; prepare talking points for members in debate; organize floor battles and work with floor leaders; are sought out for assistance by those leaders; and mobilize the grassroots for support on achieving floor success. There are, of course, limits to the floor activity that is appropriate or possible. A central finding—that caucus membership often affects voting—shows an influence on individual members that parallels that which caucuses exert on policy making as a whole.

11/ THE 104TH CONGRESS AND BEYOND

The 104th Congress will be long remembered. In January 1995, when Congress convened, the Republicans took control of both the House and the Senate for the first time in forty years. House Republicans scheduled their "Contract with America" for action on the opening day of the Congress. One of its provisions affected the caucus system: Section 222 of H. Res. 6 abolished legislative service organization status, which had been granted to a subset of congressional caucuses and which allowed them office space and central staffs. Henceforth, all caucuses would operate out of members' personal offices. Some observers predicted the end of the caucus system, but this did not happen. Caucuses continued to be active and influential. While there was some change, caucuses were able to adapt and survive.

Legislative service organization status existed only between 1979 and 1995. As described in chapter 7, during the 1980s the House Administration Committee (now House Oversight) gradually tightened regulations governing legislative service organization operations: more frequent and more specific reports were required, caucus and institute operations were separated, and caucuses were not permitted to raise or use outside monies for caucus operations. These changes received bipartisan support on the committee. Nevertheless, concern about caucus operations continued. A former senior member of the committee notes that "some LSOs were very well run, the DSG, the Wednesday Group. Others were not. . . . There were scandals." There were also funding issues, which constituents helped fuel. "Many members would come in and say 'I need more clerk-hire [for salaries] because I need to give money to more caucuses.' . . . And there would be a lot of pressure from groups at home to join caucuses, so members felt they had to use office monies for this." He continued, "When these things happen, it's time to quit and start over."

Before the 104th Congress, Pat Roberts (R-Kans.), a senior member of the House Administration Committee, had failed in his efforts to attach to legislative appropriation bills amendments abolishing legislative service organizations. After the 1994 congressional elections swept the Republicans into control of the House on an agenda of cutting back government, Roberts found support for eliminating legislative service organization status in order to clean up caucuses' alleged financial problems and cut down on congressional expenditures and staff. A former senior participant who shared some of these concerns noted that Roberts "had leadership support. John Boehner [R-Ohio], chair of the Republican Conference, supported Roberts' actions . . . although a lot of his colleagues were also trying to keep him from what he was doing." In December 1994, at an organizing meeting of all Republicans elected to the 104th Congress, Roberts' Republican colleagues approved his proposal. It became Section 222 of H. Res. 6, which was approved January 5, 1995.

Section 222 reads: "The establishment or continuation of any legislative service organization . . . shall be prohibited in the 104th Congress. The Committee on House Oversight shall take such steps as are necessary to ensure an orderly termination and accounting for funds of any legislative service organization in existence on January 3, 1995."[1] Committee regulations subsequently implemented this directive. And in February 1995 the House Oversight Committee established a new caucus designation, the congressional member organization.[2] House and bicameral caucuses that register with the committee as congressional member organizations are permitted to share official resources to carry out activities jointly, so that caucus members may share the salary of a staff aide who handles caucus matters. Congressional member organizations report their purpose, officers, and staff to the House Oversight Committee.

Why did the House abolish legislative service organizations? It may be impossible to disentangle the motives completely. As with most policy making by Congress, different concerns and goals may drive members to support a particular policy outcome. A complex mix of responses to citizens' perceptions of Congress, bipartisan concern about some caucus operations, partisan motives, and caucus vulnerability were important factors. A shift in party control and a general push for change also contributed to the change.

Leaders of the formal party and committee systems had always been wary of caucuses, although they also worked with, and were themselves members of, caucuses. Some believe that the new speaker, Newt Gingrich (R-Ga.), saw some caucuses as threats to the leadership centralization that he sought to put in place in the House. He, of course, knew how effective caucuses could be, because his own leadership of the Conservative Opportunity Society had identified him as a leader, even if a controversial one, and he launched his career within the formal party leadership system from that caucus's base. Some also believe that because some of the most influential caucuses, such as the Democratic Study Group, were entirely or primarily Democratic or took policy positions that were perceived as liberal, such as the Arms Control and Foreign Policy Caucus, the newly elected conservative House leadership hoped that abolishing legislative service organization status would make it more difficult for these groups to function. Citizen concern about congressional accountability was also a factor. Abolishing legislative service organization status would not affect the formal party or committee systems but would be a symbolic and perhaps substantive response to citizen concerns.

Roberts emphasized caucus lack of accountability and wasteful spending, which concerned members of both parties. Although some reforms had taken place, he believed "it was fourteen years too late. . . . The time for reform has passed. . . . It is much better for us to make a clean break with the past and begin anew—free of the past scandals and waste brought upon the House by these groups." In statements after the Republican Conference, Roberts noted that prior to the 104th Congress a bipartisan committee had approved reforms, "but the reform recommendations would go directly to the speaker's office, where no action was taken. . . . Why were these groups not better controlled or abolished? Simply, most of these special interests represent various segments of the Democratic party." And, he later added, "the DSG has always served as the working engine of the Democratic leadership." Eliminating legislative service organizations, especially the Democratic Study Group, would "severely damage the power structure of House Democrats."[3]

In statements and in the debate on Section 222, Democrats attacked Roberts' charges and the proposed abolition of legislative service organizations. Kweisi Mfume (D-Md.), chair of the Congressional Black Caucus, responded on December 7 that this was "an assault on diversity in the Congress and an attempt to disempower communities through congressional ethnic and philosophical cleansing." On January 4, the newly elected chair of the Black Caucus, Donald Payne (D-N.J.) argued that Section 222 "is not about reform. It is a blatant move to put a gag on minorities and others who may differ in opinion from the new majority party." And Norman Mineta (D-Calif.) noted that, if caucus work hence-

forth "requires that each caucus member duplicate within his or her individual office the work that could be done more efficiently and at a lower
cost by one person working for an LSO, then so be it. . . . The ironclad
commitment we have made to effectively providing . . . representation
will not waver."[4]

What has been the effect of abolishing legislative service organization
status? The 28 caucuses with this status that were active during the 103d
Congress lost this status. The 14 caucuses with separate office space—
many of them well known and long established—lost their space. A few
caucuses disbanded, but 25 of the 28 continued as informal caucuses. And
caucuses continued to flourish in the Senate and the House: during the
104th Congress, 161 caucuses were operating, 26 in the Senate and the
rest in the House or as bicameral groups. Fifty-six of the 161 were registered as congressional member organizations (12 of them formerly had
legislative service organization status). Eighteen of the congressional
member organizations were new caucuses, founded during the 104th Congress.[5] One close observer of caucuses concluded that the changes had
the effect of "weeding out the serious from the unserious caucuses. If the
staffer is interested but the member is not . . . the caucus goes! But, the
ones that stay are more important, because that requires personal commitment, and the staff must come from the personal staff."

Caucuses adapted to a changed environment and continued to respond
to new issues. The Republican Study Committee basically disbanded, and
its informational activities were taken over by the Republican Policy Committee. "It was one way for the leaders to get more control," an observer
said. "It was a function of all the party unity early on. Some now regret
it; they're sorry it went to the leadership."

Caucus staff of the Environmental and Energy Study Conference
started a private sector nonprofit organization, Green Sheets, to publish
information on issues and legislation previously handled by the conference. Green Sheets' publications are available to members of Congress
and to the public by subscription. Members of the caucus considered organizing for the 104th Congress but, eventually, did not do so. The Arms
Control and Foreign Policy Caucus also did not continue in the 104th.
The retirement of its long-time staff director, Edie Wilkie, wife of Don
Edwards (D-Calif.), who did not run for re-election in 1994, may have
been a factor in its demise. The Wednesday Group continued as an important forum for discussion and information exchange. It continued
some research activities but was less able to do research in depth.

CAUCUS ACTIVITY AFTER ABOLITION OF LEGISLATIVE SERVICE ORGANIZATIONS

Several caucuses illustrate the activities of caucuses that were formerly legislative service organizations and of continuing and newly established caucuses.

The Democratic Study Group

The Democratic Study Group eventually restructured after several agonizing attempts to continue operations. Initially, its publication operations were spun off to a private sector, nonprofit group called DSG Publications Inc., which was staffed by former caucus staff. But the House Oversight Committee refused to approve representatives' vouchers for the costly subscriptions and, later, issued regulations limiting payment of a subscription fee to $500 per year to newly established groups, so that "start-up operations are not primarily funded by taxpayer funds" (U.S. House of Representatives 1995). DSG Publications folded and sold the publications to Congressional Quarterly Inc., although Republicans reportedly tried to stop the sale (the staff director of the Oversight Committee is reported to have told CQ, "You don't want to buy that partisan organization").

The Democratic Study Group first registered as a congressional membership organization but then dropped that registration. In September 1995 it reorganized, becoming part of the House Democratic Caucus. The Democratic leadership took over some of the information activities of the group and provides weekly information packets to Democrats that include reviews of House actions, background information on current issues, talking points for press interviews, and constituency speeches. At this writing, the Democratic Study Group continues to have its own identity. It issues some informational material, including occasional special reports. Frequent meetings are held "to have a DSG conversation with a diverse collection of people." All Democrats are invited. The meetings are a "wide-ranging, broad-horizon way [to think about] issues and what people should be doing." During 1995–96, members of the administration were invited to speak: the U.S. trade representative, the director of the Environmental Protection Agency, and the chair of the Council of Economic Advisers. Political commentators Kevin Phillips and Mark Shields and private sector specialists Marian Wright Edelman, Ben Wattenberg, Jessica Tuchman Matthews, and Bob Greenstein of the Center on Budget and Policy Priorities have been speakers.

The Democratic Study Group considers itself separate from and independent of the Democratic leadership. A respondent said, "It is not controlled by the leaders. It is broadly and separately accountable to all Democrats of the House." One observer considers it now "basically an organization of more liberal Democrats—run by its executive committee." In late 1996, the group's restructuring appeared to be still somewhat unsettled. Its role as a forum for discussion of substantive issues was useful and well received, as were the informational materials sent to members, but the relationship with the Democratic leadership was less clearly delineated.

The Congressional Caucus on Women's Issues

The Congressional Caucus on Women's Issues presents a different picture. After losing a caucus staff and office, the caucus was "greatly limited in its ability to do things which it had previously," according to a respondent. However, it continued advocacy and an active schedule of working on issues of concern to women. A new private sector, nonprofit organization, Women's Policy Inc., staffed by former caucus staff members, was established to produce the legislative and issue information that the caucus had previously provided. Members and the public can subscribe to publications, including a highly regarded weekly, *The Source*, that reports bills introduced, congressional committee and floor activity, and executive action on issues affecting women and families. The year-end, detailed *Special Report* summarizes the action on these issues during each congressional session. In mid-1996, Women's Policy Inc. began to research and produce white papers on major pending issues; later that year it released *The Women's Health Equity Act of 1996: Legislative Summary and Overview*.

Like all caucuses in the 104th Congress, aides on the personal staffs of the co-chairs of the Caucus on Women's Issues coordinate and manage caucus matters. A staffer in each member's office is the caucus contact. These aides meet weekly to coordinate their work. Caucus members meet at least once a month. During the 104th Congress, the caucus testified on appropriations and authorizing legislation affecting women's health research, domestic violence, and education advocacy. The group also wrote to authorizing and appropriations subcommittee and committee chairs on various issues. When a bill goes to the floor of the House, "it's the same as before"; caucus members "speak and organize, and offer and oppose amendments."

When the appropriations bill for Labor and Health and Human Services came to the floor for debate in August 1995, the caucus sought to build a coalition in support of the amendment offered by James Greenwood (R-Pa.) and caucus co-chairs Connie Morella (R-Md.) and Nita Lowey (D-N.Y.) to restore funding for the Title X federal family planning program. The group sent "Dear Colleague" letters, planned floor speeches, spoke to members, and sent out fax alerts. They were successful. On a 224-to-204 vote, the House approved the amendment and overturned the committee recommendation to eliminate the funding. The caucus also drafted and introduced bills, including, in April 1996, the Women's Health Equity Act, a compendium of thirty-six bills, and two months later, the Economic Equity Act, which incorporated twenty-five bills. Abortion and family planning issues, child support in the welfare bill, and economic and health equity issues were particularly important to the caucus during 1995–96.

In addition to the focus on legislation, the caucus held briefings and meetings for members, staff, House colleagues, and outside groups. A senior staffer noted that the caucus was often asked by outside groups to arrange meetings, give briefings, work jointly on a project, or build coalitions. In a two-week period in mid-1996, caucus members and staff held a briefing on teen pregnancy in conjunction with the Population Resource Center; met with a cardiologist who was an expert on women and heart attacks; met with Susan Blumenthal, head of the Women's Health office at the Public Health Service; met with the National Osteoporosis Foundation to receive a petition to Congress; met with a group of women leaders from around the world who were visiting the United States; and met with representatives of the MTV-Women's Vote Project. The caucus successfully restructured and continues active and often successful advocacy on women's and family issues.

The Congressional Black Caucus

The Congressional Black Caucus, after a somewhat shaky start, also restructured and continues to be active on issues affecting blacks and other minorities. At the start of the 104th Congress, the caucus faced sev-

eral changes: loss of a caucus office and staff; loss of influential committee and subcommittee chair positions; loss of seats on major House committees; and the emergence of differences of opinion within the caucus.
Caucus membership had become more diverse, now drawn from rural
and suburban districts, particularly in the South, in addition to northern
urban districts. A caucus observer said: "Sanford Bishop would never vote
against peanut subsidies; Eva Clayton would never vote against tobacco
subsidies."

During the first months of 1995, caucus members considered how to
organize and operate and the issues to focus on. Caucus meetings served
a useful and important information exchange function, but coordinating
staff and providing specialized information were more difficult. The caucus registered as a congressional membership organization; senior staff in
the office of caucus chair, Donald Payne (D-N.J.), coordinated caucus
matters. The group focused on funding for programs like summer jobs,
low-income heating assistance, student aid, and affirmative action, funding that Republicans were proposing to cut. It also sought to broaden its
focus to agricultural and other issues not so specifically tied to minorities'
economic and civil rights issues.

The caucus established seven ongoing task forces, on church burning,
affirmative action, voting rights (including majority-minority districts, the
U.S. census, and voter intimidation problems), Haiti, the alternative budget, welfare reform, and health. The caucus also established temporary
brain trusts on various issues, led by caucus members who hold senior
committee positions. A brain trust briefs the caucus on the issues and on
pending committee and floor action and takes the lead in developing caucus strategy. Issue alerts sent to constituency groups identify concerns in
proposed legislation and activate a national network to contact their representatives directly. The caucus continues to develop alternative policy
proposals and an alternative budget. It opposes funding cuts that affect
its national constituency and seeks to modify legislative proposals it dis-
agrees with.

Although the caucus's influence within Congress has diminished, primarily because of the shift in party control, it continues to be a force in
agenda setting and is important within the congressional Democratic
Party. Payne was a member of the party's Leadership Group, about thirty
representatives who met daily at 5:00 P.M. to assess the events and actions
of the day and to develop strategy for the next day. The caucus has successfully adapted and restructured; a participant noted that the caucus had

been around for twenty-five years and had been a legislative service organization for only ten of those years, so the transition was made easier.

The Coalition (Blue Dogs)

The Coalition, made up of about two dozen moderate-to-conservative Democrats, got its start at the Democratic organizing caucuses after the 1994 elections. A lot of liberal members and the Democratic Leadership Council wing of the party in the House had been defeated. "Rumors were rife about party switching." Instead, members stayed in the party, but they "thought it important to have a voice." The group wanted to organize as a more formal voting bloc and knew that a swing bloc in the middle would make a difference. The Conservative Democratic Forum (Boll Weevils), to which likely Coalition members belonged, was larger and not always united. It was decided to spread the leadership of the new caucus among three co-chairs. It took a long time to organize: like "herding cats," said one participant. Members were independent; many were elected outside the party structure in their districts.

Unlike the Wednesday Group, members did not have to be invited to join but did have to be approved, as it was agreed to keep the group to twenty or twenty-five members. Some joined but were worried about the perception that the Coalition was a way station for Democratic Party switchers. (Eventually, five members did change parties.) Others did not join but came to Coalition meetings. One member joined because the senior member of his delegation told him to: "they are important in cutting deals," he said. Criteria for joining are reported to be a conservative voting record and a "bad attitude," that is, that the member is willing to stand up to "anyone." The core group of founders did not want members to join just for election purposes. Founders also saw the group as filling a void, which the Boll Weevils "didn't—and wouldn't".

The group started meeting in December 1994 and announced the formation of the caucus in mid-February 1995. Members felt that press reports of the caucus's formation portrayed them as much more combative adversaries of the Democratic leadership than they were. In fact, in announcing the group, members made clear that they might disagree with the leadership, and say so, but that they would talk with them and work with them. They would be "irritating both sides."

Early discussions focused on how the group would take formal positions. There was concern that a member's statement of personal views would be reported as the position of the Blue Dogs (as the Coalition came to be called). Although that concern has continued to cause tensions, the group has taken positions on issues and has been extraordinarily successful in influencing legislative proposals and policy outcomes. It is regarded as very influential and likely to play a significant role if the Democrats again take control of the House. Three Coalition members served on the Democrats' Leadership Group during the 104th Congress, and other members also served in leadership positions—Chet Edwards (Tex.) as chief deputy minority whip, John Spratt (S.C.) as co-chair of the Democratic Policy Committee, and Pete Peterson (Fla.) as vice chair of the Democratic Steering Committee. During the 104th Congress, Democratic leader Dick Gephardt (Mo.) worked closely with Coalition members on two major bills: welfare legislation, which was drafted by Coalition member Nathan Deal (Ga.) and adopted by the Democrats as their alternative to the Republican proposal, and the Coalition budget, adopted as the Democratic alternative to the Republican budget bill. Charles Stenholm (Tex.) of the Coalition served on the negotiating team on the budget reconciliation bill in 1995, the only member who was not a committee chair.

The Coalition took its first formal position on Deal's welfare bill. As the Coalition's co-chair for policy, Deal asked the group whether it wanted to join him in supporting the bill. At the same time, there were discussions with the Democratic leadership about alternatives to a leadership bill: "It was a balancing act, but Coalition members recognized that by forming alliances with members outside the group it would be possible to really get something done."

When the Coalition agreed to have its budget bill become the Democratic alternative, the group made changes in the leadership proposal, including savings from tax loopholes, moderate savings from welfare reform and Medicaid, and cuts in discretionary spending. The process used to reach agreement was time-intensive and based on extensive knowledge and expertise. It illustrates how the caucus system can supplement the formal committee system. Fifteen to twenty members met to debate fifteen or twenty issues. It took two hours—on two discrete issues—to finish the Medicare package. On a few issues, members voted. Most issues were decided by consensus. The group also sent surveys to its members, listing the options and asking members to indicate what they would or would not support. The responses indicated a caucus goal and became the basis for discussion on how to reach that goal.

A series of formal meetings were also held between five coalition members and five members of the Republican negotiating team, including majority whip Tom DeLay (Tex.), Budget chair John Kasich (Ohio), and Deal, who was now a Republican. Nothing came of the meetings, which "the Republicans thought were a sort of diversion, a way to put pressure on the president—and the Coalition thought so too."

As the 105th Congress began, Coalition members gained seats on the Ways and Means and Budget Committees, important positions for affecting economic legislation. Five "Blue Puppies" elected in 1996, joined the group, and minority leader Gephardt publicly praised the Coalition's work during the 104th Congress (Gugliotta 1996). The Blue Dogs were well situated to influence the work of the 105th.

Among the factors that made the Coalition an influential player on major legislation were the substantive expertise that the group brought to its activity and the strategic skill of its members. As experienced, knowledgeable senior representatives, Coalition members commanded the respect, although perhaps not the support, of leaders and colleagues. Their position as a swing bloc of votes between the parties, in addition to the substantive content of the legislation they drafted, was also critical. Caucus processes contributed to their influence. The Coalition reached out to representatives beyond their membership to develop legislative provisions that a larger group would support. They sought caucus consensus on the provisions of proposed bills. This differs from the Boll Weevils, which was its own bloc of votes only if it could keep all members on board. It did not take formal positions on issues, although individual members did—and then would seek support within the caucus. The Coalition's processes contributed to its strength. The group worked within its party and with party leaders, as would be expected of a party caucus.

Other Successful Caucuses

Other caucuses also flourished during the 104th Congress. The Progressive Caucus increased its membership to fifty. It met with Democratic leader Gephardt and, according to one observer, was "very helpful in defining the Republicans" in one-minute floor speeches and debate during 1995, when the Democrats were still in shock after the elections. The caucus was "active and effective."

The Republican Freshman Class Club played a strong supporting role in the consideration and passage of "Contract with America" legislation.

They organized early and, for most of the Congress, spoke with one voice and voted together. They pushed the Republican leadership by speaking out on issues, and they were a bloc of votes that leaders could not afford to lose. The Tuesday Lunch Bunch of moderate Republicans met regularly with the speaker and obtained modifications in Republican tax cuts and other proposals. The U.S.–Former Soviet Union Energy Caucus, a bipartisan industry caucus with its fifty members drawn largely from the oil-producing states of Texas, Oklahoma, Louisiana, Pennsylvania, and Ohio, was active in developing a draft oil-production-sharing agreement and working with oil executives and U.S. executive branch leaders to consider energy development in the former Soviet Union.

Caucus Voting in the 104th Congress

To assess the effect of caucus membership on representatives' votes on caucus issues during the 104th Congress, five caucuses were analyzed: one party caucus, the Coalition (Blue Dogs); one personal-interest group, the Progressive Caucus; and three constituency caucuses, the Congressional Black Caucus, the Congressional Caucus on Women's Issues, and the Federal Government Service Task Force. Two are long established, two are midrange, and one was formed at the start of the 104th Congress. The analysis covers votes during 1995, the first session of the 104th Congress, that were identified as important votes for a caucus, based on interview data and caucus publications supplemented by media reports. The dependent variable is support of caucus votes. Independent variables include caucus membership, party, seniority, leadership positions, membership on prestige committees, percentage of votes in the election, and committee membership and constituency variables specific to the caucus. The regression results are shown in table 11-1. (See the appendix for further discussion of the variables.)

The results of the analysis confirm and strengthen the findings on floor voting reported in the previous chapter. Most important for this study, caucus membership had a significant effect on voting for all the caucuses analyzed. In addition, this finding occurred even after the major changes at the start of the 104th Congress regarding caucus operations. Party and ideology were also significant for most caucuses (although not for the Federal Government Service Task Force). Various constituency variables were also significant for specific caucuses. Prestige committee memberships were significant for only the Progressive Caucus; and only one other

Table 11-1. Representatives' Voting, by Caucus, on Caucus Votes, 104th Congress, 1st Session: Composite Table of Regression Results (coefficients and *t*-ratios)

Variable	Federal Government Service Caucus	Women's Issues Caucus	Black Caucus	The Coalition (Blue Dogs)	Progressive Caucus
Caucus membership	0.141 (1.773)*	0.314 (4.030)***	0.256 (3.374)***	0.465 (5.921)***	0.467 (6.102)***
Party	−0.084 (−1.258)	0.430 (5.970)***	0.942 (18.309)***	0.627 (10.746)***	−0.187 (−2.837)***
Conservatism	8.614E-04 (0.824)	−0.014 (−12.701)***	−0.004 (−4.838)***	0.010 (11.097)***	−0.016 (−14.703)***
Vote margin	4.660E-04 (0.433)	−1.247E-04 (−0.108)	3.099E-04 (0.383)	−1.007E-04 (−0.127)	−3.037E-04 (−0.289)
Seniority (no. of terms)	−6.836E-04 (−0.130)	−0.007 (−1.313)	−0.002 (−0.482)	0.004 (0.961)	0.012 (2.394)*
Leader	0.118 (1.771)	0.054 (0.754)	−0.029 (−0.572)	−0.029 (−0.587)	0.084 (1.302)
Prestige committee	−0.021 (−0.440)	0.087 (1.610)	−0.006 (−0.139)	−0.035 (−0.955)	−0.115 (−2.472)*
Employed (civilian)	2.249E-06 (2.685)**	2.785E-06 (3.616)***	7.242E-08 (0.116)	7.622E-07 (1.330)	−1.406E-06 (−1.860)
Manufacturing employment	−0.450 (−1.355)	−0.485 (−1.374)	0.100 (0.419)	—	—
Percentage black	0.512 (3.351)***	0.348 (2.236)*	0.138 (1.016)	0.021 (0.186)	0.368 (2.533)*
Percentage Hispanic	0.054 (0.210)	—	−0.109 (−0.546)	−0.018 (−0.142)	0.381 (2.233)*
Percentage foreign	0.080 (0.206)	—	0.289 (0.980)	—	—
Percentage urban	−0.112 (−0.762)	0.104 (0.799)	−0.061 (−0.606)	—	−0.253 (−2.121)*
Percentage rural	—	—	—	0.105 (1.172)	—
Agriculture employment	1.208 (1.326)	1.688 (1.664)	—	—	—
Federal workers	5.014E-06 (1.295)	—	—	—	—
Commerce Committee	—	—	−0.039 (−0.747)	−0.099 (−2.042)*	—
Small Business Committee	—	−0.021 (−0.408)	−0.055 (−1.489)	—	—
Budget Committee	—	−0.072 (−1.013)	−0.086 (−1.698)	−0.008 (−0.156)	—

(Continued)

Table 11-1. *(Continued)*

Variable	Federal Government Service Caucus	Women's Issues Caucus	Black Caucus	The Coalition (Blue Dogs)	Progressive Caucus
Economic and Educational Opportunities Committee	—	0.028 (0.386)	0.043 (0.833)	0.003 (0.066)	—
Banking Committee	—	−0.021 (−0.307)	0.064 (1.303)	—	—
Agriculture Committee	—	−0.017 (−0.231)	−0.009 (−0.173)	—	—
Judiciary Committee	—	—	−0.076 (−1.368)	—	—
Constant	−0.633 (−2.239)*	−0.235 (−0.800)	−0.199 (−1.020)	−1.383 (−6.821)***	1.069 (4.437)***

Note: Except for the caucus variable (which uses a one-tailed test), all reported significance levels are for two-tailed tests. A dash indicates that a variable was not included in the regression; *t*-ratios are given in parentheses.
* $p < .05$
** $p < .01$
*** $p < .005$

committee membership, on the Commerce Committee, was significant for only one caucus, the Blue Dogs. As with the analysis of voting reported in the previous chapter, caucus membership matters in votes on caucus issues.

Adapting to Change

It seems clear from caucus activity during the 104th Congress that the caucus system adapted to a loss of legislative service organization status. New caucuses, like the Coalition, became influential players in congressional policy making. Former legislative service organizations restructured and continued caucus activity. Existing caucuses that were not legislative service organizations also continued to provide information exchange and to work toward their policy goals.

Did abolishing legislative service organization status result in savings? Office expenditures for 1994 and 1995 for a sample of members of five caucuses[6] were compared. During 1994, members of these caucuses, all legislative service organizations, could transfer monies from their office expense allowances to these caucuses for payment of staff or for other office expenditures. (Personnel and franking expenses are paid from different allowances and are not included in the analysis.) If savings occurred, members should have had lower office expense allowance expenditures in 1995 than in 1994. In the aggregate, all members in the sample from the five caucuses, as a group, spent $26,000 less in 1995 (significant at the .001 level). However, the difference is not significant for any one caucus. And there is no difference between members of legislative service organizations that had separate offices and a caucus staff and those that operated out of members' personal offices.

In a further analysis, the office expenditures and the clerk-hire (personnel) expenditures for each office were summed and analyzed. Clerk-hire is included because, although members could fund caucus staff through transfers from office expense allowances, any additional caucus staff expense in 1995 (after legislative service organizations were abolished) would have to be paid from the allowance for personnel. There is no significant difference between the 1994 and 1995 expenditures. The analysis indicates that no significant savings resulted from abolishing legislative service organization status for congressional caucuses.

There were, however, other effects. Caucuses that had separate offices and staff in 1994 were forced to restructure, which often required significant time and energy. Some activities, such as research and the publication of extensive legislative information, were cut back. And for many caucuses, operation became more difficult: they have to coordinate staff in different offices and develop systems to provide specialized information. However, as we have seen, caucuses have adapted and continue to perform their information exchange activities, to put issues on congressional and executive agendas, to coordinate members and issues, and to influence policy making.

CAUCUSES BEYOND THE 1990S

In retrospect, it should be no surprise that congressional caucuses survived the 104th's challenge to the caucus system. U.S. national policy making is a complicated process in a pluralistic society facing extraordinarily complex policy challenges. But Congress, the representative and responsive institution charged with facing those challenges, is adaptive. In the contemporary era, the development and operation of congressional caucuses evidence institutional, individual, and policy response and adaptation to changing times. These informal subunits offer members flexibility in addressing common concerns. Easier to establish than a subcommittee and less closely tied to the turf concerns of that formal subunit system, caucuses can operate actively when an issue is salient and become inactive when it is not. Caucuses can also focus on information or research or on issues that are neglected, ignored, or overlooked by committees and subcommittees.

Caucuses offer Congress and its members flexibility, enhance opportunities for representation, and serve as vehicles for integrating members' disparate efforts. A crucial element in their success is flexibility, which subunits of the formal structure do not enjoy. Flexibility helps caucuses survive changes in congressional leadership and organization and enhances their ability to meet members' goals. Caucuses permeate the formal system easily, through member overlap between caucuses and committees; through drafting legislation, building coalitions, and working with leaders; and through representation, policy, and oversight work. Caucuses are effective in agenda setting and in organizing and sharing information. Caucuses can be extraordinarily successful even though they are working through an informal structure and, as the experiences of the 104th Congress show, even when structures change. Caucuses are important, as evidenced by the attention given to these groups in the 104th.

Caucuses expand the opportunity for representation. Simply joining a caucus can be symbolic evidence of concern about an issue. Cosponsoring caucus amendments or bills can have a similar effect. In both activities, representatives demonstrate responsiveness, build trust between constituents and elected officials, and gain support for the member and for Congress as an institution. Substantive policy representation occurs when caucuses seek to influence governmental agendas or policy decisions in the executive or in Congress. Although caucuses are important in representing constituent needs and interests, caucuses are not interest groups within the Congress.[7] When members join caucuses to influence policy outcomes, they do so as representatives of citizens, not as individual citizens. Furthermore, the material benefits of caucus membership do not accrue selectively to caucus members (as would occur in an interest group) but, rather, to their constituents.

The effect of congressional caucuses on the institutional structure is both integrating and fragmenting. Caucuses integrate policy actors within and outside Congress, coordinating information, issues, agendas, committee action, and floor outcomes. Coordination contributes to efficiency and to effective policy making. In an institution that is notoriously individualistic, leaders can gain access through caucuses to an organized bloc of votes. However, caucuses also fragment the system. As subunits outside the formal system, they complicate matters by being alternate sources of information, additional communication centers, and active players on the congressional policy stage. But caucuses make a point of operating within the system. Caucus members and staff emphasize that they seek to supplement and complement, rather than to supplant, the work of the formal system.

On balance, integration outweighs fragmentation. Caucuses help manage conflict and help adversaries reach consensus or compromise. By assisting members in achieving personal goals, caucuses also serve institutional goals by carrying out the collective responsibilities of legislation, representation, and oversight. They enable members and the collective Congress to focus on and respond to concerns within Congress and in the polity at large.

In the various roles they play, caucuses reflect the complexity of American society. The experiences of caucuses in the 104th Congress are evidence that caucuses quickly respond to changing circumstances and that Congress is an adaptive organization. The caucus system continued to be important after the imposition of significant changes in the legislative environment. The continuing development of the caucus system and the establishment of new caucuses show that caucuses are here to stay. As long as caucuses assist members and the institution in carrying out their responsibilities and achieving their goals, they can be expected to remain a feature of the congressional landscape—because the caucus system works.

This study is based upon various sources of data: semifocused, open-ended interviews conducted during the Ninety-seventh through the 104th Congresses with staff directors of congressional caucuses; a telephone survey of all active caucuses during the 100th Congress; additional interviews; and congressional, caucus, and news and trade publications.

Directors of most of the active caucuses of the Ninety-seventh through the 100th Congresses and of six caucuses of the 104th Congress were interviewed. The interviews covered caucus formation, purposes, membership, organization, and activities; issues of interest and how they were pursued; interaction with committees, party leaders, the president, the White House and executive agencies, interest groups, and other policy actors; and caucus successes and failures. The interviews sought to explore the causes, operations, and consequences of the caucus system, to examine links with the formal congressional systems and with other policy actors, and to elicit reflection on caucuses.

Thirty-five additional interviews were conducted with members of Congress, leadership staff, other caucus staff, and other Senate and House staff during the Ninety-seventh through the 104th Congresses. Interviews during the 104th Congress were with senior staff of five caucuses (in addition to the six staff directors noted above) and five other members, leaders, and other staff. Interviews with members were designed to explore their views of the caucus system and their participation in it, including why they join caucuses, their level of involvement, and the costs and benefits of caucus membership. Members and other respondents were also asked about caucus-party leader interaction, to compare caucuses over time or, as in 1996, in a changed institutional context.

Interviews lasted about an hour, with some lasting as long as two or three hours. All respondents were promised anonymity, and unless otherwise noted, all quotations are from interviews.

A telephone survey of all active caucuses was conducted during the

100th Congress. Of the 107 existing caucuses in 1987, 19 were not interviewed: 10 were in the process of organizing, 4 were changing staff directors, and senior aides of 5 could not be found. Thus, eighty-eight senior staff, usually caucus staff directors, were interviewed. Six of them reported that their caucuses were organized but inactive. The remaining eighty-two interviews constitute the survey data set. The survey covered caucus purpose, structure, activities, and major issue concerns. Most interviews were conducted by telephone; a few were conducted in person. Most respondents were staff directors; all were top-level caucus aides. The survey data reported throughout the book are from the data base of 82 caucuses.

Congressional, caucus, media, and trade publications were also drawn on.

Several computer files with data on individual members of Congress permit examination of the relationship of members to the caucus system. Three data sets with information on individual members of the House were developed, one with data on all representatives in the Ninety-seventh Congress, the second on Ninety-seventh Congress freshman during the Ninety-seventh through the 103d Congresses, and the third on all 104th Congress representatives. Data entered for each Ninety-seventh Congress representative include caucus memberships, party, ideology (conservatism), seniority, election margin, committee memberships, party, and committee, including leadership, positions, constituency characteristics, and roll call votes.

A similar file for the 104th Congress includes membership in selected caucuses and data on party, committee, electoral, constituency, and roll call votes. An additional file of Ninety-seventh Congress freshmen includes data on caucus memberships, committee assignments, leadership positions, party, ideology (conservatism), electoral margin, and constituency variables for these members in the Ninety-seventh through the 103d Congresses. These files enable analysis of caucus membership patterns, caucus cohesion, and caucus effect on floor votes. The freshman file permits additional analysis regarding caucus socialization functions.

Voting analyses on votes of interest to selected caucuses in the Ninety-seventh and 104th Congresses are reported in chapters 10 and 11. The dependent variable for analyses in both chapters is the caucus support score: the sum of all votes for or against a caucus position divided by the total number of caucus votes on which the representative voted. Independent variables are caucus membership, party, seniority, party and committee leadership positions, committee memberships, and various constituency variables. For each caucus, a representative is coded as member or nonmember. Other individual variables include party (0 = Republican, 1 = Democrat); state; seniority measured by number of terms; marginality measured by the percentage of the two-party vote in the last election; and ideology (conservatism) measured by the conservative coalition support score for the Congress (97th) or the 1st session (104th), corrected for absences.

Memberships on standing committees were entered: membership on a prestige committee (Appropriations, Rules, or Ways and Means) is coded 1; other committees are 0. The leader variable is coded 1 if a representative is speaker, majority leader, whip, chief deputy, deputy, zone whip, at-large whip, regional whip, assistant whip, minority leader, whip, chief deputy, or deputy; otherwise, it is 0. District constituency variables report census data for 1980 (Ninety-seventh Congress) and 1990 (104th Congress): the percentage black, Hispanic (Spanish heritage), urban, rural, and foreign stock; the number employed in mining, manufacturing, agriculture, and the civilian labor force. The number employed in coal mining and related industries and in the federal workforce are drawn from government, industry, and workforce reports.

PROLOGUE

1. All quotations without attribution are from interviews; respondents were promised anonymity.

2. The term Blue Dogs is used by members to distinguish themselves from Yellow Dog Democrats—"a dying breed of southern Democrat so loyal to the party that, it's said, they would vote for a yellow dog over a Republican" (Calmes 1995, A28).

3. Caucus studies focus on a single caucus, or at most, several caucuses, except for Hammond 1989, 1991, 1997; Hammond, Stevens, and Mulhollan 1983, 1985; and Stevens, Mulhollan, and Rundquist 1981. Early studies of informal congressional groups (Fiellin 1962; Deckard 1972) examine state delegations. Caucus studies include Ferber 1971 on the formation of the Democratic Study Group; Groennings 1973 on the House Wednesday Group; Dilger 1982 on the Northeast-Midwest Congressional Coalition; Feulner 1983 on the Republican Study Committee; and a chapter in Gertzog 1984, 1995 on the Congressional Caucus on Women's Issues. Other studies include C. E. Jones 1987 on the Congressional Black Caucus; Thompson 1988, 1993, and 1995 on the Congressional Caucus on Women's Issues; Vega 1993 on the Hispanic Caucus; and Loomis 1979 on the Freshman Class of 1974. Loomis 1981 expands his analysis to several caucuses. Stevens, Miller, and Mann 1974, on the effect of the Democratic Study Group's whip system on caucus members' floor votes, is a sophisticated analysis of one caucus's activity and impact.

CHAPTER 1/ CONGRESSIONAL CAUCUSES AND CONGRESSIONAL CHANGE

1. See Sinclair 1989 and 1995 for somewhat similar arguments on Senate and House changes.

CHAPTER 2/ AN OVERVIEW OF CAUCUSES

1. H. Res. 1652. The bill was vetoed by the president, and a veto override did not succeed. See Olson 1987; and *Congressional Record*, Oct. 10, 1985, H20789.

2. Social clubs—voluntary associations of members with a primarily social

purpose that do not seek to affect policy—and the quasi-official task forces or other informal groups established by party leaders or committees are not included in this total.

3. A survey conducted during 1987–88 profiles the caucus system and offers a basis for subsequent examination of selected aspects of it. Of the 107 existing caucuses in 1987, 88 were interviewed. Of these, 6 were organized but inactive; the remaining 82 constitute the data set. The survey covered caucus purpose, structure, activity, and major issue concerns. Most surveys were conducted by telephone; a few were conducted in person. Most respondents were staff directors; all were top-level caucus aides. The survey data reported in this chapter and throughout the book are from the data base of 82 caucuses; organized but inactive caucuses and caucuses organizing but not yet active are not included in the data set. See the appendix for a fuller discussion of the survey. Interview data supplement the caucus survey.

4. State delegations are included in this analysis if they were accorded legislative service organization status during any Congress.

5. These data reflect rules in effect from 1979 to 1995, when some caucuses with legislative service organization status had separate offices. During the 100th Congress, twelve of the thirty caucuses with such status operated out of members' offices.

6. Some caucuses worked with private sector research institutes or foundations that focus on issues of interest and concern to the caucus. In 1989 (the 101st Congress), seven such institutes were in operation: the Congressional Black Caucus Foundation, the Northeast-Midwest Institute, the Sunbelt Institute, the Women's Research and Education Institute, the Congressional Institute for the Future, the Congressional Economic Institute (paralleling the Congressional Competitiveness Caucus), and the New Populist Forum (paralleling the Congressional Populist Caucus). The institutes are separate organizations, with varying degrees of overlap between caucus and institute leaders. In the past, some institutes used congressional office space, and some shared staff with caucuses. Institutes no longer have congressional office space and must be completely separate organizations. Under 104th Congress House Oversight Committee regulations, members of Congress may continue to serve on the boards of private, nonprofit organizations, such as institutes.

7. The data reported here contrast the eighteen Senate and thirty-four House caucuses in the data set that were organized and active during the 100th Congress (1987–88). The thirty bicameral caucuses are not included: often, most activity of bicameral caucuses takes place in the House, is directed by House caucus chairs, and is carried out by the House members of the caucus.

8. In 1995, the Democratic Study Group described itself as being "for Democratic members of the House of Representatives who wish to join together in a common effort" (Brownson 1995, 809).

9. The caucus "ideology" score is the mean conservative coalition score for all caucus members; member scores are derived from scores reported for members of the House and Senate in the *Congressional Quarterly Almanac*, 97 Cong. Scores are recomputed so that absences do not lower a member's score.

10. In the 104th Congress, the Congressional Caucus on Women's Issues restructured after new House rules eliminated legislative service organization status (and dues-paying members). The caucus returned to women-only membership, although it was likely that in the future men would again become members.

Chapter 3/ Why Caucuses Are Established

1. The first section of this chapter, on early informal groups, is based on a paper prepared by Daniel P. Mulhollan.
2. The thirteen class clubs are not included in the analysis of caucus formation. Their formation and abolition are not subject to the same forces of other caucuses: all freshmen Republicans and Democrats form class clubs; all class clubs eventually disband.
3. In the House in 1993, four new caucuses were established to assume the issue interests of the select committees that the House abolished. Caucuses are somewhat analogous to select committees, which have information and recommendation authority but cannot process and report legislation for House consideration.

Chapter 4/ The Life Cycle of Caucuses

1. This finding supports and extends findings regarding group formation (Salisbury 1969). See also literature on grassroots organizations, which are typically started by entrepreneurs.
2. Later, a House Administration (after 1995, House Oversight) Committee regulation mandated the separation of caucuses and institutes and prohibited shared staff.
3. See Kaufman (1976) for discussion of executive branch organizations.

Chapter 5/ Caucus Membership

1. Variables reported are significant at the .05 level, unless otherwise indicated.
2. Significant at the .001 level.
3. Ideology (conservatism) is measured by *Congressional Quarterly*'s conservative coalition score for each Congress, corrected for absences. See *Congressional Quarterly Almanac* (CQ Press), various editions, for conservative coalition scores.
4. This finding is significant at the .1 level. Marginal districts are those whose representative won by 55% of the vote or less.
5. For the 1976 data, see Congressional Research Service 1984. The CRS data differ from this study's data because I include only representatives (excluding from the data set delegates and resident commissioners) and because the data I report are derived from actual caucus membership lists. CRS data were obtained from the *Congressional Yellow Book* (caucus membership is self-reported information for each member) and includes both representatives and delegates. In

some instances, CRS data may underreport caucus memberships; in other instances, (because delegates are included) it may slightly overreport membership.

6. Only congressional members with the characteristics represented by these caucuses were eligible to join, so regression or logit are appropriate only if some eligibles did not join, as was the case with the Congressional Caucus on Women's Issues. All those eligible joined the Black Caucus and the Hispanic Caucus; hence, the comparison of means reported for these caucuses.

7. Rick Santorum (R-Pa.) left the House in 1995 after election to the Senate, where he continued to focus on Gang of Seven concerns.

CHAPTER 6/ CAUCUSES AND THE NATIONAL AGENDA

1. Caucuses occasionally place items on the judicial agenda: for example, the Democratic Study Group's suit against implementing the Reagan tanker-reflagging program and the Rural Caucus's suit against the impoundment of funds.

2. Using the Pearson chi-square, the differences on public agenda setting and attention to the congressional or administrative agendas are significant at the .001 level.

3. Walker 1976 makes this distinction. In a typology of Senate agenda items (98), he develops a continuum from required (periodically recurring problems) to discretionary (the chosen problems). Also see Walker 1977.

4. In August 1987, 110 members of Congress—led by Lowry and the Democratic Study Group—filed suit in the District of Columbia U.S. District Court to require the president to adhere to the procedures of the War Powers Resolution; the effect would have been to include Congress in the decision on escorting reflagged tankers. The suit was dismissed by the court "because of the constraints of the equitable discretion and political question doctrines" (*Lowry v. Reagan*). This was an unusual caucus approach, especially for the Democratic Study Group, but it shows the effect of strategic flexibility on policy-driven caucus activity.

5. In 1995 (the 104th Congress), Democrats split the committee into the Steering Committee and the Policy Committee.

CHAPTER 7/ CAUCUSES AND PARTY LEADERS

1. After legislative service organizations were abolished in 1995, Democratic Study Group publication activities were eventually divided. Some were sold to the *Congressional Quarterly,* and in September 1995 some were assumed by the House Democratic leadership. An alternate model is that of the Republican Study Committee, which disbanded after the legislative service organization designation was abolished. Its information activities were taken over by the Republican Party Conference.

2. The data reported here group House and bicameral caucuses together and compare that group with Senate caucuses. All bicameral caucuses with office space were housed on the House side; several received legislative service organization status between 1979 and 1995. Interview data indicate that bicameral cau-

cuses often focus more on the House and that House operations of bicameral caucuses are generally more structured than are Senate operations.

3. For discussion of the Boll Weevils during the 1980s, see Lorenzen 1992.

4. "Work with party leaders" is defined as active caucus participation in support of leadership activities, including leadership meetings and whip counts. Survey results are reported in table 7-1. Table 7-2 reports on House caucuses for which there is interview response data regarding work with party leaders. The interviews permit in-depth analysis of caucus-leader interaction. Senate caucuses are not included in this analysis because most Senate caucuses include leaders as members, and in addition the less structured Senate rules result in less formal caucus work with party leaders.

Chapter 8/ Working with the Executive Branch

1. This refers to contractors who qualify for minority preferences under Section 8(a) of the Small Business Investment Act of 1958, as amended by PL 95–507 (1978).

2. Establishing a regional petroleum reserve in the Northeast remains an issue. During the 1980s some argument revolved around whether the strategic petroleum reserve law (the 1975 Energy Policy and Conservation Act) required establishing a regional reserve. Members of Congress from the Northeast continued to push for it and put the issue on committee agendas. In the 102d Congress (1991–92), a provision establishing a New England regional reserve was included in a major energy bill and was approved by the House; it was later dropped by the House-Senate conference committee.

3. Only one regional caucus, the TVA Caucus (its members are from Tennessee Valley Authority states), differs significantly in its approach. The Tennessee Valley Authority generates its own data and has permanent authorization, so it has very little occasion for contact with the executive or with Congress. According to a TVA Caucus senior staff aide, there is "occasional contact with the White House" and "some work, occasionally, on appropriations." Because of its permanent authorization, the TVA is only very rarely affected by legislation on the floor.

Chapter 9/ Working with Congressional Committees

1. Dellums, Conyers, and Clay became ranking minority members in the 104th Congress. Clay was ranking member of the Economic and Educational Opportunities Committee (formerly, Education and Labor) after the Post Office and Civil Service Committee, which he had chaired in the 103d Congress, was made a subcommittee of the Government Reform and Oversight Committee (formerly, Government Operations).

2. The question was, What were the two most important issues the caucus worked on in 1987? The respondent was asked to identify the locus of work on each issue named (e.g., Congress, the executive) and the stage of the legislative process (e.g., precommittee, committee).

3. In 1995, a House Oversight Committee regulation prohibited caucuses from holding hearings.

CHAPTER 10/ CAUCUSES AND CONGRESSIONAL FLOOR ACTION

1. The data may understate caucus floor activity. One session does not completely capture the range of activity, and several respondents who reported no floor activity in 1987 described having made such efforts at other times. A few caucuses also report coordinating strategy on amendments with other caucuses or with groups of party members.

2. The Populist Caucus "focuses on questions of economic equity and justice . . . promotes legislation concerned with agriculture, small business, taxation, interest rates, and energy. Its goal is to ensure a 'fair shake' for America's common people and small business, and to revive populism as a full force in America's political debate" (*Congressional Yellow Book 1986*, VI-40).

3. The caucus was less successful during the 103d Congress and more successful during the 104th, after the shift in party control.

4. The Vietnam Era Veterans in Congress Caucus was initially included in the analysis. It was dropped because two of the three roll call votes were nearly unanimous (more than 90% of the votes cast were in one direction), and the votes were therefore excluded from the data set analyzed. On the third roll call, the vote split was almost 90–10%. Several other measures of concern to the caucus were passed by voice vote. Caucus amendments were incorporated into omnibus bills at the committee level, and these bills had overwhelming support from the committee and, indeed, most of the House when the legislation came to the floor. This success rate is anomalous, and there is virtually no variance between the caucus and the rest of the House on any of these votes.

5. A difference-of-proportions test was used to estimate statistical significance. A one-tailed test is reported in the text, significant at the .05 level unless otherwise indicated.

6. The literature on congressional voting behavior is extensive. See, e.g., Cherryholmes and Shapiro 1969; Turner and Schneier 1970; McRae 1970; Brady, Cooper and Hurley 1979; Collie 1984, 1988; Clausen 1973; Poole and Rosenthal 1987; Kingdon 1989; Rohde 1991; Cox and McCubbins 1993. Note that Kingdon, in his important study of voting behavior, does not include caucuses. I argue that the (newly developed) caucus system has become an element that can affect the floor voting of caucus members.

7. Regression is the appropriate technique to use, as the dependent variable is continuous.

8. If caucus membership and the specific caucus-relevant variable are both significant, both have a direct effect on caucus members' votes. If one of the two is significant, the nonsignificant variable may have an indirect effect through the significant variable. Policy preferences might best be captured by the use of DE-NOMINATE. However, for this analysis, *Congressional Quarterly*'s conservative

coalition score, based on more than a hundred roll call votes on a variety of issues, seemed appropriate.

9. Because the ideology variable for each member was his or her conservative coalition score (see note 8), caucus votes that were also conservative coalition votes were deleted from the analysis.

10. The significance level reported for all variables except the caucus membership variable is two-tailed; that for caucus membership is one-tailed (the hypothesis is that caucus members support the caucus position on roll call votes). There are no expectations as to direction for the other variables. For the three national constituency caucuses, only full members (blacks, Hispanics) or executive committee members (women) were included in the analysis. The nine Republican members of the Democratic Study Group during the Ninety-seventh Congress were included in the analysis (extensive reporting on the issue through DSG information would be likely to persuade members to a DSG position). The three national constituency caucuses do not make available such extensive information to their members. The Democratic Study Group and the Environmental and Energy Study Conference seem somewhat analogous: the Environmental Conference is explicitly an information-providing caucus and does not take caucus positions on issues; nevertheless, caucus membership was a significant variable in vote support for caucus issues, presumably because of the information members receive.

11. Although Rural Caucus membership was not significant in the aggregate regression analysis of Rural Caucus votes, logit regression reveals that caucus membership was significant on some individual votes.

12. If the Rural Caucus is included ($p \leq .1$), caucus membership was significant for six of the nine constituency caucuses (67%).

CHAPTER 11/ THE 104TH CONGRESS AND BEYOND

1. On a party-line vote of 227 to 201, House members refused to send H. Res. 6 back to committee. It then approved Title II of the bill, including Section 222, by voice vote. See H. Res. 6, Rules of the House, Title I, Contract with America: A Bill of Accountability; Title II, General, Section 222, Abolition of Legislative Service Organizations (*Congressional Record*, daily ed., v. 141, Jan. 4, 1995, H30 for Sec. 222; H83–989 for debate; H89–90 for motion to recommit and voice vote on adopting Title II, including Sec. 222).

2. A congressional membership organization is defined as "an informal organization of Members who share official resources to jointly carry out activities. . . . [It has] no separate corporate or legal identity apart from the Members who comprise it . . . is not an employing authority, and no staff may be appointed by, or in the name of a CMO. A CMO may not be assigned separate office space" (Congressional Member Organization Regulations, Committee on House Oversight, February 8, 1995). Later regulations prohibit caucus use of the frank or of office allowances to purchase caucus stationery.

3. See "Statement of Congressman Pat Roberts Regarding Abolishment of

LSOs," December 6, 1994, released by his office; and news release, Pat Roberts, December 6, 1994.

4. For Mfume, see K. Cooper 1994; for Payne, see *Congressional Record*, Jan. 4, 1995, H85; for Mineta, see ibid., H89.

5. Information derived from Congressional Research Service 1996; *Congressional Yellow Book 1996;* and author's data.

6. These were the Automotive Caucus, the Black Caucus, the Caucus on Women's Issues, the Hispanic Caucus, and the Democratic Study Group.

7. For a more detailed discussion of caucuses and interest groups, see Hammond, Stevens, and Mulhollan, 1983; for discussion of caucuses and representation, see Stevens, Mulhollan, and Rundquist, 1981.

REFERENCES

Abramson, Paul R., John H. Aldrich, and David W. Rohde. 1986. *Change and Continuity in the 1980 Elections*, rev. ed. Washington: CQ Press.

Aldrich, John H. 1989. "Power and Order in Congress." In *Home Style and Washington Work: Studies of Congressional Politics*, ed. Morris P. Fiorina and David W. Rohde. Ann Arbor: University of Michigan Press.

Asher, Herbert B. 1983. "Voting Behavior Research in the 1980s: An Examination of Some Old and New Problem Areas." In *Political Science: The State of the Discipline*, ed. Ada Finifter. Washington: American Political Science Association.

Barnes, Gilbert Hobbs, and Dwight Lowell Dumond, eds. 1934. *Letters of Theodore Dwight Weld, Angelina Grimké, and Sarah Grimké, 1822–1844*. New York: D. Appleton-Century.

Barry, John M. 1989. *The Ambition and the Power: The Fall of Jim Wright: A True Story of Washington*. New York: Viking.

Baumgartner, Frank R., and Bryan D. Jones. 1991. "Agenda Dynamics and Policy Subsystems." *Journal of Politics* 53:1044–74.

———. 1993. *Agendas and Instability in American Politics*. Chicago: University of Chicago Press.

Bell, Gerald D. 1967. "Formality versus Flexibility in Complex Organizations." In *Organizations and Human Behavior*, ed. Gerald D. Bell. Englewood Cliffs, N.J.: Prentice Hall.

Bell, Rudolph M. 1973. *Party and Faction in American Politics: The House of Representatives, 1789–1801*. Westport, Conn.: Greenwood.

Berry, Jeffrey M. 1989. *The Interest Group Society*, 2d ed. Glenview, Ill.: Scott-Foresman.

Biaggi, Mario. 1980a. Representative Biaggi of New York, speaking before the Massachusetts State Board of the Ancient Order of Hibernians and Ladies Auxiliary (inserted into remarks by Representative Mavroules of Massachusetts). 96 Cong., 2 sess. *Congressional Record*, June 10, 13937.

———. 1980b. Representative Biaggi of New York, speaking before the Ancient Order of Hibernians National Convention. Reprinted. 96 Cong., 2 sess. *Congressional Record*, Aug. 18, 21841.

Bogue, Allan G., and Mark Paul Maclaire. 1975. "Of Mess and Men: The Boardinghouse and Congressional Voting, 1821–1842." *American Journal of Political Science* 19:207–30.

Bond, Jon R., and Richard Fleischer. 1990. *The President in the Legislative Arena*. Chicago: University of Chicago Press.

Brenner, Philip, and William M. LeoGrande. 1991. "Congress and Nicaragua: The Limits of Alternative Policy Making." In *Divided Democracy: Cooperation and Conflict between the President and Congress*, ed. James A. Thurber. Washington: CQ Press.

Brownson, Ann L., ed. 1995. *Congressional Staff Directory*. Mount Vernon, Va.: Staff Directories.

Bullock, Charles S., III, and Burdett A. Loomis. 1985. "The Changing Congressional Career." In *Congress Reconsidered*, 3d ed., ed. Lawrence C. Dodd and Bruce I. Oppenheimer. Washington: CQ Press.

Calmes, Jacqueline. 1986. "Class of '82: Redefining Democratic Values." *Congressional Quarterly Weekly Report* 44:1269–73.

———. 1995. "Conservative 'Blue Dog' Democrats in the House." *Wall Street Journal*, March 28.

Capper, Arthur. 1922. *The Agricultural Bloc*. New York: Harcourt Brace.

Center for Congressional and Presidential Studies. 1984. *Setting Course*. Washington: American University.

Cherryholmes, Cleo H., and Michael J. Shapiro. 1969. *Representatives and Roll Call Votes: A Computer Simulation of Voting in the Eighty-eighth Congress*. Indianapolis: Bobbs-Merrill.

Clausen, Aage. 1973. *How Congressman Decide: A Policy Focus*. New York: St. Martin's.

Cobb, Roger W., and Charles D. Elder. 1983. *Participation in American Politics: The Dynamics of Agenda Building*, 2d ed. Baltimore: Johns Hopkins University Press.

Cobb, Roger W., Jennie Keith-Ross, and Marc Howard Ross. 1976. "Agenda Building as a Comparative Political Process." *American Political Science Review* 70:126–38.

Collie, Melissa P. 1994. "Legislative Structure and Its Effects." In *Encyclopedia of the American Legislative System*, vol. 2, ed. Joel H. Silbey. New York: Scribner's.

Congressional Quarterly Almanac. 1981, 1987. Washington: CQ Press.

Congressional Research Service. 1984. *Selected Data on Congressional Member Organizations*. Washington.

———. Various years. *Caucuses and Legislative Service Organizations: An Informational Directory*. Washington.

———. Various years. *Formal and Informal Congressional Groups: Summary Data*. Washington.

———. Various years. *Informal Congressional Groups and Member Organizations*. Washington.

Congressional Yellow Book. Various years. Washington: Washington Monitor.

Conservative Opportunity Society. N.d. "1987: Laying the Groundwork." Washington.

Cooper, Joseph. 1970. *The Origins of the Standing Committees and the Development of the Modern House*. Houston: Rice University.

———. 1975. Review of *The Washington Community, 1800–1828*, by James Sterling Young. *Capitol Studies* 3:167–71.

———. 1977. "Congress in Organizational Perspective." In *Congress Reconsid-*

ered, 1st ed., ed. Lawrence C. Dodd and Bruce I. Oppenheimer. New York: Praeger.

———. 1981. "Organization and Innovation in the House of Representatives." In *The House at Work*, ed. Joseph Cooper and G. Calvin MacKenzie. Austin: University of Texas Press.

Cooper, Joseph, and David W. Brady. 1981. "Institutional Context and Leadership Style: The House from Cannon to Rayburn." *American Political Science Review* 75:411–25.

Cooper, Joseph, and Melissa P. Collie. 1981. "Structural Adaptation in the House: Multiple Reference and Interunit Committees in Organizational Perspective." Paper prepared for annual meeting of the American Political Science Association, New York.

Cooper, Joseph, and Rick K. Wilson. 1994. "The Role of Congressional Parties." In *Encyclopedia of the American Legislative System*, vol. 2, ed. Joel H. Silbey. New York: Scribner's.

Cooper, Kenneth J. 1994. "Plan to Curb Caucuses Draws Plenty of Heat." *Washington Post*, Dec. 8.

Cox, Gary W., and Mathew D. McCubbins. 1993. *Legislative Leviathan: Party Government in the House*. Berkeley: University of California Press.

Cunningham, Nobel E. 1981. "Congress as an Institution, 1800–1850." Paper prepared for Project '87 Conference, Washington.

Deckard, Barbara. 1972. "State Party Delegations in the U.S. House of Representatives: A Comparative Study of Group Cohesion." *Journal of Politics* 34:199–222.

Deering, Christopher J., and Steven S. Smith. 1985. "Subcommittees in Congress." In *Congress Reconsidered*, 3d ed., ed. Lawrence C. Dodd and Bruce I. Oppenheimer. Washington: CQ Press.

Dilger, Robert J. 1982. *The Sunbelt/Snowbelt Controversy: The War over Federal Funds*. New York: New York University Press.

Dillon, Merton L. 1974. *The Abolitionists: The Growth of a Dissenting Minority*. Dekalb: Northern Illinois University Press.

Dodd, Lawrence C. 1977. "Congress and the Quest for Power." In *Congress Reconsidered*, 1st ed., ed. Lawrence C. Dodd and Bruce I. Oppenheimer. New York: Praeger.

———. 1981. "Congress, the Constitution, and the Crisis of Legitimation." In *Congress Reconsidered,* 2d ed., ed. Lawrence C. Dodd and Bruce I. Oppenheimer. Washington: CQ Press.

———. 1986a. "The Cycles of Legislative Change: Building a Dynamic Theory." In *Political Science: The Science of Politics*, ed. Herbert F. Weisberg. New York: Agathon.

———. 1986b. "A Theory of Congressional Cycles: Solving the Puzzle of Change." In *Congress and Policy Change*, ed. Gerald C. Wright Jr., Leroy N. Rieselbach, and Lawrence C. Dodd. New York: Agathon.

———. 1993. "Congress and the Politics of Renewal: Redressing the Crisis of Legitimation." In *Congress Reconsidered*, 5th ed., ed. Lawrence C. Dodd and Bruce I. Oppenheimer. Washington: CQ Press.

————. 1995. "Placing Congress in Theoretical Time: Three Perspectives on the Republican Revolution." *Newsletter of the Legislative Studies Section of the American Political Science Association* (Dec.).

Donovan, Beth. 1993. "Fractures in Freshman Class Weaken Impact on House." *Congressional Quarterly Weekly Report* 51:807–10.

Eulau, Heinz, and Vera McCluggage. 1981. "Standing Committees in Legislatures." In *Handbook of Legislative Research*, ed. Malcolm E. Jewell. Cambridge: Harvard University Press.

Fenno, Richard F. 1973. *Congressmen in Committees*. Boston: Little, Brown.

Ferber, Mark. 1971. "The Formation of the Democratic Study Group." In *Congressional Behavior*, ed. Nelson W. Polsby. New York: Random House.

Fessler, Pamela. 1992. "When It's Time to Choose Sides, Clinton Picks from the Home Team." *Congressional Quarterly Weekly Report* 50:3789–93.

Feulner, Edwin J. 1983. *Conservatives Stalk the House: The Republican Study Committee, 1970–1982*. Ottawa, Ill.: Green Hill.

Fiellin, Alan. 1962. "The Function of Informal Groups: A State Delegation." *Journal of Politics* 24:72–91.

Fiorina, Morris P., and David W. Rohde, eds. 1989. *Home Style and Washington Work: Studies of Congressional Politics*. Ann Arbor: University of Michigan Press.

Foerstel, Karen. 1994. "DSG Report Kicks Off Anti-Filibuster Efforts." *Roll Call*, June 13.

Gertzog, Irwin N. 1995 (1984). *Congressional Women: Their Recruitment, Integration, and Behavior*. New York: Praeger.

Gigot, Paul. 1993. "Potomac Watch." *Wall Street Journal*, Oct. 22.

Gilligan, Thomas W., and Keith Krehbiel. 1988. "Complex Rules and Congressional Outcomes: An Event Study of Energy Tax Legislation." *Journal of Politics* 50:625–54.

————. 1989. "Asymmetric Information and Legislative Rules with a Heterogeneous Committee." *American Journal of Political Science* 33:459–90.

————. 1990. "Organization of Informative Committees by a Rational Legislature." *American Journal of Political Science* 34:531–64.

Groennings, Sven. 1973. "The Clubs in Congress: The House Wednesday Group." In *To Be a Congressman: The Power and the Promise*, ed. Sven Groennings and Jonathan P. Hawley. Washington: Acropolis Books.

Gugliotti, Guy. 1996. "'Blue Dog' Democrats May Have Their Day in a Kinder Gentler Congress." *Washington Post*, Nov. 24.

Haas, John Eugene, and Thomas E. Drabek. 1973. *Complex Organizations: A Sociological Perspective*. New York: Macmillan.

Hammond, Susan Webb. 1989. "Congressional Caucuses in the Policy Process." In *Congress Reconsidered*, 4th ed., ed. Lawrence C. Dodd and Bruce I. Oppenheimer. Washington: CQ Press.

————. 1990. "Committee and Informal Leaders in the U.S. House of Representatives." In *Leading Congress: New Styles, New Strategies*, ed. John J. Kornacki. Washington: CQ Press.

————. 1991. "Congressional Caucuses and Party Leaders in the House of Representatives." *Political Science Quarterly* 106:277–94.

————. 1997. "Congressional Caucuses in the 104th Congress." In *Congress Reconsidered*, 6th ed., ed. Lawrence C. Dodd and Bruce I. Oppenheimer. Washington: CQ Press.

Hammond, Susan Webb, Daniel P. Mulhollan, and Arthur G. Stevens Jr. 1985. "Informal Congressional Caucuses and Agenda Setting." *Western Political Quarterly* 38:1044–74.

Hammond, Susan Webb, Arthur G. Stevens Jr., and Daniel P. Mulhollan. 1983. "Congressional Caucuses: Legislators as Lobbyists." In *Interest Group Politics*, ed. Allan J. Cigler and Burdett A. Loomis. Washington: CQ Press.

Hatzenbuehler, Ronald L. 1972. "Party Unity and the Decision for War in the House of Representatives, 1812." *William and Mary Quarterly* 29:367–68.

————. 1976. "The War Hawks and the Question of Congressional Leadership in 1812." *Pacific Historical Review* 45:2.

Henderson, Herbert James. 1974. *Party Politics in the Continental Congress.* New York: McGraw-Hill.

Horsman, Reginald. 1964. "Who Were the War Hawks?" *Indiana Magazine of History* 60.

House Wednesday Group. 1992a. "Insiders and Outsiders: American Firms Tackle the Tokyo Loop." Washington.

————. 1992b. "Beyond Revisionism: Towards a New U.S.-Japan Policy for the Post-Cold-War Era." Washington.

————. 1994. "Market-Oriented Environmental Policies." Washington.

Hurley, Patricia A., and Rick K. Wilson. 1989. "Partisan Voting Patterns in the U.S. Senate, 1977–86." *Legislative Studies Quarterly* 14:225–50.

Jones, Bryan D. 1994. *Reconsidering Decisionmaking in Democratic Politics: Attention, Choice, and Public Policy.* Chicago: University of Chicago Press.

Jones, Charles E. 1987. "Testing a Legislative Strategy: The Congressional Black Caucus's Action-Alert Communications Network." *Legislative Studies Quarterly* 12:221–37.

Jones, Charles O. 1981. "House Leadership in an Age of Reform." In *Understanding Congress*, ed. Frank H. Mackaman. Washington: CQ Press.

————. 1994. *The Presidency in a Separated System.* Washington: Brookings.

Kaufman, Herbert. 1976. *Are Government Organizations Immortal?* Washington: Brookings.

King, David C. 1994. "The Nature of Congressional Committee Jurisdictions." *American Political Science Review* 88:48–62.

Kingdon, John. 1989. *Congressmen's Voting Decisions*, 3d ed. Ann Arbor: University of Michigan Press.

————. 1995. *Agendas, Alternatives, and Public Policies* 2d ed. New York: HarperCollins.

Krehbiel, Keith. 1991. *Information and Legislative Organization.* Ann Arbor: University of Michigan Press.

Latimer, Margaret Kincaid. 1955. "South Carolina—A Protagonist of the War of 1812." *American Historical Review* 61:914–29.

Loomis, Burdett A. 1979. "The Congressional Office as a Small (?) Business: New Members Set Up Shop." *Publius* 9:35–55.

———. 1981. "Congressional Caucuses and the Politics of Representation." In *Congress Reconsidered*, 2d ed., ed. Lawrence C. Dodd and Bruce I. Oppenheimer. Washington: CQ Press.

———. 1988. *The New American Politician: Ambition, Entrepreneurship, and the Changing Face of Political Life*. New York: Basic Books.

Lorenzen, Edward. 1992. "The Evolution of a Caucus: The Role of the Conservative Democratic Forum in the U.S. House of Representatives." Senior Thesis, American University.

Lowry v. Reagan, 676 F. Supp. 333 (D.D.C. 1987), aff'd, No. 87–5426 (D.C. Cir. 1988).

Mackaman, Frank, ed. 1981. *Understanding Congress*. Washington: CQ Press.

MacNeil, Neil. 1963. *Forge of Democracy: The House of Representatives*. New York: David McKay.

Maisel, Louis Sandy. 1981. "Congressional Information Sources." In *The House at Work*, ed. Joseph Cooper and G. Calvin MacKenzie. Austin: University of Texas Press.

Mayhew, David R. 1974. *Congress: The Electoral Connection*. New Haven: Yale University Press.

Miller, Warren, and Donald Stokes. 1963. "Constituency Influence in Congress." *American Political Science Review* 68:169–86.

Morrison, David. 1995. "So What's in the New Era?" *National Journal*, Jan. 28.

Novak, Robert. 1995. "Enemies Within," *Washington Post,* Jan. 16.

Olson, David M. 1987. "U.S. Trade Policy: The Conditions for Congressional Participation." Paper prepared for annual meeting of the American Political Science Association, Chicago.

O'Neill, Tip, and William Novak. 1987. *Man of the House: The Life and Political Memoirs of Speaker Tip O'Neill*. New York: Random House.

Oppenheimer, Bruce I. 1977. "The Rules Committee: New Arm of the Leadership in a Decentralized House." In *Congress Reconsidered*, 1st ed., ed. Lawrence C. Dodd and Bruce I. Oppenheimer. New York: Praeger.

Ornstein, Norman J., Robert L. Peabody, and David W. Rohde. 1985. "The Senate through the 1980s." In *Congress Reconsidered*, 3d ed., ed. Lawrence C. Dodd and Bruce I. Oppenheimer. Washington: CQ Press.

Pancake, John S. 1955. "The 'Invisibles': A Chapter in the Opposition to President Madison." *Journal of Southern History* 21:17–37.

Perkins, Bradford. 1961. *Prologue to War: England and the United States, 1805–1812*. Berkeley: University of California Press.

Pitney, John J., Jr. 1988a. "The Conservative Opportunity Society." Paper prepared for annual meeting of the Western Political Science Association, San Francisco.

———. 1988b. "The War on the Floor: Partisan Conflict in the U. S. House of Representatives." Paper prepared for annual meeting of the American Political Science Association, Washington.

Politics in America. Various editions. Washington: CQ Press.

Rice, Stuart. 1924. *Farmers and Workers in American Politics.* New York: Columbia University Press.

Richardson, Sula. 1993. *Caucuses and Legislative Service Organizations of the 103rd Congress, 2d Session: An Informational Directory.* Washington: Congressional Research Service.

———. 1996. *Informal Congressional Groups and Member Organizations of the 104th Congress: An Informational Directory.* Washington: Congressional Research Service.

Riker, William. 1982. *Liberalism against Populism: A Confrontation between the Theory of Democracy and the Theory of Social Choice.* San Francisco: W. H. Freeman.

Risjord, Norman K. 1961. "1812: Conservatives, War Hawks, and the Nation's Honor." *William and Mary Quarterly* 18:196–210.

Rohde, David W. 1989. "'Something's Happening Here; What It Is Ain't Exactly Clear': Southern Democrats in the House of Representatives." In *Home Style and Washington Work: Studies in Congressional Politics,* ed. Morris P. Fiorina and David W. Rohde. Ann Arbor: University of Michigan Press.

———. 1991. *Parties and Leaders in the Postreform House.* Chicago: University of Chicago Press.

Rohde, David W., and Kenneth Shepsle. 1987. "Woodrow Wilson and Congressional Leadership." *Congress & the Presidency* 14:111–34.

Ryan, Mary P. 1971. "Party Formation in the United States Congress, 1789–1796: A Quantitative Analysis." *William and Mary Quarterly* 28:523–42.

Salisbury, Robert. 1969. "An Exchange Theory of Interest Groups." *Midwest Journal of Political Science* 13:1–32.

Schlaifer, Robert. 1969. *Analysis of Decisions under Uncertainty.* New York: McGraw-Hill.

Schlozman, Kay Lehman, and John T. Tierney. 1986. *Organized Interests and American Democracy.* New York: Harper and Row.

Selznick, Philip. 1949. *TVA and the Grass Roots: A Study in the Sociology of Formal Organization.* Berkeley: University of California Press.

Shaiko, Ronald. 1992. "Leadership by Other Means: Political Networks in Congress." Paper prepared for annual meeting of the Northeastern Political Science Association, Philadelphia.

Shepsle, Kenneth A. 1986. "Institutional Equilibrium and Equilibrium Institutions." In *Political Science: The Science of Politics,* ed. Herbert Weisberg. New York: Agathon.

Shepsle, Kenneth A., and Barry Weingast. 1987a. "The Institutional Foundations of Committee Power." *American Political Science Review* 81:85–104.

———. 1987b. "Why Are Congressional Committees Powerful? *American Political Science Review* 81:935–45.

Sinclair, Barbara. 1981. "The Speaker's Task Force in the Post-Reform House of Representatives." *American Political Science Review* 68:667–81.

———. 1983. *Majority Leadership in the U.S. House.* Baltimore: Johns Hopkins University Press.

———. 1989. *The Transformation of the U.S. Senate*. Baltimore: Johns Hopkins University Press.

———. 1995. *Legislators, Leaders, and Lawmaking: The U.S. House of Representatives in the Postreform Era*. Baltimore: Johns Hopkins University Press.

Smith, Steven S. 1989. *Call to Order: Floor Politics in the House and Senate*. Washington: Brookings.

———. 1990. "Informal Leadership in the Senate: Opportunities, Resources, and Motivations." In *Leading Congress: New Styles, New Strategies*, ed. John J. Kornacki. Washington: CQ Press.

Stevens, Arthur G., Jr., Arthur H. Miller, and Thomas E. Mann. 1974. "Mobilization of Liberal Strength in the House, 1955–1970: The Democratic Study Group." *American Political Science Review* 68:667–81.

Stevens, Arthur G., Jr., Daniel P. Mulhollan, and Paul S. Rundquist. 1981. "Congressional Structure and Representation: The Role of Informal Groups." *Legislative Studies Quarterly* 6:415–37.

Stewart, James Brewer. 1970. *Joshua R. Giddings and the Tactics of Radical Politics*. Cleveland: Case Western Reserve University Press.

Stockman, David Allan. 1986. *The Triumph of Politics: How the Reagan Revolution Failed*. New York: Harper and Row.

Thompson, Joan Hulse. 1988. "The Women's Rights Lobby in the Gender Gap Congress, 1983–84." *Commonwealth*, 19–35.

———. 1993. "The Family and Medical Leave Act: A Policy for Families." In *Women in Politics: Outsiders or Insiders?* ed. Lois Lovelace Duke. New York: Prentice-Hall.

———. 1995. "The Congressional Caucus for Women's Issues." In *Women's Issues Interest Groups*, ed. Sarah Slavin. Denver: Greenwood.

Timberlake, Richard H. 1978. "Repeal of Silver Monetization in the Late Nineteenth Century." *Journal of Money, Credit, and Banking* 10:39.

Turner, Julius, and Edward Schneier. 1970. *Party and Constituency: Pressures on Congress*. Baltimore: Johns Hopkins Press.

U.S. House of Representatives. 1977a. *Administrative Reorganization and Legislative Management*. Vol. 2, *Work Management*. 95 Cong., 1 sess., H. Doc. 95-232. Washington: GPO.

———. 1977b. *Final Report of the Commission on Administrative Review*. Vol. 1, *Work of the Commission*. 95 Cong., 1 sess., H. Doc. 95-272. Washington: GPO.

———. 1982. *Hearing*. Committee on House Administration, Ad Hoc Subcommittee on Legislative Service Organizations. 97 Cong., 2 sess. Committee Print.

———. 1987. *Report*. Committee on House Administration, Ad Hoc Subcommittee on Legislative Service Organizations. 100 Cong., 2 sess. Committee Print.

———. 1992. "Creating a Temporary Ad Hoc Joint Committee on the Organization of Congress to Study and Recommend Reforms in the Operations of Congress." 102 Cong., 2 sess. H. Con. Res. 192.

———. 1994. "Rural Children: Increasing Poverty Rates Pose Education Challenges." Briefing Report to the Chairwoman, Congressional Rural Caucus.

———. 1995. "Policy for Subscriptions and Publications." Committee on House Oversight, 104 Cong.

———. 1995–96. *Regulations and Policy Statements Regarding Caucuses.* Committee on House Oversight. 104 Cong.

Vega, Arturo. 1993. "Congressional Informal Groups as Representative Responsiveness." *American Review of Politics* 14:355–73.

Walker, Jack L. 1976. "Setting the Agenda in the U.S. Senate." In *Policymaking Role of Leadership in the Senate.* Papers prepared for the Commission on the Operation of the Senate, 94 Cong., 2 sess. Committee Print.

———. 1977. "Setting the Agenda in the U.S. Senate: A Theory of Problem Selection." *British Journal of Political Science* 7:423–45.

———. 1991. *Mobilizing Interest Groups in America.* Ann Arbor: University of Michigan Press.

Waller, Douglas C. 1987. *Congress and the Nuclear Freeze.* Amherst: University of Massachusetts Press.

Young, James Sterling. 1966. *The Washington Community, 1800–1828.* New York: Columbia University Press.

INDEX

ABM (antiballistic missile) Treaty, 61
Addabbo, Joseph, 187
Administration Committee, House (now House Oversight), 8, 159, 209, 233; and LSOs, 112–13, 233
Adoption, Congressional Coalition for, 46
Africa Subcommittee of House International Affairs Committee, 185
Agency for International Development, 139
agendas, caucuses and, 81–87, 108; industry caucuses, 105–7; national constituency caucuses, 96–100; party caucuses, 87–92; personal-interest caucuses, 92–96; regional caucuses, 100–103; state/district caucuses, 103–5
Agent Orange, 99, 141, 143, 144, 170, 188
Agent Orange, Presidential Task Force on, 141
Agricultural Forum, 49, 75
Agriculture, Department of, 56, 136, 149, 150, 151, 172
Agriculture Committees, House and Senate, 150, 152, 156, 159, 173, 183, 184, 193, 205; members in caucuses, 163–64
Aid to Families with Dependent Children (AFDC), 52
Air and Space Caucus, Senate, 43
Alcohol Fuels Caucus, 115
Appropriations Committee, House, 117, 173, 174, 188, 197, 229; members in caucuses, 163–65; mentioned, 2, 4; in 104th Congress, 76, 120
Appropriations Committee, Senate, 28, 145
Arab Boycott, Task Force to End the, 43–44
ARCO, 46
Armed Services Committee, House (now National Security), 77, 157, 159, 163, 164, 172
Armed Services Committee, Senate, 28
Armey, Richard, 76

Arms Control and Foreign Policy Caucus (was Peace through Law), 41, 157, 192, 204, 205, 207; activities of, 62, 165, 166, 172, 185, 191; Central America Task Force, 78, 128–29, 189; and congressional leadership, 127–29; dissolution of, 212; mentioned, 93, 118; in 104th Congress, 211; structure of, 21, 22, 31, 32
Army Corps of Engineers, 101
Arts and Humanities, Presidential Task Force on the, 138
Arts Caucus, 21, 32, 115, 138; activities of, 29, 62, 182
Australia, 144
Auto Industry Task Force (now Automotive Caucus), 51, 58
Automotive Caucus (was Auto Industry Task Force), 62, 107, 164, 238; and Chrysler Corporation, 58, 106

B-1 Bomber, 139
B-2 Stealth Caucus, 43
Balanced Budget, Congress and Leaders United for a, 95
Balanced Budget Amendment, 6, 90, 95, 189
Balanced Budget Caucus, 43, 192, 205
Baltic States and the Ukraine, Ad Hoc Monitoring Committee on, 104
Baltimore Conference III, 1986, 122
Banking, Finance and Urban Affairs Committee, House (now Banking and Financial Services), 164, 193
Banking, Housing and Urban Affairs Committee, Senate, 172
Bateman, Jim, 113
Baucus, Max, 61
Beard, Edward, 63
Beef Caucus, 30, 35

249

Library of Congress Cataloging-in-Publication Data

Hammond, Susan Webb.
  Congressional caucuses in national policy making / Susan Webb Hammond.
    p. cm.
  Includes bibliographical references and index.
  ISBN 0-8018-5682-5 (alk. paper)
    1. United States. Congress—Caucuses. 2. Political planning—United States. I. Title.
JK1108.H36 1998
328.73'076—dc21   97-25890
                                                                                CIP